Walking Oxford

Vicky Wilson

Walking Oxford

Written by Vicky Wilson
Photography by Andrew Kershman and Susi Koch
Edited by Sophie Lazar
Book design by Lesley Gilmour and Susi Koch
Illustrations by Hannah Kershman

First published in 2021 by
Metro Publications Ltd
www.metropublications.com

Metro® is a registered trade mark of Associated Newspapers Limited. The METRO mark is under licence from Associated Newspapers Limited.

Printed and bound in Turkey. This book is produced using paper from registered sustainable and managed sources.

© 2021 Metro Publications
British Library Cataloguing in Publication Data. A catalogue record for this book is available from the British Library.

ISBN 978-1-902910-67-3

Walking Oxford

Vicky Wilson

Archway to the Bodleian Library

Contents

View from the University Church of St Mary

Introduction

I started exploring Oxford when my daughter moved here a few years ago. Like most visitors, the first things I went to see were the colleges – the famous dreaming spires (or more precisely, crocketed pinnacles) stacked up within the city centre. But Oxford is much more than that, and I hope this book will lead the reader beyond the halls and chapels of the many colleges and the majestic buildings of the University to discover a richer and more diverse story.

The first two walks here – 'North of the High' and 'South of the Broad' – take in most of the colleges as well as the major University buildings and the town's picturesque medieval lanes. Four of the most significant colleges are treated separately in the 'Four Colleges & a Cathedral' walk. The 'East of St Giles' walk embraces monuments to the religious controversies that feature so prominently in Oxford's story as well as the science area, with the pioneering Museum of Natural History and Pitt Rivers Museum and the many laboratories that are still at the forefront of research. 'West of Carfax' explores a formerly industrial area, still containing many (now repurposed) workshops and warehouses on the banks of streams that fed breweries and powered mills. The once dilapidated but now gentrified terraces of the 'Jericho' walk were developed in the mid-19th century for workers at Oxford University Press and the Lucy & Co. iron foundry, along with philanthropic institutions such as churches and schools. 'North Oxford' surveys a suburb of eclectic late-Victorian villas commissioned for the families of Oxford fellows and the business owners made rich through trade with the University, with many households run by women determined to provide educational opportunities for their sex. Finally, 'Along the Thames' follows the course of the waterways that made Oxford a centre for trade from its Anglo-Saxon origins beside a ford for driving oxen.

While the eight walks in this book are not narrowly themed, instead drawing attention to the often mind-boggling variety of points of interest in Oxford's streets, each does explore the particular circumstances that shaped the area it covers – whether the evolving culture of the University, the growth and decline of industry, or social change. Perhaps more than any other British city outside London, Oxford has proved a magnet for eccentric, often extraordinarily dedicated individuals – many but by no means all of them rich and privileged. I hope their stories also come through in these pages.

Finally, in case you grow tired of exploring streets and lanes, Oxford offers several green areas and waterside walks. Port Meadow, accessed from Walton Well Road in Jericho, is 120 hectares of grazing land bounded by the Thames to the west and the canal to the east. University Parks, between Keble and Lady Margaret Hall, is some 30 hectares planted with specimen trees stretching along the banks of the Cherwell. You can also walk north up the canal from the station to Wolvercote, north up the Thames to the ruins of Godstow Abbey or south to Iffley with its magnificent 12th-century church.

Vicky Wilson

A practical note

Most of the walks within *Walking Oxford* are approximately circular, and none involves public transport. There are only minor overlaps between them, and doing them all will take you along the city's most interesting and attractive streets and past most of its significant monuments. All can be done without entering any buildings – though descriptions of the interior of accessible spaces such as churches are given in case you wish to go inside. Tours of the colleges are separated off in boxes, but even if you are not going in, it is worth reading the opening paragraphs, which describe what you can see from the street. Opening times can change unexpectedly, so if a visit to a particular college is a priority, it's best to check before you set out by phoning the porter's lodge. It's worth knowing that sometimes you can gain entry even if the closed board is up just by asking.

Note: Larger maps of each walk are available to download and print. Just visit our website
www.metropublications.com

Acknowledgements

My thanks to Andrew Kershman and Susi Koch for commissioning this book and for all their hard work – including the beautiful photographs.

Nancy Wilson and Kat Kwok have been invaluable in sharing their knowledge of the city, as well as accompanying me on most of the walks, commenting on discoveries and points of interest and taking reference photographs.

I am extremely grateful to Suzanne Tarlin and David Watkinson, who have 'road-tested' the walks for me, drawing my attention to things that have intrigued them, posing useful questions and, of course, correcting my lefts and rights.

And finally, thank you to Tom Neville for walking the walks, then reading the walks – and for offering much-appreciated advice and support throughout.

Recommended reading

For a general history of Oxford and a love letter to its traditions, personalities and eccentricities, see Jan Morris' *Oxford* (OUP, 1965). Geoffrey Tyack's *Oxford: An Architectural Guide* (OUP, 1998) has provided insights not only to the city's buildings but to its social history. Peter Howard and Helena Webster's *Oxford* (Ellipsis, 1999) is an easily digestible introduction to Oxford's architecture and Paul Sullivan's *The Secret History of Oxford* (The History Press, 2013) brought many lesser-known places to my attention. Inevitably, I consulted many websites but none was more useful than the wonderful oxfordhistory.org, which is full of more information than I could possibly use as well as pointers to other sources. And finally, for North Oxford I am grateful to Tanis Hinchcliffe, both for her in-depth study of the area (*North Oxford*, Yale, 1992) and for an illuminating conversation about the suburb and its female pioneers.

Merton Street

AREA MAP

Port Meadow

Botley Park

BOTLEY ROAD

Oatlands Road
Recreations
Ground

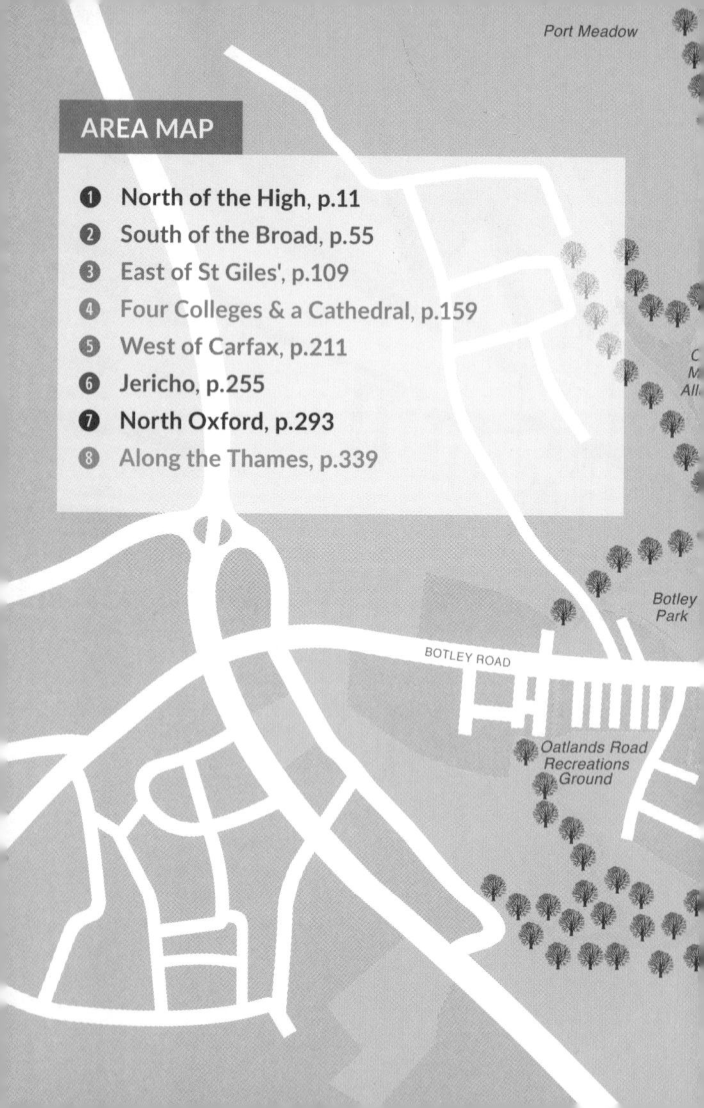

New College Lane

1
North of
the High:
from medieval to moderne

North of the High

1. Botanic Garden entrance
2. Jewish Cemetery memorial
3. Penicillin memorial
4. Daubeny Building
5. Morris showroom
6. Plaque to the 'Catholic Martyrs'
7. John Chessell Buckler
8. Holywell Music Room
9. Bath Place
10. Turf Tavern
11. Jane Burden
12. Bridge of Sighs
13. Edmond Halley
14. New College gateway
15. Provost's Lodgings
16. St Peter-in-the-East

St Edmund Hall
17. Front Quadrangle
18. Hall of residence
19. Kelly and Emden student accommodation
20. Graveyard of St Peter-in-the-East
21. St Edmund

22. Queen's Lane Coffee House
23. Grand Café
24. Sarah Cooper
25. Examination Schools
26. Ruskin School of Art
27. William Morris cycle shop
28. Eastgate Hotel
29. The Queen's College
30. University College
31. Robert Boyle

All Souls
32. Front Quadrangle
33. Chapel
34. North Quadrangle

35. Radcliffe Camera
36. Hertford College

Wad
Coll

PARKS ROAD

43

BROAD STREET   41   42
BROAD STREET   40
                            38 37
             39
Exeter College

BRASENOSE LN

TURL STREET   Brasenose
                   College

ST MARY'S PASSAGE

HIGH STREET

ALFRED ST

BEAR LN

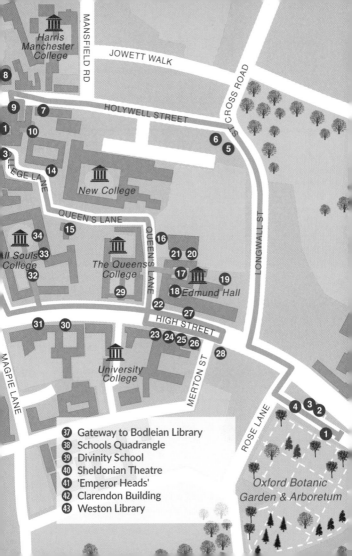

MANSFIELD RD

JOWETT WALK

Harris
Manchester
College

ST CROSS ROAD

HOLYWELL STREET

8

9

7

1

10

3

COLLEGE LANE

14

New College

QUEEN'S LANE

15

All Souls
College

34

33

32

The Queens
College

16

QUEEN'S LANE

21

20

17

19

18 Edmund Hall

LONGWALL ST

29

22

27

HIGH STREET

31

30

23 24 25 26

28

University
College

MERTON ST

MAGPIE LANE

ROSE LANE

4 3 2

1

Oxford Botanic
Garden & Arboretum

37 Gateway to Bodleian Library
38 Schools Quadrangle
39 Divinity School
40 Sheldonian Theatre
41 'Emperor Heads'
42 Clarendon Building
43 Weston Library

North of the High: from medieval to moderne

Start: Botanic Garden
Finish: Weston Library
Distance: 1.6 miles

*'The High Street is one of the world's great streets.
It has everything.'*
Nikolaus Pevsner, *Oxfordshire*

Describing a gentle curve from Magdalen Bridge to the city's central crossroads at Carfax, Oxford's High Street, known locally as The High, consists of a number of impressive set-piece buildings interspersed with relatively modest housing, often with shops or cafés at street level. This walk takes in the section from Magdalen College (pronounced 'maudlin') in the east to the University Church of St Mary the Virgin two-thirds of the way along as well as some of the medieval lanes and 17th-century streets that grew up within and just outside the old city walls to the north. The route ends with the magnificent Georgian buildings that form the heart of the University – the Radcliffe Camera, Bodleian Library, Sheldonian Theatre and Clarendon Building. Magdalen and New College can be visited as part of this walk if you have time and energy: they are described in detail as part of the 'Four Colleges' walk (pages 179 and 189).

The walk begins opposite Magdalen College outside the entrance to the ❶ **Botanic Garden** (open November to February, 9–16; March, April, September and October, 9–17; May to August, 9–18 but not included in the walk). The oldest in Britain, the Botanic Garden was founded in 1621 as a physic garden to grow medicinal herbs 'for the glorification of the works of God and for the furtherance of learning'. Funds were supplied by Henry Danvers, 1st Earl of Danby. The fantastic sandstone main gateway, designed by aptly named royal master-mason Nicholas Stone, who was also responsible for the striking porch of the University Church (see page 99), is based on a Roman triumphal arch, with three overlapping pediments above four columns with vermiculated rustication – appropriate for a garden as the pattern is intended to resemble the tracks of worms. The statues – of Charles I and Charles II in the side niches and Danby in the central pediment – were added towards the end of the 17th century.

Part of the Botanic Garden site was a Jewish cemetery that had been used from just after 1177, when Jews were first granted permission to bury their dead outside London, until 1231, when the area was appropriated by the Hospital of St John. To the right of the outside of the main gateway a plaque in Hebrew and English installed in 1931 commemorates the dead: the first line of the Hebrew text, 'For a stone shall cry out from the wall', refers to the fact that gravestones and bones were dug up during construction of the wall and that graves may still lie beneath the gardens.

The Jews were subsequently given a piece of adjacent wasteland that served as a cemetery for only 60 years before they were expelled from England in 1290. A ❷ memorial erected in 2012 in front of the rose garden that lies between the Botanic Garden and the High Street marks the site. The path known as Deadman's Walk, which once linked the cemetery to the heart of the Jewish community around St Aldate's, runs west from Rose Lane at the far end of the garden.

Behind the Jewish memorial is a stone plinth commemorating the ❸ scientists who discovered penicillin. The New York Lasker

Foundation, which funded the monument, specified that it should be placed in a rose garden – presumably because the first patient to be successfully treated with the drug at the Radcliffe Infirmary was suffering from an infected wound caused by a rose thorn. In addition to the usually credited Ernst Chain, Norman Heatley and Howard Florey, the memorial honours the scientific contributions of Florey's first wife Mary Ethel, who supervised the clinical trials, and his research assistant and second wife Margaret Jennings. Designed by pioneering landscape architect Sylvia Crowe (1901–1997), the garden echoes a traditional physic garden, with planting surrounded by low box hedges.

Walk to the spreading tree near the garden's centre. Opposite it on the ❹ **Daubeny Building**, originally a laboratory built from 1834 with vermiculated relief that echoes that of the Botanic Garden gateway, is a plaque inscribed 'Sine experientia nihil sufficienter sciri potest' (Without experience nothing can be known sufficiently). This is from the *Opus Majus* of philosopher and Franciscan friar Roger Bacon (aka Rogerius Baconus or Doctor Mirabilis), written in 1267 at the request of Pope Clement IV to explain his work in grammar, logic, mathematics, physics, philosophy and his empiricist approach to the natural sciences.

Emerge from the garden and turn left along the High then right up **Longwall Street**, named for the 12th-century city wall that used to run along its western flank (and can still be seen within the grounds of New College, see page 195) rather than the 15th-century wall of Magdalen College that now bounds the street to the east. Today Magdalen owns the first building in the street and the rickety-looking **nos 1–3** (with the overhanging jetty), dating from the mid-17th century, as well as **nos 4–7**, built about a century later.

The grander pink house at **no. 8**, remodelled in the mid-18th century, belongs to New College – along with the rest of the street to **no. 20**. The highly articulated 1960s buildings next door were constructed on what was formerly its garden. Now combined into a single building, the prettily painted houses with the wrought-iron balconies and wooden shutters at **nos 9–12** were mostly occupied

Longwall Street

Sacher Building

5

by college servants and porters after they too were remodelled in the mid-18th century. **No. 14**, with its double doorway leading to outbuildings, was the home of a stable-keeper and flyman; after his daughter inherited the business, her husband was prosecuted a number of times for 'driving cabs furiously' before going bankrupt. The adjacent Sacher Building, designed in the 1960s by David Roberts (1911–82), best known for his influential buildings and teaching career at 'the other place' (Cambridge), is student accommodation accessed from New College: the Longwall frontage, its masonry echoing the wall opposite, is given over to circulation with rooms facing the quieter courtyard at the back.

The large red-brick building at no. 21 Longwall was built by ❺ **car manufacturer William Morris** (later Lord Nuffield, 1877–1963; see box on page 228) in 1910 on the site of disused livery stables and the former offices of *Jackson's Oxford Journal*. Described as 'Oxford's new motor palace', it contained repair shops, lock-up garages and an extensive showroom. The prototype of the Morris Oxford car was assembled here in 1912: when production moved to Cowley two years later, the building became a service and distribution centre, with Morris' own office – described by Jan Morris in 1965 as a time capsule still containing a desk diary, blotter, bottle of stale medicine and cigarette advertisements illustrating 'harmlessly amorous situations' – on the first floor. The building, with a small display of Morris memorabilia in the showroom windows, is now accommodation for New College.

Thanks largely to the expansion of the University, the population of Oxford tripled from about 3,000 in the 1550s to more than 10,000

a century later, by which time it was one of the richest towns in England. **Holywell Street** – like Longwall sited just outside the city walls – was developed in its present form at about that time, with new houses, many of them timber-framed, built singly or in pairs. The modest terrace of **nos 99–100**, on the north side, typifies the way the street might have looked in the early 17th century. Houses such as the much more substantial building opposite (**no. 1**) were remodelled in the late 18th century with flat frontages and grander entrances like the recessed porch here with an elegant neoclassical window above. In the early 1950s **no. 99** was home to *Lord of the Rings* author J. R. R. Tolkien and his wife after they had left North Oxford (see page 330).

On the wall of **no. 100** is a ❻ **plaque to the 'Catholic Martyrs'** – two priests and two laymen, including Humphrey Pritchard, a servant at the Catherine Wheel Inn where the men were arrested – who were executed for their faith in 1589 at the nearby Holywell Gallows. The priests were hung, drawn and quartered with their heads displayed at Oxford Castle and their quarters on the four city gates.

Robinson Tower

7

Holywell Street

The imposing buildings on the south side of the street were designed for New College from 1872 by George Gilbert Scott, who had already worked at Exeter. The overscaled, castellated Robinson Tower contained quarters for a married tutor, New College being one of the first to allow tutors to wed. The range was extended eastwards in 1896 by Basil Champneys, architect of the Indian Institute (see page 60) and subsequently the Rhodes Building at Oriel (see page 98).

Nos 2 and **3** on the north side, the latter with an impressive Georgian porch supported on heavy scrolls, were girls' boarding schools for periods during the 19th century, as were many other houses in the street. Together with the buildings from **nos 1–20** they are now owned by Merton College. **Nos 6** and **7** have been one large dwelling since the 18th century – hence the lack of a second front door. **Nos 13** and **13a**, once two separate cottages accessed from a central passageway and still with their original upper-floor windows, offer another glimpse of how the street might originally have looked.

If you are ready for a break, **no. 15** houses Japanese restaurant Edamamé, which serves lunch from Wednesday to Sunday (food is good but service is brisk, so this is not a place to linger). **Nos 28** and **29** are part of Harris Manchester College: the crests include those of pottery manufacturers Josiah Wedgwood and Thomas Bentley, benefactors of the college, which was originally in Warrington in Cheshire. **No. 65**, opposite, has windows supported by carved brackets of grotesque beasts, one of which is dated 1639. Jane Burden (see below) gave this as her address on her marriage certificate to artist William Morris, though in fact her impoverished family lived in a house in the yard behind.

On the wall of **no. 58** is a blue plaque to architect ❼ **John Chessell Buckler** (1793–1894), who managed the Magdalen estates, worked on several Oxford colleges and came second to Charles Barry in the competition to rebuild the Palace of Westminster following the fire of 1834. **Nos 31** and **32** (opposite), both with fine doorcases, originally backed on to livery stables owned by Brasenose College.

JANE BURDEN
Mrs William Morris
1839 - 1914
Pre-Raphaelite Muse
and
Embroiderer
was born in a dwelling
in this passage
19th October 1839

The beautifully simple white building at No. 34 – easily mistaken for a Nonconformist chapel – is the **8** **Holywell Music Room**, designed by St Edmund Hall vice-principal Thomas Camplin in 1748 as the first room in England solely for public performances of music. James Wyatt, architect of the Radcliffe Observatory (see page 263), probably remodelled the interior in the 1780s: the space is dominated by a Dutch organ flanked by simple white urns on a low stage at the far end of the building, with tiers of seating rising in a horseshoe around the entrance. The ornate chandeliers were hung in Westminster Hall for the coronation of George IV in 1820 and presented by the king to Wadham College, in whose grounds the Music Room stands.

Turn left opposite the Holywell Music Room into **9** **Bath Place**, a picturesque cobbled alley surrounded by a cluster of 17th-century cottages built by Flemish weavers on the outside of the city wall. Novelist Dorothy L. Sayers (1893–1957) lived here in the late 1910s, working as a publishing assistant for Basil Blackwell and writing some of her first poems. The cottages were converted into a bed and breakfast in the early 1960s and Elizabeth Taylor and Richard Burton stayed here while the latter was performing at the Oxford Playhouse.

Walk through the last doorway on the left to the **10** **Turf Tavern**, dating back to 1381 and built against the city wall, a section

22

of which you can still see in the courtyard. The pub claims patrons as diverse as Elizabeth Taylor and Margaret Thatcher, Oscar Wilde and Ernest Hemingway, Stephen Hawking and Thomas Hardy as well as cast members from the Harry Potter films; future US President Bill Clinton, at Oxford in the late 1960s, was said not to have inhaled while drinking here. Morse and Lewis also return frequently to the Turf to prod their brains into action with a pint or two in the TV adaptations of Colin Dexter's detective novels.

Cross the courtyard and skirt the city wall to **St Helen's Passage**, where a plaque on the right marks the birthplace of ⑪ **Jane Burden** (1839–1914). The daughter of an impoverished groom, Jane was spotted at the theatre when she was eighteen by poet and painter Dante Gabriel Rossetti and artist Edward Burne-Jones, then a student of theology at Exeter. She agreed to sit for a series of murals based on Arthurian myth commissioned by John Ruskin to decorate the Oxford Union – where she met William Morris (1834–96), who was part of the team. The couple married in St

Michael at the Northgate in 1859 and Jane was educated to become a gentleman's wife, possibly serving as the inspiration for Eliza Doolittle in family friend George Bernard Shaw's play *Pygmalion*. The marriage was not altogether happy – Morris was attracted first and foremost by Jane's dark, haunting beauty while she found his wild enthusiasms and irascibility difficult to deal with, retreating into defensive silence and eventually an affair with Rossetti (Henry James described her as 'an apparition of fearful and wonderful intensity... this dark silent medieval woman with her medieval toothache').

Emerge from St Helen's Passage into **New College Lane**. To your right is what has become known as the **⑫ Bridge of Sighs** – though in fact it more closely resembles Venice's Rialto Bridge. Linking new residential buildings for Hertford College (see below) to the existing campus, it was designed in 1913–14 by Thomas Graham Jackson, architect of the Examination Schools and Ruskin School of Art (see below) as well as much of Brasenose.

View from St Helen's Passage

Turn away from the bridge. On a pillar to the garden wall of no. 7 New College Lane is a minimalist plaque with the name **⑬ Edmond Halley** (1656–1742) and an engraving of a comet. An astronomer, mathematician, physicist and translator (from Greek and Arabic), Halley is considered to be the founder of geophysics, a pioneer in social statistics for his work on calculating annuities, and an important figure in navigation and meteorology. He observed the comet that bears his name in 1682 and in 1684 computed its orbit. In 1691 he was unsuccessful in his bid to be appointed

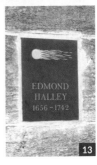

EDMOND HALLEY
1656 ~ 1742

13

Savilian Professor of Astronomy because of his freethinking religious beliefs and rejection of a literal interpretation of the scriptures. He is thought to have moved into no. 7 soon after being finally appointed Savilian Professor of Geometry in 1703; the rooftop observatory (still visible) was built for him in about 1705.

Continue walking along New College Lane, its twists and turns and high, largely windowless walls giving a powerful sense of what the city might have looked like in medieval times, with its monastic and literally inward-facing institutions constructed to frustrate prying eyes and keep the riotous public at bay. The stretch with the **14** **gateway to New College** at its end has the college's cloister wall on the left and on the right (with the old double wooden door) a barn to store produce from its estates. Resembling a fortress watchtower, the entrance was the first of many Oxford college gatetowers. The niches hold statues of the angel of the Annunciation and the founder on either side of the Virgin

Mary: allegedly, the low doorway below was a Catholic ruse to force visitors to bow their heads before the Madonna.

Turn right under the arch into **Queen's Lane**. On your right are the wildly crocketed pinnacles of All Souls, followed by the disciplined simplicity of The Queen's College ⑮ **Provost's Lodgings**, designed in 1958 by Raymond Erith, who also worked extensively at Lady Margaret Hall: the robust ashlar-faced block, square in plan, reflects the spirit of the surrounding buildings in presenting a

near-blank face to the lane. Also on the right, behind the wall, is the grandly classical Queen's College library (1692–95), with its tall arched windows. Above the elaborately carved pediment, an eagle standing on a globe holds a shield with the college arms of three eagles, inspired by the name of its founder, Robert de Eglesfield, chaplain to Queen Philippa (c. 1310–69), consort of Edward III (the walk will lead you round to the front of the college for a clearer view and more information is given below). The near-windowless, rough stone building opposite is New College's 14th-century latrine block – still used for that purpose today.

On the left of the final stretch of lane before the High Street is the church of ⑯ **St Peter-in-the-East**, founded possibly in Saxon times as a place of prayer or thanksgiving

for travellers departing or entering the city via the nearby East Gate (see below). The current building, its plain stone walls relieved only by a frieze of quatrefoils, was begun in the 1130s, with the tower added in the 1300s. The church is now the library of St Edmund Hall and through the railings beyond it you can see a statue of St Edmund of Abingdon (c. 1174–1240), who gave the institution its name.

Oxford and its University

Originating in the 8th century as a settlement around a 'ford for oxen' near the confluence of the Thames and Cherwell at what is now Folly Bridge, Oxford was sited at an important crossroads between the Midlands and London and Wales and the south-east. Following the Norman conquest of 1066, by which time it was one of England's largest towns, its governor Robert d'Oilly strengthened its fortifications and built a castle housing a monastic community that became one of the country's first places of formal education.

The University itself grew up over the following century, with groups of scholars congregating around famous teachers. It received its first charter in 1214 and soon gained the patronage of both king and pope, who benefited from its output of clerics or clerks to serve both Church and state. Students lived in small groups in academic halls, with lectures given in schools: undergraduates (from the age of sixteen) studied for seven years to gain a Bachelor of Arts, with a doctorate (usually in theology, but also in law or medicine) taking some sixteen years. The first colleges were founded in the 1260s by rich, often childless benefactors to educate a handful of fellows under a head variously (and still) referred to as a master, president, provost, rector or warden. Substantial endowments of land as well as gifts from subsequent benefactors supplied ample revenue to expand into often magnificent buildings including the halls in which members dined and the chapels in which they were to pray in perpetuity for the founder's soul. Accommodation was usually in rooms shared by up to four scholars with adjacent individual study cubicles.

During the Middle Ages, the University – its members answerable only to ecclesiastical law – sought to enforce its authority on the town, which increasingly depended on it economically. Both town and University grew rapidly from the mid-16th century, with the urban population more than tripling to 10,000 by the time Charles I made Oxford his capital during the Civil War. The University expanded its remit to preparing students for professional and public life as well as fostering scientific study: from the 1660s an ambitious institutional building programme produced the grand classical masterpieces stretching north from Radcliffe Square.

The 18th century brought increasing complaints of students' idleness, drunkenness and lack of scholarship but Parliamentary commissions from 1850 forced through reforms to the curriculum, with teaching of science boosted by the foundation of the University Museum; examinations, which had so far been largely oral and increasingly discredited; and admissions, with non-Anglican students accepted from 1871, a level of education for women pioneered soon afterwards and fellows allowed to marry from 1877.

Though the largest industrial employer remained Oxford University Press, the 19th century saw the arrival of the canal and railway and a smattering of manufacturing. A suburb of workers' housing (Jericho) was built to the west of the city centre and a new suburb for the middle classes (including fellows and their families) established to the north. Between the wars Oxford became one of the fastest growing British towns, largely thanks to the presence of Morris Motors. William Morris (later Lord Nuffield) became the first of many industrialists and businessmen to found new colleges and Oxford continues to attract donors from business and finance.

Today Oxford (since 1929 encompassing the suburbs of Cowley, Headington, Iffley and Wolvercote) has a population of about 150,000, 70 per cent of whom are employed in 'knowledge-intensive industries', living side by side with some 34,000 students (24,000 at the University of Oxford and the remainder at Oxford Brookes). Its other major industry is tourism, which attracts some 7 million visitors each year.

St Edmund Hall

Queen's Lane, OX1 4AR

www.seh.ox.ac.uk

Open daily, 10–16; it is worth asking at the porter's lodge even if the board claims the college is closed

Known affectionately as 'Teddy Hall' and incorporated as a college only in 1957, St Edmund Hall is the sole survivor of the medieval Oxford halls established to house and educate undergraduates. The first documented reference to its existence dates from 1317 but it is thought to have been founded up to a century earlier. Though other Oxford colleges date to the mid-13th century, most did not admit undergraduates until the 16th, supporting St Edmund Hall's claim to be the oldest society to accommodate and teach undergraduates of any university. Recent alumni and college members include broadcasters Samira Ahmed, Robin Day and Jeremy Paxman; politician Keir Starmer; and comedians Terry Jones, Stewart Lee and Al Murray.

The entrance to St Edmund Hall is one of the most unassuming of Oxford's colleges. Above the inconspicuous doorway is the college crest (four modest Cornish choughs in contrast to Queen's rapacious eagles) and a chronogram ('sanCtVs edMVndVs hVIVs aVLae LVX' – 'St Edmund, light of this hall') – an example of an abstruse Oxford convention whereby adding (and sometimes subtracting) the capital letters translated into Roman numerals gives a date, in this case 1246, the year of Edmund's canonisation. A one-time Archbishop of Canterbury and devout ascetic, Edmund was an expert in mathematics, dialectics and theology and was allegedly the first university lecturer to teach the philosophy of Aristotle.

From the entrance, visitors step into an intimate **⓱ Front Quadrangle** with a medieval well at its centre. The entrance range, dating from 1635–59, contains the dining hall and master's lodging, marked by the oriel window to the south. To your left, with a sundial (again featuring a chough) on its wall, is a medieval-looking **⓲ hall of residence**: the west side (nearest the entrance) was built between 1581 and 1600 and the east side in 1746 but only a mortar joint marks the hiatus. The chapel opposite the entrance, built in the 1680s, has an elegant classical façade given a touch of monumentality by giant Corinthian columns. The east window (visible to visitors only from the inside) was designed by Edward Burne-Jones and William Morris in 1865; fragments of medieval glass were set into the southernmost windows facing the quadrangle in the 1950s. With space at a premium, the upper floor was planned as a library, its function denoted by the carved stacks of books supporting the pediment above the door. This was the first Oxford library to be built with shelves along the walls and the last to be furnished with chains to secure precious books from theft. To the right is a cottage dating from 1609, above which rise a startling, brutalist concrete cylinder and part of a block with quirky gables that seem to echo the dormers of the older residences. This is the **⑲ Kelly and Emden student accommodation**, squeezed into a tight site by architects Kenneth Stevens Associates in 1968.

Walk through Staircase 1 at the western end of the 1600 residence to the **⑳ graveyard of St Peter-in-the-East**. Ahead is the emaciated figure of **㉑ St Edmund** poring over a book, cast in bronze by Rodney Munday in 2007. Two headstones just before you reach the church porch deserve mention: on the left lies James Sadler, the first English aeronaut who in 1784 ascended in a balloon from Christ Church Meadow (see page 178); on the right lies Sarah Hounslow, mother of six children and presumably unique in having died on 31 February, in 1835.

Sections of the south wall of the former church (facing the graveyard) date from the 12th century, though the two-storey porch is from some 400 years later; the grotesques below the frieze include a frog, lamb, cat and grasshopper. To the east is the entrance to the crypt, which survives largely intact from 1120; the plain east end has two pyramid-capped staircase turrets, also dating from the 12th century. The north chapel was added by Edmund c. 1230 and the tower, now a bookstore with a fellows' room in the lit portion at the top, was built a century or so later. A charming garden to the north has planting among the headstones, and from here you can appreciate the flowing tracery of the library's expansive windows and the light that floods the interior from both sides.

Continue to the High Street and turn left. On the corner is the ㉒ **Queen's Lane Coffee House**, which claims to be the oldest established coffee house in Europe – though the grander ㉓ **Grand Café** opposite, bizarrely, claims to be the oldest in England. In fact, it seems that the Queen's Lane Coffee House, launched in 1654 by Cirques Jobson, a Levantine Jew from Syria, is the oldest coffee house in continuous operation; the Grand Café was established only in the 1990s but is on the site of the Angel Inn, where a Jewish immigrant from Lebanon named Jacob set up a coffee house in 1650. Either way, Oxford was the first English city to enjoy a distinctive coffee-house culture, with the first establishments known as 'penny universities' as they charged a penny admission for access to newspapers, conversation with scholars and students and the opportunity to enjoy the newly imported drink.

From the 1850s to 1919 the building that now houses the Grand Café and No. 83 next door were occupied by the Cooper family, who ran a grocery business on the ground floor. In 1874 ㉔ **Sarah Cooper** (commemorated by a blue plaque) decided to try to sell off the surplus from the marmalade she had been making for her family: it proved so successful that by 1900 manufacture had moved to the Jam Factory in Park End Street (see page 215) and Cooper's Oxford Marmalade, still claiming to use Sarah's original recipe, continued to be produced in Oxford by her descendants until

the mid-1960s. The building at No. 83 dates from the 17th century: its origins as the Angel Inn presumably explain why the Ionic columns that flank the triple window have an image of Bacchus on their capitals.

Still on the opposite side of the street, the striking example of Victorian eclecticism next door to no. 83 is the **㉕ Examination Schools**, designed by Thomas Graham Jackson, whose win in the 1875 competition launched his career as one of the most influential and prolific of Oxford University architects. A former pupil of George Gilbert Scott (author of the much less successful New College buildings on Holywell Street, see above), Jackson rejected the neo-gothic style of his mentor in favour of designs inspired by Elizabethan and Jacobean country houses – here an elaborate porch in the form of a Serliana topped by a balustrade, pediment and pinnacles and embellished by a frieze of vines, birds and squirrels, leads to a lavishly decorated hall lit by vast windows (the cost, unsurprisingly, was triple the initial estimate).

25

The need for the new building was driven by the introduction of written papers to replace discredited oral exams (their lack of rigour is exemplified by an anecdote about parodist and poet Charles Stuart Calverley, whose alleged response in the 1850s to the question 'With what feelings ought we to regard the Decalogue' was the stab in the dark 'With feelings of devotion mingled with awe'; 'A very proper answer', responded the Master of Balliol, unaware that his pupil had no idea he was referring to the Ten Commandments). The panels on either side of the central arch here depict a nervous candidate undergoing a *viva* on the left and successful students at their graduation ceremony, where even today they kneel in front of the vice-chancellor to be hit on the head with a Bible. (The walk will lead you back along the other side of the street, where you can yourself examine these in more detail.) Students still sit exams in the two halls on the first floor, dressed in sub fusc (black and white) and academic gowns.

The adjacent building, now the ㉖ **Ruskin School of Art**, was built by Jackson five years later. It originally housed the Delegacy for Non-Collegiate Students, set up to make an Oxford education accessible to those who could not afford to live in college. The Ruskin School of Drawing, as it was initially known, was established by John Ruskin (1819–1900) in 1871, soon after he had been appointed Oxford's first Slade Professor of Art, to encourage artisanship and technical skills as well as the study of the 800 drawings and watercolours he had collected to illustrate his lectures (now in the Ashmolean). His admiration for the Venetian gothic in architecture had a lasting impact on Oxford, realised most fully in 1860 in the University Museum of

Natural History (see page 135). Committed to recognising the labourer as a creative member of society and manual labour as an honourable pursuit, Ruskin also put his ideas into practice in less successful schemes such as a plan of 1874 for students including Arnold Toynbee and Oscar Wilde to dig a road across the swamp that separated the villages of Upper and Lower Hinksey ('like a bad lecture it ended abruptly – in the middle of the swamp... [with] Ruskin going away to Venice', wrote Wilde).

Almost opposite the junction between the two buildings, on the north side of the street where you are walking, is no. 48, now Fitrite shoes, which from 1900 to 1908 was **㉗ William Morris' cycle-repair business**. You can read a brief tribute on the glass of the door. A cycling enthusiast who held seven speed championships, Morris had launched his cycle-repair business at the age of sixteen from his parents' house before moving to the High. He began developing motorcycles in 1901 and soon sold the bicycle business to set up Morris Garages, where initially he sold, hired and repaired cars in a purpose-built showroom at no. 21 Longwall (see above and box on page 228).

Opposite the end of the Ruskin, across Merton Street, is the **㉘ Eastgate Hotel**, built in 1900 in a style that pays tribute to a 17th-century coaching inn known as the Flying Horse that stood on the site. Depicted in the cartouche between the building's first-floor windows, the East Gate itself – demolished in 1771 – straddled the High at this point.

Cross the road and return up the other side, crossing again at the junction with Queen's Lane. Though ㉙ **The Queen's College**, which stands on the corner, is usually closed to the public, you can often glimpse the classical buildings of the Front Quadrangle by climbing the steps and looking through the gateway. Topped by a cupola sheltering a statue of Queen Caroline, consort of George II, who financed the rebuilding of the college in the first half of the 18th century, the entrance and screen wall facing the High were designed by Nicholas Hawksmoor, who also worked extensively at All Souls (see below).

Established in 1341 to accommodate a Provost and eighteen fellows as well as a number of 'poor boys' (the first undergraduates specifically mentioned in the statutes of an Oxford college), Queen's retains several eccentric traditions linked to founder Robert de Eglesfield. For instance, the annual 'Boar's Head Gaudy' – initially for students from Cumberland and Westmoreland, Eglesfield's home counties, who could not get home for Christmas – commemorates a heroic student who fought off an angry boar by thrusting a work of Aristotle down its throat and then brought it back to college to be cooked. During the 'Needle and Thread Gaudy', the bursar presents each guest with a needle and thread (*aiguille* and *fil*, a pun on Eglesfield) and exhorts them to be thrifty in mending their gowns. Alumni and college members include playwright Thomas Middleton, astronomer Edmond Halley, critic Walter Pater, and more recently comedian Rowan Atkinson, neurologist Oliver Sacks and World Wide Web inventor Tim Berners-Lee.

Almost opposite The Queen's College, and also usually closed to the public, is ㉚ **University College**, rumoured to have been founded by Alfred the Great but in fact established by former Archbishop of Rouen William of Durham, who is said to have led a group of rioting Parisian students to Oxford. Set up in 1249, it is one of the three oldest

Oxford colleges (along with Merton and Balliol). Alumni and college members include politicians Clement Attlee, Bill Clinton, Bob Hawke and Harold Wilson; writers Armando Iannucci, C. S. Lewis, Andrew Motion, V. S. Naipaul and Percy Bysshe Shelley; actors Warren Mitchell and Michael York; and physicist Stephen Hawking.

The long street frontage stretching from Logic Lane, which the college owns, dates from the 17th and early 18th centuries: above the main gateway is a statue of benefactor Queen Anne. At the western end of the site is a plaque marking the location of the house and physic garden where apothecary **Robert Boyle** (1627–91) discovered the law that states the inversely proportional relationship between the volume and pressure of a gas. He was assisted by Robert Hooke (1635–1703), later to identify biological cells, design new types of telescopes and microscopes and work with Christopher Wren on rebuilding London after the Great Fire of 1666.

What looks from the outside like a low-level domed observatory now houses the Shelley Memorial, a sculpture of 1892 by Edward Onslow Ford depicting the naked poet, washed up dead on the Italian seashore, resting on a marble slab. Shelley (1792–1822) was expelled from the college in 1811 for writing a pamphlet called 'The Necessity for Atheism'.

A little further along on the opposite side of the street is the entrance to All Souls.

All Souls
High Street, OX1 4AL
www.asc.ox.ac.uk
Open Monday to Friday, 14–16,
except over Christmas, Easter and August

All Souls was founded in 1438 by Henry Chichele, Archbishop of Canterbury and ambassador to Henrys IV, V and VI, for the study of law and theology as well as to train an 'unarmed militia' to serve Church and country, not least by praying daily for the souls of the founder and those who had died in the recent Hundred Years' War (the college's full name is 'The College of All Souls of the Faithful Departed, of Oxford'). Essentially a research institution, All Souls has no undergraduates but only a warden and fellows – according to Jan Morris, writing in 1978, its members 'need not do anything at all... though they are mildly expected to dine in college sometimes, sleep in the bed that awaits them there, and be looked after by a college scout'. The buildings fronting the High – a two-storey range with a castellated gateway – as well as the rest of the ㉜ **Front Quadrangle** date mostly from 1438–43: the alternation of two-light and single-light windows indicates the original juxtaposition of sleeping quarters shared by two fellows with smaller individual study spaces.

Opposite the entrance and topped by a fine set of crocketed pinnacles is the ㉝ **chapel**, in which the fellows fulfilled their daily duty of prayer. As at New College, where Chichele

41

had studied and on which All Souls is modelled, there is an antechapel with two pairs of soaring gothic arches: some of the delicately drawn stained glass here dates back to the mid-15th century. A heavily gilded baroque reredos, designed in 1716 by court painter James Thornhill (who was also working at nearby Blenheim Palace), divides the antechapel from the chancel with its original hammer-beam roof – the first of its kind in Oxford – decorated with gilded angels. The reredos was destroyed during the Reformation and as at New College it was remodelled in the 1870s to designs by George Gilbert Scott, with at least one of its figures based on a contemporary college member: in stance and features, these are romantic Victorian evocations of knights and noblemen rather than medieval crusaders. The colouring of the original medieval reredos can be detected behind some of the heads.

Emerge through an arcade into the impressive **❸❹ North Quadrangle**, built in 1716–34 in characteristically idiosyncratic style by Nicholas Hawksmoor at the request of fellows who resented the cramped conditions of their 15th-century quarters. Oxford diarist Thomas Hearne describes the members of All Souls at the time as 'persons of great fortunes and high birth and of little morals and less learning': certainly Christopher Codrington, who financed the magnificent library that mirrors the chapel and adjacent hall, made his fortune from a West Indian sugar plantation, as a plaque at the entrance acknowledges. The sundial at its centre, designed in 1658 by alumnus Christopher Wren, was said to be so accurate that Oxford watchmakers set their watches by it.

Hawksmoor's intention was to create a dramatic public space with views of the new Radcliffe Square. Certainly his gatetower with its pineapple-topped dome as well as the two soaring towers in the eastern range offer unsettling juxtapositions of elements and disturb the sense of scale.

Turn right up **Catte Street**. At the back of the University Church, in a vaulted chamber dating from the 1320s, is an excellent café, the Vaults & Garden.

In addition to his work on All Souls (visible through an iron gateway on the right side of Catte Street if you have not visited the college), Nicholas Hawksmoor was initially engaged as architect of the iconic ㉟ **Radcliffe Camera** or Radcliffe Library, endowed by Dr John Radcliffe (1650–1715), a *bon viveur* and physician to Queen Anne who frequently boasted about how little medical theory he had read. The fortune Radcliffe left was allegedly amassed through the strategy of rejecting patients who seemed terminally ill so as not to damage his reputation for healing as well as advocating fresh air, good diet and exercise rather than medical intervention in an age when so-called cures were as likely to kill.

Hawksmoor conceived the building as the centrepiece of a new academic area he referred to as the Forum Universitatis. Following his death in 1736, the library was completed by his assistant James Gibbs, who was allowed to make only stylistic alterations to the concept of a circular structure with an open colonnade at ground level, topped by a reading room (the *camera*) with a high domed ceiling and an arcade running around its perimeter with bookshelves on the outer face. Drawing on his training in Italy (whose architecture Hawksmoor knew only from books), Gibbs embellished the original design, making it lighter, more sculpturally expressive and more playfully baroque. The ground-floor colonnade was enclosed in 1862.

Continue up Catte Street to ❸❻ **Hertford College** (usually closed to the public) on the right, recognisable by the carving of a deer (or hart) on the shield above the door: together with the three other colleges that feature a stag as part of their crest (Magdalen, Lincoln and Jesus) members of Hertford meet annually to feast on venison. Hertford was founded in 1740 on the site of the medieval Hart Hall but most of its present buildings date from its expansion by Thomas Graham Jackson around the turn of the 20th century.

Evelyn Waugh attended from 1922–24, leaving without a degree after a career marked by flamboyantly drunken behaviour, intense homosexual affairs and a bitter feud with his history tutor. Nevertheless, he immortalised the college in his novel *Brideshead Revisited* (1945) and several scenes from the 1981 TV adaptation starring Jeremy Irons were filmed here, some in Waugh's own rooms. Other famous alumni and college members include authors John Donne, Jonathan Swift and Gavin Maxwell; philosopher Thomas Hobbes; Harlem Renaissance figurehead Alain Locke; politicians Henry Pelham and Charles James Fox; and TV presenter Fiona Bruce.

Opposite Hertford is the **37** **gateway to the Bodleian Library** (open Monday–Saturday, 9–17; Sunday, 11–17), its massive oak door embellished with the crests of the colleges in existence when the library was established in 1602 by Thomas Bodley, a diplomat at the court of Elizabeth I. Bodley had grown rich by marrying the widow of a wealthy pilchard merchant (you can see Bodley's initials among comical masks above the main window on the Catte Street frontage). Second in size only to the British Library and in possession of some 13 million books, the Bodleian has been entitled to a copy of every work published in the UK since its founder made an agreement to that effect with the Stationers Company in 1610. No works are lent out to readers (both Charles I and Oliver Cromwell had requests politely refused) and anyone using the facilities still has to swear an oath not to 'bring into the Library or kindle therein any fire or flame'.

Since its inception in the mid-15th century in a single chamber built above the Divinity School (see below) to house books donated by Humfrey,

Duke of Gloucester (younger brother of Henry V), and the major expansion initiated by Bodley after most of this bequest was destroyed or dispersed by the Dean of Christ Church following the Reformation, the library's premises have gradually expanded through the acquisition of the Radcliffe Camera in the mid-19th century, underground vaults dug beneath Radcliffe Square in 1909–12 and the construction of the Weston Library in the 1930s (see below). Access to the Schools Quadrangle is free; a kiosk at the entrance sells tickets for guided tours and self-guided tours offering access to the Divinity School.

The **38** **Schools Quadrangle**, built in the 1610s in an essentially gothic style with a strikingly pinnacled and castellated roofline and extravagant gatetower, is one of Oxford's most impressive spaces. The western range opposite the gatetower (the Proscholium), with the entrance to the library at its centre, took its delicate network of blind arcading (as well as its flamboyant roofline) from the pre-existing Divinity School, which it adjoins at right angles: inside, the library on the first floor was the first in England to have shelves arranged floor to ceiling against its walls, with the upper levels accessed from galleries. The other ranges around the quad were conceived by Bodley to provide 'better built scholes... than those ruinous little rooms' that had previously served for lectures and examinations. The ground-floor halls (moving clockwise from the gateway) were to contain the schools of Logic, Music, Natural Philosophy, Moral Philosophy, Grammar & History, and Metaphysics, with Astronomy, Rhetoric, Anatomy & Medicine, Law, Greek, and Arithmetic & Geometry above: the names of the schools are given in Latin above their entrances. The third storey was originally intended for the display of the Bodleian's many portraits, making it the first public art gallery in Britain.

47

In front of the Proscholium stands a swaggering statue of the third Earl of Pembroke, one of the complex's chief benefactors, cast by Hubert Le Sueur from a portrait by Rubens and presented to the University by the subject's great-nephew: allegedly the two mistrustful scholars who accepted the gift at dinner at the family seat in Wiltshire took the head with them back to Oxford the next morning, leaving the body to follow later, as you can see from the cut mark above the ruff. The gatetower opposite, its upper storeys built to safeguard the University's financial deposits, features a statue of James I presenting a copy of his collected writings to a woman representing the University (where, of course, women were still unable to study) with an allegory of Fame blowing his (own) trumpet. Known as the Tower of the Five Orders, it has columns rising through the orders of Tuscan, Doric, Ionic and Corinthian to Composite, offering an easily digestible lesson in architectural history.

Exit the quadrangle to the north (opposite the Clarendon Building, see below) and turn left to find the **❸❾ Divinity School**, begun in the 1420s as a single-storey building where theology was taught and examined, with an upper floor added to house the library of Humfrey, Duke of Gloucester. A masterpiece of late gothic, it has the pinnacles and castellation echoed in the later ranges surrounding the Schools Quadrangle and a façade made up almost entirely of glazing set into delicate tracery. Christopher Wren added the central doorway in 1669 (you can see his initials above it) to create a ceremonial route for new graduates, who still leave the Sheldonian Theatre by a side door, wearing their commoners' gowns, don new gowns and hats in Convocation House (where the University's ruling body originally met) adjoining the Divinity School, then process through the Divinity School to the door of the Sheldonian opposite, entering the theatre to thunderous applause. The bizarre ceremony during which students kneel before the vice-chancellor to be bumped on the head with a Bible is depicted on a plaque on the façade of the Examination Schools (see above).

Inside, the Divinity School's chief wonder is its exquisite stone-vaulted roof, studded with 455 carved bosses bearing the arms or

initials of University officers and donors – in effect a library of calling cards for Oxford's 15th-century great and good. The space was used as the Hogwarts infirmary, with the room above featuring as the 'restricted' section of the school library (where Harry is caught by caretaker Filch) in the film of *Harry Potter and the Philosopher's Stone*.

Also by Wren, the **40 Sheldonian Theatre** is not a theatre at all but was built as a secular space to celebrate the success of members of the University after Archbishop Laud (1573–1645) objected to the disrespectful and often blasphemous speeches given at ceremonies in the University Church. Designed two decades after Laud's execution on unproved charges of treason, this was Wren's first major work, a not entirely successful D-shaped building based on the Theatre of Marcellus in Rome (which the architect knew only from pictures), with a cupola added in 1838 by Edward Blore. Appropriately for Oxford's first classical building, the façade opposite the Divinity School resembles the entrance to a Palladian church, though decorated with an un-Palladian fussiness. Bizarrely, however, it is the rear of the building that faces Broad Street and offers the main entrance for visitors (self-guided and guided tours including the cupola are available; check website for opening times). Here you can discern the layout of the interior: a full-height central hall, lit by the clerestory, has a horseshoe of seating raised on tiers above the ground-level corridor that runs around the perimeter of the drum. With the foundation stone laid only four years after the Restoration of the monarchy, the royal coat of arms occupies a prominent place

above the doorway. Inside, the ceiling of the main space is painted with an allegory of learning and religion triumphant after the turmoil of the Civil War.

On plinths between the railings on Broad Street are a series of **41** **'Emperor Heads'**, variously interpreted as representing Roman emperors, the apostles, philosophers or simply herms (boundary markers topped by the head of a god). Installed when the theatre was built, they were remodelled in 1868 and again in the early 1970s by sculptor Michael Black. Each head has a different beard, and the one to the left of the stairs (viewed from the theatre) has a wren chiselled in its hair in honour of the architect.

To your right is the **42** **Clarendon Building**, a typically eccentric work designed by Hawksmoor in 1712–13 for Oxford University Press. OUP's offices had been in the roofspace of the Sheldonian with its clattering presses in the basement, so printing had to stop every time a ceremony was held. The publisher's new home – a perhaps unique example of an 18th-century baroque industrial building – was financed mainly from profits from the *History of the Great Rebellion* (1702–04) by the 1st Earl of Clarendon, whose statue – looking very pompous, with his great work literally cast in

stone – stands in the central niche on the side facing you (the west side). The flamboyant statues on the roof, some by James Thornhill, represent the muses.

Walk to the monumental central temple front and through a passageway – which once separated OUP's Learned and Bible divisions – into **Broad Street**. The even more monumental Doric portico here was to form a triumphal entrance to Hawksmoor's planned University quarter. The Clarendon Building became the University Registry when OUP moved to Walton Street in the 1820s (see page 266) and was given to the Boldeian in 1975. It is the site of most student and staff demonstrations and in 2018 the press featured much criticised images of the chalked slogan 'Happy International Women's Day' being washed off the steps by a female cleaner overseen by two male security staff.

Opposite the Clarendon Building is the fortress-like ⓭ **Weston Library**, built by Giles Gilbert Scott (grandson of George Gilbert Scott, see above) to accommodate 5 million books: it was opened in 1940 by George VI, who broke the key as he tried to get in. Conceived largely as a warehouse, with a central steel-framed book stack rising through eleven storeys (three of them underground)

wrapped by lower levels of offices, it is connected to the main Bodleian site by a tunnel under Broad Street with a conveyor belt to transport books. Much criticised for its austerity – plain masonry façades, sparsely decorated with classical and moderne motifs and pierced with a regular arrangement of mullioned windows – it was successfully remodelled in 2015 by WilkinsonEyre to open up the ground floor to the street. You can take a well-deserved break in the café in the new entrance hall with its backdrop of book stacks. ●

Visit...

Bodleian Library
Broad Street, OX1 3BG
www.bodleian.ox.ac.uk

Botanic Garden
Rose Lane, OX1 4AZ
www.obga.ox.ac.uk

Holywell Music Room
Holywell Street, OX1 3SD
www.coffeeconcerts.com

Sheldonian Theatre
Broad Street, OX1 3AZ
www.sheldonian.ox.ac.uk/visit

Weston Library
Broad Street, OX1 3BG
www.bodleian.ox.ac.uk/weston

Eat/Drink...

Bodleian Café
Weston Library,
Broad Street OX1 3BG
www.benugo.com

Edamamé
15 Holywell Street, OX1 3SA
www.edamame.co.uk

Grand Café
84 High Street, OX1 4BG
www.thegrandcafe.co.uk

Queen's Lane Coffee House
40 High Street, OX1 4AP
www.qlcoffeehouse.com

Turf Tavern
4-5 Bath Place, OX1 3SU

Vaults & Garden Café
1 Radcliffe Square, OX1 4AH
www.thevaultsandgarden.com

Jesus College

2
South of the Broad:

town & gown

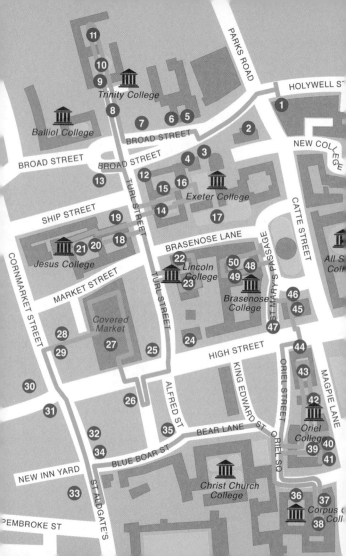

South of the Broad

1. Indian Institute
2. Clarendon Building
3. 'Emperor Heads'
4. History of Science Museum
5. Blackwell's
6. White Horse
7. Kettell Hall

Trinity College
8. Front Quadrangle
9. Chapel
10. Durham Quadrangle
11. Garden Quadrangle

12. Anthony Gormley
13. Oxfam shop

Exeter College
14. Front Quadrangle
15. Chapel
16. Palmer's Tower
17. Fellows' Garden

Jesus College
18. First Quadrangle
19. Chapel
20. Hall
21. Second Quadrangle

Lincoln College
22. First Quadrangle
23. Chapel Quadrangle

24. All Saints
25. The Mitre

26. Kemp Hall
27. Covered Market
28. Golden Cross
29. No. 3 Cornmarket
30. Carfax Tower
31. Swindlestock Tavern
32. Oxford Town Hall
33. Post Office
34. Museum of Oxford
35. Bear Inn

Corpus Christi College
36. Front Quadrangle
37. Chapel
38. Main garden

Oriel College
39. First Quadrangle
40. Hall
41. Chapel
42. Library
43. Third Quadrangle

44. Rhodes Building
45. University Church of St Mary
46. Annie Rogers
47. St Mary's Passage

Brasenose College
48. Old Quadrangle
49. Hall
50. Chapel

REET

South of the Broad: town & gown

Start: Indian Institute
Finish: Brasenose College
Distance: 1.8 miles

'There is probably not a single yard in any part of the classic High Street between St Martin's [Carfax] and St Mary's [the University Church] which has not, at one time or another, been stained with blood. There are historic battlefields where less has been spilt.'
Hastings Rashdall, *The Universities of Europe in the Middle Ages*

View south from the University Church of St Mary

Many of Britain's towns experience strained relations between their general and university populations, but perhaps none as violently or consistently as Oxford, where the colleges not only hold considerable land, property and wealth, but also benefit from a web of powerful connections that reaches far beyond the city walls. The first recorded incident in the battle between town and gown took place in 1209, when two Oxford scholars – trainee clerics, like all students at that time – were hanged by townsmen for murder: members of the University fled en masse before returning five years later after the pope intervened to impose severe financial penalties on the populace. In 1355 a brawl in a tavern at Carfax sparked the St Scholastica Day riot, in which 63 students and 30 townspeople were killed. And even as late as 1867 a battle between what the *Daily Telegraph* described as 'rough bargees and railway labourers glad to "lick a lord", and... students [ready to] thrash a cad' required military intervention.

In the 17th century even Charles I recognised that the University was 'an Ocean or Great Sea of Privilege', with rights to arrest citizens for 'noctivating' (walking the streets at night) and perhaps most importantly to hear court cases – no doubt weighted against the citizenry by being conducted largely in Latin. The University's dominance was even enshrined in its right to political representation: between 1603 and 1950 it had two MPs – elected by all Oxford graduates, wherever they lived – to the town's one.

Starting in Broad Street (known as the Broad), this walk visits strongholds of both town and gown, including Carfax, the Town Hall and the former courts of justice on the one hand and on the other the University Church of St Mary and several colleges. Whatever time of year or day you choose, it is inevitable that colleges will be closed: information is given about each in the hope that you will be able to access some of them, and even if the 'closed to visitors' signs are up, it's always worth asking at the porter's lodge. If you are lucky enough to be spoiled for choice, Exeter, Corpus Christi and Oriel are top recommendations, followed closely by Brasenose and Trinity.

The walk starts at the former ❶ **Indian Institute** on the corner of Catte Street and Holywell Street. The institute was founded in the late 19th century with support from Queen Victoria, several Indian princes and the colonial authorities to further Indian scholarship through the establishment of a museum, lecture theatres and a library. With insufficient funding for upkeep, however, the programme was soon reduced and 30 years later a collection of rotting taxidermy and artefacts was donated to the Pitt Rivers Museum (see page 138). In the 1970s – to accusations of racism from the Oxford Student Union and protests from the Indian government – the building was given to the University Modern History Faculty. It now houses the Oxford Martin School, founded by technology guru James Martin with the largest single donation ever made to the University to foster cross-disciplinary research into global issues.

Designed by Basil Champneys, architect of the Rhodes Building (see page 98), the institute was completed in 1896: its original purpose can be guessed from Indian-inspired detailing such as the frieze of water buffalo, lions and elephants on the turret at first-floor level and the elephant weather vane that tops the Mughal-style dome. On the left, just inside the porch, you can still see a brass plate proclaiming in Sanskrit and English that the building was inaugurated by the 'High-Minded Heir Apparent Albert Edward, Son of the Empress of India' with the hope that 'the learning and literature of India be ever held in honour'.

Formerly known as Horsemonger Street and once the site of Oxford's horse market, **Broad Street** itself – like Holywell Street (see page 19) – was developed in the 1600s, a time of rapid expansion for the city. Like Holywell Street too, it runs alongside the site of the ditch outside the former city wall, much of whose stone was used to build its houses.

Walk along Broad Street past the ❷ **Clarendon Building** with its monumental temple-front portico, designed in 1712–13 by Nicholas Hawksmoor to house the offices and printing presses of Oxford University Press. The ❸ **'Emperor Heads'** between the railings in front of the neighbouring Sheldonian Theatre, built by Christopher Wren in 1669 to host University ceremonies, were installed when the theatre was completed: they have been variously interpreted as apostles, Roman emperors, philosophers or simply herms (boundary markers topped by the head of a god). For more information on both of these, see pages 50 to 51.

Behind the final four heads stands the ❹ **History of Science Museum** (open Tuesday to Sunday, 12–17), designed in 1679 by master-mason Thomas Wood (who was responsible for the carving on the Sheldonian) with rooms for scientific teaching and research at ground level and a museum – the original Ashmolean – above. The funding for what was probably Europe's first public museum came from astronomer and alchemist Elias Ashmole, who had been accused of appropriating the renowned collection of botanist John Tradescant the Younger through a fraudulent will (Tradescant's widow Hester claimed her husband had signed the document unread when drunk; after Ashmole moved in next door, she was found drowned in the garden pond). Much of the collection was transferred to the new University Museum of Natural History (see page 135) in the 1860s and the rest to the new Ashmolean; the History of Science Museum was built up from a collection of scientific instruments donated in 1924 by Lewis Evans, son of Arthur Evans, archeologist and inspirational keeper of the Ashmolean for a quarter of a century from 1884.

The museum frontage on Broad Street is domestic in scale and feel: as with the Clarendon and Sheldonian, the grand entrance faces away from the public thoroughfare. To find it, walk through the small arched gateway at the museum's eastern end, where a palatial porch with paired Corinthian columns supports a curved pediment, above which are beautifully carved stone panels. The aged stone wall topped with urns adjoining the museum to the south is the boundary of Exeter (see below).

Cross the road to ❺ **Blackwell's** at 48–51 Broad Street, founded in 1879 by Benjamin Henry Blackwell – not a University man, but the son of the city's first public librarian. The original shop – only 3.5 metres square – has now expanded to include the largest bookselling room in the world, the Norrington Room, excavated below the quadrangle of Trinity College in the 1960s. Enter through the Recent Fiction department and follow signs that take you down a narrow staircase to a space like a gladiatorial arena, with a series of tiers descending to a central stage where the ancient discipline of philosophy faces off against gender studies. Furnished with battered leather chairs, the Norrington is a haven for both bibliophiles and people-watchers, with customers ranging from solitary scholars with long reading lists to chatting couples and excited children.

Between the shop's book and music divisions is the ❻ **White Horse**, one of Oxford's oldest pubs (and reputedly male-only until 1973), made more famous recently as a location for several episodes of the *Inspector Morse* TV series, based on the books by local author Colin Dexter. The stone house next door is ❼ **Kettell Hall**, built in 1620 to house undergraduates by Trinity president Ralph Kettell, whose strategy for maintaining good relations between town and gown was to provide 'excellent beer, not better to be had in Oxon', ensuring his students got drunk only on college premises. No doubt Morse would have approved.

Trinity College

Broad Street, OX1 3BH

www.trinity.ox.ac.uk

Open daily, 10.30–12 and 13–16

Trinity College was founded in 1555 by devout Catholic Thomas Pope to ensure his soul would be prayed for by its members: having accumulated considerable wealth when in charge of the estates of monasteries dissolved during the Reformation, he perhaps felt he needed some insurance in the afterlife. The site, with its extensive gardens, originally accommodated Durham College, established in the late 13th century for students from Durham's Benedictine cathedral priory. Alumni and college members include Cardinal (now Saint) John Henry Newman; politicians Anthony Crosland, William Pitt the Elder, Sian Berry, Jacob Rees-Mogg and Jeremy Thorpe; art historian Kenneth Clarke; and writers Patrick Cockburn and Terence Rattigan.

Unusually, the ❽ **Front Quadrangle** can be seen through magnificent wrought-iron entrance gates. The buildings to the left (west), including a polychromatic chapel designed by William Butterfield in the 1850s, belong to neighbouring Balliol. To the east stands a range of student accommodation built in the 1880s – along with the president's lodging to the north – by the University's most prolific architect, Thomas Graham Jackson: the neo-Jacobean façades have an eclectic wealth of elements (Tudor chimneys, fussily decorated Dutch gables, Renaissance doorways flanked by fluted columns) crammed together at reduced scale.

Luckily Jackson's plans to demolish the row of cottages that form the Broad Street frontage and now contain the porter's lodge – dating from 1680 but entirely rebuilt in 1970 – were frustrated by objections from, among others, artist William Morris, who claimed they were 'in their way as important as the more majestic buildings to which all the world makes pilgrimage'. Trinity's ❾ chapel, next to the president's lodging, was the first in Oxford to be built using classical principles: on completion in 1694 it became a famous tourist attraction, even making it on to the itinerary of Tsar Peter the Great, and it is still considered to be the best piece of late-17th-century ecclesiastical architecture in Oxford.

Designed by an unknown architect, the chapel was perhaps influenced by Wren's newly completed Sheldonian: certainly Wren was consulted on details such as the windows and cornice and is said to have contributed the idea for the urns on the parapet, with their dynamic copper flames. The baroque interior includes an exquisitely carved wooden screen with putti on the antechapel side and fruit and flowers within; a ceiling painting of the Ascension surrounded by delicately moulded plasterwork; and behind the altar a simple marquetry sunburst framed by carvings of fruit and flowers said to be by Grinling Gibbons.

To the left of the altar is the tomb of Thomas Pope (the only founder's tomb within an Oxford college); to the right is an alcove that allowed the president's wife, formerly the only woman in college, to worship in private, protected by what are said to be Oxford's first sash windows.

Beyond the chapel is the ❿ Durham Quadrangle, with the old library, a remnant of the original Durham College dating to 1421, on the right.

The ⓫ Garden Quadrangle beyond consists of a north range (facing you as you enter) designed by Wren in the 1660s as a freestanding residential building: the mirroring structure to the west was added soon afterwards and the blocks were given a third storey in the early 1800s. From here you can access the extensive college gardens.

Return to Broad Street and take a moment to admire the wonderfully eclectic, brightly painted façades of the buildings on its south side, mostly dating from the early to mid-1700s.

On the roof of the single conspicuously 20th-century block – built in 1964 as accommodation for Exeter College, with Blackwell's Art & Poster Shop at street level – is a 2-metre-tall bronze statue by ⑫ **Anthony Gormley**. This was installed in 2009, in the face of objections to its nudity by local councillors who had presumably never visited an art gallery.

Continue walking west, crossing the road to look at no. 17, the world's first ⑬ **Oxfam shop**, established in 1947. Oxfam began life as the Oxford Committee for Famine Relief, launched in 1942 by a group of Quakers, social activists and academics in protest at the British government policy of preventing food supplies from reaching starving citizens in German-occupied Europe, in particular Greece. A green plaque to the left of the window commemorates the shop's opening and a blue plaque to Oxfam co-founder Cecil Jackson-Cole (1901–79) sits on the façade.

Return along the street to Blackwell's Art & Poster Shop and turn right down **Turl Street** (The Turl), its name allegedly derived from the twirling gate that until 1722 punctuated the city wall at the junction with Ship Street. As long as you don't mind being the only customer without a laptop, the Turl Street Kitchen on the right makes a good pitstop: profits support the Oxford Hub, founded in 2007 to connect and help students to engage in social action and volunteering.

Turl Street

Further down the street on the left is the entrance to Exeter.

Exeter College

Turl Street, OX1 3DP

www.exeter.ox.ac.uk

Open daily, 14–17 – if the door is closed within these hours, try pushing it open and asking at the porter's lodge

Founded in 1314 by Bishop of Exeter Walter de Stapledon, the college suffered two centuries of poverty before being generously re-endowed in 1556 by alumnus William Petre, who had managed to survive as secretary of state to Henry VIII, Edward VI, Mary I and Elizabeth I. More recent alumni and college members include writers Tariq Ali, Martin Amis, Alan Bennett, Imogen Stubbs, J. R. R. Tolkien and Will Self; artists William Morris and Edward Burne-Jones; actor Richard Burton; broadcasters Russell Harty and Ned Sherrin; and athlete Roger Bannister. Unsurprisingly, Exeter was the model for Jordan College in alumnus Philip Pullman's *Northern Lights* trilogy (1995–2000).

Exeter's 17th-century street frontage was remodelled in the 1830s. But below the parapet beyond the gatetower is a much more recent addition: running north to south are bosses of a marigold, archer, roundel, eye of God, lion, yew and Neptune; then the date 1993; then bells, a unicorn, lamb & flag, espiscopal crozier and rector. Together (in a typically coded Oxford tribute) their initials form the name of literary critic Marilyn Butler (1937–2014), rector from 1993 to 2004 and the first female head of any Oxbridge college.

The ⑭ **Front Quadrangle** is where Morse suffered his fatal heart attack in the TV adaptation of *The Remorseful Day* (2000). The hall on the right (south) dates from 1618 but the space is dominated by the magnificent ⑮ **chapel** opposite, designed in the 1850s by George Gilbert Scott and funded in part through the sacrifice of a year's salary by each of the college's fellows. Inspired by the 13th-century gothic Saint-Chapelle in Paris, the exterior has full-height buttresses topped by statues of saints alternating with lofty windows with geometric tracery. Inside is a single space with soaring fan vaulting interspersed with somewhat lurid stained glass; a series of byzantine mosaics form the backdrop to the altar. To the right of the chancel, the medieval romanticism of Scott's source is complemented by a sentimental if skilful tapestry designed in 1890 by Morris and Burne-Jones that recasts the characters of the Adoration of the Magi as Pre-Raphaelite 'stunners'. On the left inside the door is a bust of Tolkien, who was an undergraduate here from 1911 to 1915.

Back in the quadrangle, at the far (east) end of the chapel is **16 Palmer's Tower**, a gatehouse of 1432 (named after the rector at the time) that once formed part of the city wall. Walk through it to see the vaulted ceiling with painted angels and arrive in the Margery Quadrangle, where you find the other side of the Blackwell's Art & Poster Shop building, designed with the rest of the quad in 1964 by architect and planner Lionel Brett, 4th Viscount Esher.

The true glory of Exeter, however, is the **17 Fellows' Garden** accessed through a door marked by a discreet wooden sign near the centre of the range opposite the entrance. (Again, do not be afraid to push the door open.) The secluded space – a central grassy area surrounded by a curved path with a meander at one end based on Hogarth's line of beauty – recalls the history of the colleges as monastic retreats as well as exemplifying the privileged environment enjoyed by present-day students. Walk to the far end – past Scott's castellated and crocketed library, where you can glimpse fan vaulting similar to that of the chapel through the screens of glazing – climb the stairs and keep walking clockwise for breathtaking views of the Radcliffe Camera and University Church.

Almost opposite Exeter across the Turl is the entrance to Jesus College.

Jesus College
Turl Street, OX13DW
www.jesus.ox.ac.uk
Open daily, 14–16.30

Jesus College was established in 1571 as Oxford's first Protestant college and is the only one founded in the long reign of Elizabeth I. Though the queen accepted the honorary title of founder and her portrait dominates the hall, Jesus was in fact funded by Welsh clergyman Hugh Price – and the vast majority of its subsequent principals have been Welsh. Alumni and college members include T. E. Lawrence (Lawrence of Arabia); politicians Norman Washington Manley (former president of Jamaica), Pixley ka Isaka Seme (founder of the ANC) and Harold Wilson; broadcaster Magnus Magnusson; and college administrator Nancy Wilson.

Part of Jesus' austere Turl Street frontage dates from the mid-16th century, though it was extensively remodelled in the 18th and 19th. Above the gothic main doorway are the Prince of Wales feathers and to the right is the college arms of three stags on a green background. Just inside (where you might expect a doormat) is a plaque informing us that 'the first women to study at Jesus College crossed this threshold in 1974'.

The charmingly irregular ⑱ **First Quadrangle** was built largely in the early 1600s, with the castellated parapet added a century later.

The modest ⑲ **chapel** on the right was remodelled by George Edmund Street in the mid-19th century, though the barrel-vaulted roof, screen and pulpit are all 17th century. A bust of T. E. Lawrence lurks behind the door of the antechapel; to the right of the altar is Guido Reni's *St Michael Overcoming Satan*. The principal's lodging beyond the chapel is distinguished by a richly ornamented shell hood above the doorway, added in about 1700; the rooms inside are said to have set a new standard in luxury for accommodation for heads of colleges.

Opposite the main entrance is the ⑳ **hall**, one of the first to have a chimney breast rather than a central hearth. Welsh dragons feature on the elaborately carved Jacobean screen and the plasterwork above the high table; among many portraits, the only woman (apart from Elizabeth I) is historian Felicity Heal.

The uniform ㉑ **Second Quadrangle**, its Dutch gables like rows of dragons' teeth, was built between 1646 and 1713.

Continue along Turl Street to the entrance to Lincoln.

Lincoln College
Turl Street, OX1 3DR
www. lincoln.ox.ac.uk
Open 14–16, weekends 11–17

Lincoln was founded in 1427 by Richard Fleming, then Bishop of Lincoln, as a 'little college of true students of theology who would defend the mysteries of Scripture against those ignorant laymen who profane with swinish snouts its most holy pearls'. Intended as a bastion of Catholicism against the Lollards – followers of John Wycliffe (*c.* 1320–84) who railed against the papacy, the veneration of saints, requiem masses and monasticism among other sacred tenets – three centuries later Lincoln was to welcome as a fellow John Wesley (1703–1791), founder of Methodism and another rebel against the established Church. Other alumni and college members include writers John Le Carré, William Davenant, Dr Seuss and Edward Thomas; physician and Oxford benefactor John Radcliffe; and scientist Howard Florey.

Even if the college is closed to visitors, the entrance in the castellated gatetower – rebuilt like the rest of the Turl Street frontage in the early 19th century – is often open to reveal the intimate **㉒ Front Quadrangle**, its original 15th-century buildings largely intact and now covered in Virginia creeper. The quadrangle forms the end point of the annual Ascension Day 'beating the bounds' ritual, in which clergy and parishioners re-mark the boundaries of the parishes of St Michael at the Northgate and the University Church of St Mary by chalking on the remaining boundary stones (including one that stands near the lifts inside Marks & Spencer). A connecting door between Lincoln and Brasenose is opened for only ten minutes, with Brasenose students offered a free glass of homebrew in recompense for the long-ago murder by a town mob of a Brasenose student refused sanctuary by the Lincoln porter.

Inside the Front Quadrangle, in a niche on the wall to the right (south), is a bust of Wesley; above the door to the hall, to the left of the range opposite the entrance, is the grotesquely grinning Lincoln imp, a replica of the original designed in 1899 by Thomas Graham Jackson after a figure in Lincoln cathedral. In the hall, which dates from 1437, is an open timber roof, well preserved early 18th-century panelling and an elaborately carved stone fireplace surround with the initials of the college founders.

The **㉓ Chapel Quadrangle** (entered through an arch in the south range) dates from the early 17th century. A plaque on the Turl Street range to the right marks the rooms thought to have

been occupied by Wesley from 1726: it was here, in conjunction with a group of like-minded University members known as the Holy Club, that he formulated the tenets of Methodism, named to reflect the order within its disciples' lives.

The chapel (opposite the entrance to the quad) has a fine cedarwood screen, a barrel-vaulted ceiling adorned with gilded emblems and on the front pews beautifully carved statues (dating from 1680) of St Peter and St Paul and the four apostles, as well as the pulpit Wesley preached from. The glorious painted windows, installed when the chapel was built in 1629, are the work of Flemish master Abraham van Linge.

Continue down Turl Street towards the **High Street**. At the corner on the left is the Lincoln College library, housed since the 1970s in the former church of **㉔ All Saints**, built in the first decade of the 18th century possibly to designs by Henry Aldrich, dean of Christ Church. The rusticated tower is topped by a steeple based on Wren's St Mary-le-Bow with elements contributed by Hawksmoor. The front and rear of the building mirror each other with high arched windows topped by a clerestory and pedimented porches flanked by Corinthian columns.

㉕ The Mitre, opposite the library across Turl Street, has been owned by Lincoln since 1475: it takes its name from the college founder's headgear, displayed prominently above the High Street entrance in a façade that dates from 1631. Once an important coaching inn, with services running daily to London, Bristol and Bath, since 1969 its upper floors have been student accommodation. In *Gaudy Night* (1935) Dorothy L. Sayers has her hero Lord Peter Wimsey stay at the Mitre while helping mystery writer Harriet Vane – visiting her old college (based on Somerville, which Sayers attended from 1912–15) – to solve a crime involving poison-pen letters. At the end of the book she accepts his marriage proposal – given in Latin, of course ('Placetne Magistra') – in New College Lane.

Continue walking west along the High, pausing to admire the ornate façade of no. 126 (Bubbleology) on the other side of the

25

street: the first-floor window is a rare survival of a glazing pattern fashionable in 17th-century Oxford known as an Ipswich window. Cross the road and follow signs down an alley to the Chiang Mai Kitchen, located in **㉖ Kemp Hall**. One of a number of important dwellings off the High sited on garden plots, with no formal street frontage, this impressive (and impressively well-preserved) house was built for alderman William Boswell in 1637 (the date is carved above the front door). From 1870 until the completion of the new Town Hall and police headquarters in St Aldate's 30 years later (see below), Kemp Hall served as a police station, with a library and offices on the ground floor, a dormitory for fourteen constables above and three lock-up cells: until 1937 the alley was known as Blue Lamp Alley. The premises have been a restaurant since 1928, with a stint as La Sorbonne, employing chef Raymond Blanc in the early 1970s. The interior still has its original layout, with domestic-scale rooms, heavy wooden beams and stone fireplaces – as well as excellent Thai food.

Return to the High Street and take a moment to look at the stripped-back classical façade of the **㉗ Covered Market** opposite, designed in 1774 by John Gwynn, a civil engineer who was also responsible for Magdalen Bridge. A response to the University and town's common project to clear 'messy and unsavoury stalls' from the streets around Carfax, by 1794 the market housed 40 stalls for butchers (moved from Butcher's Row in nearby Queen Street), 40 for poultry, bacon, eggs and cheese, and a large area for fruit and vegetables; subsequently fishmongers moved in from part of St Aldate's known as Fish Street. Initially the roofed stalls were connected by open walkways, with the present timber roofing and clerestory windows added in the late 19th century. Cross the road, enter through one of the four doorways and wander.

To continue the walk, exit to the west, signposted Golden Cross. (If you find yourself disorientated, return to the High Street, turn right into Cornmarket Street at Carfax and Golden Cross is on your right.)

The site of a 12th-century coaching inn, **28 Golden Cross** forms a surprisingly tranquil retreat from the often uncomfortable bustle of the area. The two-storey range to the north (on your right if you have your back to Pizza Express) was built in the late 15th century and still has its original oriel windows; the three-storey range opposite with the gabled bays was rebuilt in the 17th century; the flat-fronted, pink-painted building housing the entrance to Pizza Express dates from the early 19th century. It is well worth buying a coffee at Pizza Express (or just asking to look inside). Above the entrance in the main building is a room with finely carved wooden panelling and a frieze of fruit and flowers. But to find a truly extraordinary interior, walk all the way through to the upper floor of Golden Cross' 15th-century range where you'll find alarmingly leaning walls, low wooden beams, original fireplaces and – best of all – several sections of early 16th-century wall painting with strange hybrid creatures, some with animal heads and naked human breasts, surrounded by elaborate arabesques.

The Oxford Movement

On 14 July 1833 John Keble, a fellow of Oriel and author of *The Christian Year*, a phenomenally popular book of devotional verses, preached a sermon on 'National Apostasy' at the University Church of St Mary. The unlikely trigger was parliamentary legislation to reduce the number of bishoprics in Ireland. But Keble saw this interference in the prerogatives of the Church as a symptom of a nation and institution in crisis: the state acting as though it were superior to the Church.

An informal group of young fellows (notably John Henry Newman, centre, and Edward Pusey, centre left) formed around the slightly older Keble (centre right) at Oriel, setting out their views in a series of *Tracts for the Times* – hence their nickname of Tractarians. Among other things, these polemical texts attacked doctrinal liberalism, lack of attention to the Church's heritage and political threats to its pre-eminence (including disestablishmentarianism, the separation of Church and state). Tractarianism was often seen as the antithesis of the contemporary Evangelical movement, but in fact the two had much in common, particularly the insistence on the importance of preaching and the idea that religion affected every aspect of life.

Over a period of just eight years 90 tracts were published, increasingly asserting the importance of Anglicanism's Catholic heritage, the beauty of ritual in worship and personal holiness. The tracts were seen both as attacks on the dignity of the established Church and on established authority itself.

Their effect was amplified by Newman's genius as a preacher, delivering sermons with the zeal of a prophet from the pulpit of St Mary's. Unsurprisingly, the University authorities were keen to disassociate themselves from the controversy.

The final tract of 1841, written by Newman, argued that nothing in the Church of England's Thirty-nine Articles of Religion – which members of the University had to accept, effectively barring the institution to Jews, Roman Catholics and Dissenters – was in fact contrary to the Council of Trent, which had defined Catholic doctrine in reaction to the Reformation. This was too much for the University: no more tracts were produced and in 1842 Newman left Oxford, converting to Roman Catholicism in 1845 (and achieving sainthood in February 2019).

His withdrawal from the city weakened the Oxford Movement, and his conversion to Roman Catholicism effectively signalled its end. However, by this time its concerns had become a national phenomenon, encouraging new interest in liturgical practice and church architecture, notably in the work of Augustus Welby Pugin, also a Catholic convert. Looking back to a golden age of the English Church, Pugin promoted gothic as the only proper style for churches.

Although the Oxford Movement faded away, Pusey, Newman's lieutenant, continued to promote its High Church ideals, founding Keble College in 1870 following the relaxation of rules governing students' religion. Like the Tractarians, Pusey's followers had a lasting influence on the Church of England, with the adoption of a range of Catholic practices including confession and the rise of ritualism – granting the Oxford Movement a kind of afterlife.

Emerge on to **Cornmarket Street** and turn left. Next door, ㉙ **no. 3** (currently occupied by Vodaphone) is a timber-framed 16th-century building with a smart 18th-century front. This is the former Crown Tavern, run from the 1590s until 1614 by John Davenant. It is known that Shakespeare stayed here on visits to Oxford and was the godfather (some say father) of John's son William, who became a playwright. Painted rooms on the upper floors, managed by the Oxford Preservation Trust, are occasionally open to visitors.

Continue down Cornmarket Street to Carfax, Oxford's city-centre crossroads, taking its name from the Latin *quadrifurcus* (four forks) or French *carrefours* (four ways). ㉚ **Carfax Tower** (open daily, November to February, 10–15; March and October, 10–16; April to September, 10–17) is all that remains of St Martin's church – the official City Church used for civic ceremonies and the burial site of many mayors, in rivalry with the University Church of St Mary. The body of the original 12th-century building, which stretched from the present tower towards the High, was demolished in 1820 when it became unstable; its replacement was pulled down in 1896 to improve traffic flow. Plans to heighten and embellish the 14th-century tower to rival the spires of the University were rejected and it was restored less flamboyantly by the ubiquitous Thomas Graham Jackson, who moved the door from west to east, turning the tower back to front, and added the feeble

stair-turret and buttresses. Today, no tower in central Oxford can be built higher. On the east side is a copy of the original church clock, with 'quarterboys' who hammer out the quarter hours.

Also to the east is an arched gateway with a verdigris relief of St Martin tearing his cloak to give half to a beggar. Go through the arch and on the north face of the tower is an inscription commemorating the peace of 1814 – referring to the short-lived break in hostilities between England and France when Napoleon was imprisoned on Elba. Continue past the café along the rickety passageway, its roof punctured by two mature trees, to the remnants of St Martin's graveyard at the back of the tower, where tombstones are stacked against the wall.

Re-emerge to the front of the tower: facing you on **St Aldate's** is the Santander Bank, where an inscription to the left of the entrance commemorates the ㉛ **Swindlestock Tavern** that stood here from 1250 to 1709. This was the starting point for what became the bloodiest conflict between town and gown, the St Scholastica Day riot of 10 February 1355, sparked when a group of students complained to the landlord of the aptly named tavern about the weakness of his wine and then threw a jug of it at his head. Reinforcements for both sides were summoned by the bells of St Mary's and St Martin's. Tensions escalated after the mayor called in 2,000 men from outside the city, who advanced crying 'Slea, slea... Havock, Havock... Smyt fast, give gode knocks' to ransack the colleges and eventually kill 63 students. Edward III rebuffed the mayor's appeals and sided with the University, ordering the town's officials to swear an oath recognising its pre-eminence and to truncate St Martin's tower to make it less effective as a stronghold. Heaping humiliation on humiliation, 63 citizens were required to pay a penny fine and bow in penitence to the vice-chancellor of the University in an annual ceremony at St Mary's that continued until 1825.

THIS WAS THE SITE OF THE
SWINDLESTOCK TAVERN
1250–1709

31

Walk down St Aldate's. Formerly known as Great Jewry (and its current name probably taken from a corruption of 'old gate' rather than an obscure Gloucestershire saint), the street lay at the heart of the Jewish community from c. 1080, when Jews first arrived in the city, until their expulsion two

centuries later. A synagogue was built to the south, near where Christ Church's Tom Tower now stands (see page 164): poorer residents were concentrated around this area with the grandest houses facing Carfax. ❸❷ **Oxford Town Hall**, on the left, stands on the site of expropriated Jewish houses including that of the family of Moses of Oxford ('the mighty one', died c. 1268), whose writings on the Torah and Jewish law were for centuries standard scholarly works. Extensive cellars – for storage, clandestine worship and/or refuge – linked properties along the street, including Jacob's Hall, home to an important financier and banker, where the Santander Bank now stands. The street's Jewish heritage is commemorated by a carved inscription at eye level at the south end of the Town Hall façade.

The present Town Hall – replacing a previous incarnation built in 1751 when the last of the seized Jewish properties were demolished – was commissioned in 1895 as an expression of civic pride after Oxford was granted county borough status. Designed, following a competition, by young architect Henry Thomas Hare, it included council chambers, halls for concerts and meetings, and a library, with a police station and courts entered from Blue Boar Street at its southern end. The foundation stone on the southernmost corner, laid on the wedding day of the future George V, was quickly replaced when the nominated builder went bankrupt. The opening of the new building by the future Edward VII in 1897 was hardly less auspicious: police brought in from outside Oxford attacked a crowd of rowdy students with batons, resulting in the arrest of a young law don who became the cells' first overnight guest.

The virtuoso façade on St Aldate's assembles a number of seemingly random elements – arched and oriel windows, an elaborate frieze, an arcaded parapet guarded by griffins, richly embellished Jacobean gables and turrets with ogee caps – around an impressive frontispiece topped by the royal coat of arms and a diminutive statue of Queen Victoria. Above the door is Oxford's coat of arms: an ox fording the Thames flanked by an elephant and beaver (symbols of 17th-century city worthies), under a leopard with a crown and Tudor rose (granted to Oxford by Elizabeth I after a visit of 1566). Disconnected motifs from the emblem decorate the lead drainpipes and inside, at the top of the mock-baronial staircase, is a brightly painted, clearer version. If you are allowed access, it's worth taking a quick look at the staircase, the main hall with its heavily moulded plaster ceiling and the wood-panelled council quarters.

Almost opposite the Town Hall is a ㉝ **Post Office** built in 1880: the large wooden post boxes on the pavement outside straddle a void that allowed letters to drop directly into the building's basement.

Turn into **Blue Boar Street** to see the entrance to the former public library on the corner, with the motto 'Studies serve for delight, for ornament and for ability' (from philosopher Francis Bacon's 1625 essay) over the doorway; the building now houses the ㉞ **Museum of Oxford** (open Monday to Saturday, 10–17). Beyond is the entrance to the former law courts, with a broken

pediment that holds the scales of justice and an inscription in Latin from Virgil's *Aeneid* that translates as 'Be warned, learn justice, and do not despise the gods'.

Continue along Blue Boar Street: according to a plaque beside the law courts, the street was laid out by Christ Church in 1533 and the college's boundary wall, with elegant 1960s buildings by Powell & Moya, runs along the southern side.

The ㉟ **Bear Inn**, possibly named after its 16th-century landlord's unusual pet, is housed in the ostler's house of what was once a substantial coaching inn. The pub's present-day fame stems from a collection of more than 4,500 snippets of neckties that landlord Alan Course began amassing in 1952 in exchange for half pints of beer. The pub's landlords were consulted about the provenance of a tie by Inspector Morse in the 1996 novel *Death Is Now My Neighbour*; part of the collection, neatly arranged in glass cases lining the walls and ceiling, can be glimpsed through the windows.

Continue along **Bear Lane**. On the left (marked by stone plaques on either side of the arched entrance) is Quartermaines Stables, established by Samuel Quartermaine in the early 19th century. The college crest is that of Lincoln, which has turned the site behind into student accommodation. Continue to King Edward Street and turn right into **Oriel Square**. Walk past the gateway to Oriel College and then turn left into **Merton Street**: on your right is the entrance to Corpus Christi College.

35

Corpus Christi College
Merton Street, OX1 4JF
www.ccc.ox.ac.uk
Open daily, 13.30–16.30

The modest frontage of Corpus Christi is decorated with numerous gilded representations of the college emblem of a pelican taking blood from its breast to feed its young – standing for Christ shedding his blood for mankind, in a reference to the college name. The lower two storeys of the entrance range date from the college's foundation in 1517, with the upper floor added two centuries later.

Corpus Christi was founded by Richard Fox, Bishop of Winchester and diplomat in the service of Henry VII – for whom he brokered the heir to the throne's marriage to Catherine of Aragon – as well as of Henry VIII. On the advice of a colleague who had anticipated the upheavals of the Reformation, Fox decided not to make Corpus Christi a training ground for monks but rather a place of Renaissance learning in the humanities and sciences, where 'the scholars night and day may make wax and sweet honey to the honour of God, and the advantage of themselves and all Christian men'. Erasmus was an early visitor and great admirer of the well-stocked trilingual (Latin/Hebrew/Greek) library. In the 19th century Corpus Christi was one of the first to recruit students through open competition; alumni and college members include philosopher Isaiah Berlin; writers Robert Bridges and Vikram Seth; art historian John Ruskin; and British politician brothers Ed and David Milliband.

The door to the **36** **Front Quadrangle** is usually open. Facing the gatetower is a frontispiece of 1817 with a statue of Fox surveying his legacy – according to legend, he was blind by the time of the quad's completion and fellows led him around its perimeter twice so he would not be offended by its small size. The central pelican sundial, dating from 1581, is the work of

mathematician Charles Turnbull, author of a treatise on the celestial globe. Here the pelican stands on a sphere (representing the cosmos), with below it coats of arms including that of Fox (facing his statue). The complicated device includes several sundials as well as calculators to reckon feast days, a perpetual calendar to find the day of the week on a given date, and a means of telling the time by moonlight.

Accessed through a passageway embellished by one of Oxford's earliest fan vaults, the Corpus Christi Front Quadrangle is made up of largely original residential two-storey ranges, with the hall on the left (east). Walk through a passage in the south-east corner and on your left is the **37** **chapel**. The screen and stalls date from the late 17th century and effigy monuments of presidents John Spenser (1607–14) and his predecessor John Rainolds (the instigator and part-translator of the 1611 King James Bible) face off across the aisle. The pre-Reformation eagle lectern with its candleholders is the oldest in Oxford.

Walk along the colonnade with its many memorials then double back and take the passage to a charming small garden. At the far side is an entrance to the **38** **main garden**, fronted by the Fellows' Building of 1706, a three-storey freestanding block of the kind Wren pioneered at Trinity (see above) with a pediment and four Ionic pilasters marking its central bays. The design has been attributed to Henry Aldrich. At the end of the garden is a raised terrace with views over Christ Church Meadow on one side and the cathedral on the other; to the right is a bastion and part of the old town wall alongside the Rick Mather-designed MBI Al Jabber auditorium, a minimalist pavilion with a generous roof terrace built in 2009.

Retrace your steps to the entrance to Oriel College.

Oriel College
Oriel Square, OX1 4EW
www.oriel.ox.ac.uk
Open daily, July to mid-April, 14–16

Oriel College was founded in 1324 by Adam de Brome, a rector at the University Church of St Mary, as the House of the Blessed Mary, before being refounded two years later by Edward II and renamed King's College. The name Oriel, which soon took hold, derives from La Oriole, a house on the site. Originally occupying several medieval halls, the college was uniformly redeveloped in the first half of the 17th century: the castellated gatetower, appropriately, features an oriel window above the heavy oak doors. Alumni and college members include explorer Walter Raleigh; naturalist Gilbert White; Oxford Movement theologians John Keble, John Henry Newman and Edward Bouverie Pusey; writers Matthew Arnold and J. I. M. Stewart (Michael Innes); historians Christopher Hibbert and A. J. P. Taylor; dandy Beau Brummel; and colonialist Cecil Rhodes.

The **39** **First Quadrangle** is dominated by a central porch opposite the entrance: above the parapet of Jacobean strapwork and lettering are statues of doomed kings Edward II (gruesomely murdered, at least according to legend, with a red-hot poker) and Charles I (decapitated), with the Virgin and Child standing serenely above. A flight of steps leads to the panelled **40** **hall** with its magnificent hammer-beam roof and central lantern, originally unglazed to allow smoke from the fire below to escape. The gothic windows are embellished with the arms of the great and good – as well as Cecil Rhodes (see below) at the bottom of the last window before the bay on the left. Founder Adam de Brome appears in the top row of the first window on the right. The heavy cartouches over the other doorways around the quadrangle support the arms of major donors.

The **④ chapel**, still with its original 17th-century furnishings including a finely carved communion rail, is entered from the quadrangle by a discreet door to the right (south) of the hall. Climb the stair to the left of the entrance to access the memorial to Oxford Movement leader, cardinal and now saint John Henry Newman (1801–90) (see box, page 84), located in a bay that once formed part of the rooms he occupied as college chaplain (1826–31 and 1833–35); allegedly one of his predecessors used the space as a larder but Newman dedicated it to private prayer.

Emerge into the quadrangle and take a passageway in the north range to the Second Quadrangle: at the far end is the **④ library**, a handsome, palazzo-like building with giant Ionic columns above a rusticated base designed by Radcliffe Observatory architect James Wyatt in 1788. Unusually, the arcaded ground floor was intended not as an open colonnade but as an enclosed space providing common rooms for the college's fellows (an innovation for Oxford): you can glimpse the well-upholstered life within through the windows.

Take the path to the left of the library into the **④ Third Quadrangle**. The tall stone building to your right is the former hall and chapel of the medieval St Mary Hall, rebuilt in the 1640s; the simple timber-framed, white-painted building adjoining it dates from 1743. Opposite it, in total contrast, is an elaborate range built a century later with castellation, an extravagant oriel (fronting the principal's drawing room) and doorcases graced by angels. Facing the entrance to the quadrangle (to the north) is the back of the Rhodes Building, dating from 1911 (see below).

Carter House

Return to Oriel Square and head north up **Oriel Street**. On the right are college walls and buildings and on the left a row of brightly painted houses dating mainly from the early 18th century: many still have projecting jetties at first-floor level but have been refronted in Georgian style. Some obviously had shops or businesses at street level, with early 19th-century records showing premises occupied by booksellers, bookbinders, picture framers, shoemakers, saddlers and tailors. The deep blue house – now known as 'Carter House' – was restored in 1984 for Oriel with funding from former Rhodes scholar William Nelson Turpin, whose connections with the former US president's home state of Georgia led to a request to name it in his honour.

Cross the **High Street** and look back at the **44** **Rhodes Building**, on the corner of Oriel Street and the High, built by Basil Champneys in 1911 – as perhaps a few Oxford dons might be able to deduce from the chronogram above the door, where the sum of the capitalised Roman numerals within the Latin inscription gives the date. A bombastic chunk of Edwardian baroque, the building was financed by a bequest from Cecil Rhodes (1853–1902), the imperialist diamond-mining magnate who served as president of the South African Cape Colony from 1890 and in 1895 gave his name to a swathe of appropriated African territory around the Zambezi River (Rhodesia, now Zimbabwe). Rejected by University College, Rhodes joined Oriel for a term in 1873 and graduated eight years later, having taken time off to return to South Africa to manage his business interests. Though the Oriel president complained on his admission that 'all the colleges send me their failures', the Rhodes legacy of £100,000 was no doubt graciously received. The scholarship that bears his name was set up to promote unity (or perhaps to consolidate power) between the British Empire, the United States and Germany, in the belief that 'Wherever you turn your eye – except in science – an Oxford man is at the top

of the tree'. Despite several campaigns to rid Oxford's High Street of his presence, at the time of writing Rhodes' besuited image still stands in a niche at the top of the building's elaborate frontispiece, lording it over statues of Edward VII and George V, inexplicably clothed in armour, flanked by former Oriel provosts.

The twisted Solomonic columns on either side of the Rhodes statue are presumably a homage to the porch of the **⑮ University Church of St Mary** (open Monday to Saturday, 9.30–17; Sunday, 12–17) across the High. Until the Sheldonian Theatre was built in 1669 (see page 50), St Mary's lay at the heart of the University, used for meetings of academics (the Congregation), degree ceremonies and examinations. The bizarrely eclectic, baroque entrance, with its statue of the Virgin and Child in an elaborate shell niche within a broken pediment surmounted by oversized angels, was added in 1637, possibly by Nicholas Stone, who created the gateway to the Botanic Garden. The oldest part of the present church is the tower, which dates from c. 1280; the spire, with its ornate pinnacles and statues of saints, was added about 50 years later. It's worth buying a ticket to climb to the top for the stunning views over Oxford, from privileged bird's-eye views into nearby quadrangles to the distant hills that surround the city.

45

Inside the church, all that remains of the early foundation is the Brome chapel to the left (north) of the entrance, probably dating from *c.* 1320 and named after Oriel founder and St Mary's rector Adam de Brome, whose tomb lies within it. Nearby in the nave is a column mutilated to erect a platform on which the condemned Thomas Cranmer (1489–1556) made his final speech before his execution (see box, page 123); on the wall beside it is a plaque recently updated to commemorate both Protestant and Catholic martyrs. Across the nave is the pulpit used by John Henry Newman when he was vicar of St Mary's from 1828 to 1843, before his conversion to Catholicism two years later (see box, page 84).

As the church's structure began to crumble in the second half of the 15th century, its chancel and then nave were rebuilt with University funding in a splendour unaffordable by the town's parishioners. At a slight angle to the nave (apparently symbolising the head of Christ leaning towards the good thief on the Cross), the chancel is collegiate in atmosphere, with a screen of beautifully carved fluted columns and rows of heavily woodworm-scarred stalls. Behind the altar is a wonderfully lifelike *Madonna and Child* by Simon Vouet (1590–1649) against a simple backdrop. The stained-glass window directly south-east of the chancel, with its glowing blues and purples, was commissioned from Augustus Pugin (co-designer of the Palace of Westminster) in 1843 by comic actor George Bartley in memory of his son Thomas, a student at Exeter, who kneels in his scholar's gown in the bottom left panel. The wall on the south side of the nave contains several striking memorials set among scenes from the Passion sculpted after designs by Eric Gill. Back near the entrance is the chair still used by the chancellor of the University.

Exit through the Brome chapel and north porch to a stunning view of the Radcliffe Camera – or if you have not visited the church, walk up **Catte Street**. The eastern section of the back of

View from the University Church of St Mary onto Brasenose College

the church (on the Catte Street side) was formerly Congregation House, dating from the 1320s and used for meetings of the University Congregation, with the upper floor housing the first University library. The large windows were added during the 15th-century rebuilding of St Mary's to unify its exterior: it is only if you peep – or take a break – inside the stone-vaulted ground-floor Congregation chamber now occupied by the excellent Vaults & Garden café that you get a sense that this

46

is probably the oldest surviving university (as opposed to collegiate) building in Europe.

In the gardens behind the church, to the left of the exit, is a curved stone bench with a lengthy Latin inscription to 46 **Annie Rogers** (1856–1937), who in 1873, as A. M. A. H. Rogers, won scholarships to Balliol and Worcester only to be rejected when it was realised she was a woman. She was given a copy of the works of Homer as a consolation. Rogers gained a first in examinations equivalent to those of male students in 1877 but was not formally awarded a degree until 1920 (see box, page 316). Meanwhile, she taught some of Oxford's female students as well as campaigning and working on their behalf.

Skirt the railings behind the bench and walk down 47 **St Mary's Passage**, past a solitary lamppost. On the right is a door with a lion's head carved on a wooden panel, below a porch supported by two gilded Pan figures or fauns. It is alleged that one snowy morning C. S. Lewis emerged from St Mary's to be confronted with the elements that inspired his *Chronicles of Narnia* series (1950–56) – the lamppost that marks the entrance to a snow-bound kingdom featuring a lion deity (Aslan) and friendly faun (Mr Tumnus). Return towards the Radcliffe Camera with the entrance to Brasenose College on your left.

47

Brasenose College

Radcliffe Square, OX1 4AJ
www.bnc.ox.ac.uk
Open Monday to Friday, 10–11.30 and 14–16.30; Saturday and
Sunday, 9.30–10.30 and 14–16.30 termtime and 10–11.30 and
14–16.30 vacations

Brasenose was founded in 1504 by lawyer Richard Sutton and
Bishop of Lincoln William Smythe, both from the north-west
of England, with which the college maintained strong links.
Its name probably derived from a nose-shaped brass (brazen)
knocker on the door to the medieval Brasenose Hall on the
college site, which was allegedly stolen by rebellious students
and taken to Stamford in Lincolnshire in 1333: the college
authorities recovered it (or what they thought might be it) in
1890 by buying the house to which it was attached. The knocker
is now safely stowed in the hall, and above the door is a more
recent cartoon face with a huge nose.

Town-and-gown disputes involving Brasenose include tales of 16th-century fellow William Sutton, who got into a brawl with constabulary investigating his affair with the wife of a Chipping Norton tradesman; student H. J. Radcliffe, who in 1827 gave a passing prostitute – later found dead – a teapot of brandy; and, according to Jan Morris, a student killed by a butcher's knife in 1857, whose memorial reads 'Inter Tumultum Plebis Obdormivit' (He Fell Asleep Among the Tumult of the People). Alumni and college members include Ashmolean founder Elias Ashmole; highwayman John Clavell (expelled for stealing a silver plate); archeologist Arthur Evans; writers John Buchan, Helen DeWitt, J. G. Farrell and William Golding; literary critic Walter Pater; comedian Michael Palin; politicians David Cameron, John Profumo and Malcolm Turnbull; and cricketer Colin Cowdrey.

The four-storey gatetower on Radcliffe Square, its panelled front topped by a statue of the Virgin and Child, leads to the **48** **Old Quadrangle**, built in 1509, with a third storey added a century later. The sundial to the right dates from 1719: it's worth walking past it to the far end of the quadrangle for the view of the dome of the Radcliffe Camera and the spire of the University Church. Opposite the sundial is the **49** **hall** with its prominent oriel window: the panelling was installed in 1684 and the vaulted plaster ceiling created in the 1750s. The Brasenose knocker takes pride of place behind the high table, below a truly majestic version of the royal coat of arms; opposite it is a much smaller rendering of the Brasenose arms in a beautifully carved frame of fruit and flowers. A passage to the left of the gatetower leads to the intimate Chapel Quadrangle, built in the 1650s. The library (to the left)

and 50 **chapel** (straight ahead) originally had a continuous open cloister: that of the library was filled in at the start of the 19th century, perhaps by architectural maverick John Soane, which would explain unusual features such as the paired oval windows. Until the 1750s the cloister was a burial ground and you can still see gravestones underfoot in the chapel colonnade, along with several memorials (one with a skull flanked by putti decorously dabbing their eyes with handkerchiefs).

This was the last Oxford chapel to be built to a T-plan and its exuberant exterior mixes gothic with classical – gothic windows flanked by pilasters topped by a parapet with urns and crockets. In the antechapel, to the right of the entrance, is a memorial to Walter Pater (d. 1894; see page 315): his profile is flanked by Dante, Plato, Leonardo and Michelangelo. To the left is a life-size portrait of the 'Childe of Hale' (John Middleton), a giant of 9 feet 3 inches who visited Brasenose in 1617 with his landlord, a former student. The unusual marble reredos in the chancel dates from the 1730s but the most spectacular feature is the fan-vaulted ceiling of 1659, inexplicably painted in a way that conceals its lightness as part of Thomas Graham Jackson's restoration of the 1890s. Beyond the Chapel Quadrangle is the eclectic New Quadrangle, built by Jackson between 1882 and 1911.

Turn left at the far end of the college into **Brasenose Lane**, a picturesque alley between Brasenose and Exeter with a central cobbled gutter that was once an open sewer. At the end of the lane, turn right along Turl Street to get back to the Broad. ●

Visit...

Carfax Tower
Queen Street, OX1 1ET
www.experienceoxfordshire.org/
venue/carfax-tower/

History of Science Museum
Broad Street, OX1 3AZ
www.hsm.ox.ac.uk

Museum of Oxford
St Aldate's, OX1 1BX
www.museumofoxford.org.uk

Oxford Covered Market
High Street, OX1 3DZ
www.oxford-coveredmarket.co.uk

University Church of St Mary
High Street, OX1 4BJ
www.universitychurch.ox.ac.uk

Eat/Drink...

Bear Inn
6 Alfred Street, OX1 4EH
www.bearoxford.co.uk

Chiang Mai Kitchen
130A High Street, OX1 4DH
www.chiangmaikitchen.co.uk

Fernandos Café
Carfax Tower, OX1 1EP
fernandoscafeoxford.com

Jericho Coffee Traders
105 High Street, OX1 4BW
www.jerichocoffeetraders.com

Pizza Express
8 Golden Cross, OX1 3EX
www.pizzaexpress.com/oxford-
golden-cross

Turl Street Kitchen
16–17 Turl Street, OX1 3DH

Vaults & Garden Café
1 Radcliffe Square, OX1 4AH
www.thevaultsandgarden.com

The White Horse
52 Broad Street, OX1 3BB
www.whitehorseoxford.co.uk

3
East of St Giles':
from religion to reason
& back again

East of St Giles'

1. St Aloysius
2. St Giles
3. West side of St Giles'
4. Eagle and Child
5. Pusey House
6. Blackfriars
7. Martyrs' Memorial
8. St Mary Magdalen
9. Martyrs' cross

Balliol College
10. Front Quadrangle
11. Chapel
12. Gates
13. Hall

14. Cabmen's shelter

St John's College
15. Front Quadrangle
16. Chapel
17. Canterbury Quadrangle
18. Gardens

19. St Giles' House
20. Lamb & Flag
21. University Museum of Natural History
22. Pitt Rivers Museum
23. First chemistry laboratory
24. Radcliffe Science Library
25. Inorganic Chemistry Laboratory
26. Rhodes House

27. Earth Sciences Building
28. Dyson Perrins Organic Chemistry Laboratory
29. Chemistry Research Laboratory
30. Rothermere American Institute

Mansfield College
31. Main Quadrangle
32. Chapel
33. Eleanor Roosevelt

34. Civil War plaque
35. Siew-Sngiem Clock Tower
36. King's Arms

Wadham College
37. Front Quadrangle
38. Chapel
39. Fellows' Garden

40. University Department of Agriculture

Keble College
41. Liddon Quadrangle
42. Chapel
43. Newman Quadrangle
44. Hayward Quadrangle

45. Clarendon Laboratory's Townsend Building
46. Beecroft Building
47. James Legge

WALK

East of St Giles':
from religion to reason & back again

Start: St Aloysius
Finish: University Parks
Distance: 3.6 miles

The University of Oxford was founded in the late 12th century as a religious institution under the ultimate control of the pope, with its scholars monks or trainee clergy, its headquarters the University Church of St Mary, its academic robes versions of ecclesiastical vestments and many of its colleges established to guarantee continuing prayers for their founders' souls. The University has been at the centre of some of England's most radical religious controversies – from the burning of the Oxford Martyrs, who refused to accept a return to Catholicism in the 1550s, through the establishment of Methodism two centuries later, to the Oxford Movement's attempts to return the Anglican Church to its Catholic roots a century after that.

But Oxford has also been a centre for science, with pioneers ranging from the 13th-century advocate of empiricism Roger Bacon to mid-17th-century founders of the Royal Society such as Robert Boyle, Robert Hooke and Christopher Wren. More recently, it has fostered the careers of many Nobel Prize winners, from Howard Florey for his role in the development of penicillin in 1945, through Dorothy Hodgkin for the advancement of X-ray crystallography in 1964 to Oliver Smithies for his discoveries about DNA in 2007.

This walk begins and ends in a part of Oxford still steeped in religion as well as taking in the University's modern science area. Between the two is the University Museum of Natural History, founded in 1860 to combat the educational focus on theology and the humanities through an institution that would increase our 'knowledge of the great material design of which the Supreme Master-Worker has made us a constituent part'.

Start at the north end of **St Giles'**, at the church of ❶ **St Aloysius** (usually open 7–19), built in 1875 by J. E. Hansom, inventor of the hansom cab. The narrow frontage – in yellow brick to save money – is given presence by the stair turret and huge rose window. Inside, the impressive aisled nave with its vaulted ceiling culminates in a spectacular reredos with two tiers of more than 50 saints topped by a frieze of angels and 20 saints' heads; the Lady Chapel to its right, restored in 2007, gives an idea of the original decorative scheme.

Back near the entrance is a holy water stoop presented in memory of poet Gerard Manley Hopkins, who was a curate here from 1878–79. The relic chapel on the right, decorated with images from its time as a baptistery, bears witness to recent changes in Vatican policy: dismantled in 1970 following the modernising Second Vatican Council, with most of its contents destroyed, it was restored in the 1990s and now houses two cabinets of 'relics of the month'.

In 1993 St Aloysius became only the third Oratory in the UK, part of a movement established in England by John Henry Newman (1801–90, canonised in 2019, with a shrine beside the relic chapel) in which groups of priests live in communities without vows. *Lord of the Rings* author J. R. R. Tolkien (1892–1973) and his family worshipped at St Aloysius and in 2017 a mass was held in the church to support his canonisation.

Cross the road to the church of ❷ **St Giles** (open Monday to Friday, 12–14), consecrated in 1200 by St Hugh, Bishop of Lincoln. Much of the fabric, including the tower and chancel, is original or 13th century, though the walls of the nave were raised to their present height in the 1500s. Walk through the churchyard, where some of the yew trees are said to predate the church: just beyond its bounds is a sundial presented in 1985 to commemorate the twinning of Oxford with the West German capital of Bonn. Since medieval times, St Giles' Fair – described by poet John Betjeman in *An Oxford University Chest* (1938) as 'about the biggest fair in England... thick with freak shows, roundabouts, cake-walks, the whips, and the witching waves [amusement rides]' – has been held in the street each September to celebrate the feast of St Giles.

Cross the road again to **Little Clarendon Street**, on the same side as the Oratory. If you need a break already – or wish to return later, when the walk brings you up the other side of St Giles' – George & Davis, on the left of Little Clarendon Street, has excellent ice-cream.

Continue south along the ❸ **west side of St Giles'**, a mix of shops, religious buildings and homes where members of the University and of various churches have lived as neighbours. Probably dating from the late 18th century, **no. 31**, now a delicatessen, was from 1885 until 1960 a butcher's shop famed for its Royal Oxford Sausages; the ground floors of the two pretty early 19th-century houses adjoining it were from the 1840s to the 1960s respectively a baker's and a cabinet-maker's. The more formal, taller terrace of **nos 34–36** was built in 1828 by Daniel Evans, who lived at no. 34 and let the other two houses out: behind them was his builder's yard, accessed from Little Clarendon Street. In the early 1820s Evans had been embroiled in arguments over the future of Magdalen College, when he was ordered first to demolish and then to rebuild part of the cloister (see page 184); the firm established by his stonemason son-in-law Joshua Symm – which still operates in Oxford – was responsible for many of the city's prestigious 19th-century buildings including the main Post Office on St Aldate's, the

No. 37

No. 38

No. 39

No. 40

remodelling of the entrance to Pembroke and restorations of the Bodleian Library, Sheldonian Theatre and Christ Church Cathedral. Unusually for builders, both men are commemorated by a blue plaque, as is Annie Rogers, the first woman to be awarded a full Oxford degree and first female don (see page 103), who lived at no. 35 in the last decade of the 19th century. In 1933 the terrace was sold to the First Church of Christ, Scientist: a church was built in the garden behind and in 2004 the organisation added the pavilion-style reading room you can glimpse through the gateway.

The handsome house with the pedimented doorway at **no. 37** was built in 1790 by retired carpenter and twice mayor Vincent Shortland on what was formerly his timber yard. From 1894 until 2004 it was home to 'Dr Lee's Readers' – science professors and lecturers funded through an endowment from Dr Matthew Lee (1695–1755). Also on land belonging to Shortland, the even grander **no. 37a**, strangely without a front door, is now Ertegun House, the headquarters of a scholarship programme for humanities graduates funded by Ahmet Ertegun, founder of Atlantic Records, and his wife Mica, founder of interior design firm MAC II.

No. 38 was built in 1830, with the top storey and dormers added by St Ursula's Convent, which owned the building from 1910. Since 1922 it has housed St Benet's Hall, established at the end of the 19th century to provide accommodation for Benedictine monks from Ampleforth Abbey in Yorkshire while they studied at Oxford. Above the first door of the more modest house at **no. 39**, dating from the mid-19th century, is the coat of arms of Samuel Wilberforce, Bishop of Oxford from 1845 to 1869 and the son of anti-slavery campaigner William Wilberforce. Known as 'Soapy Sam' after prime minister Benjamin Disraeli described him as 'unctuous, oleaginous, saponaceous', he is best remembered for his part in a debate at the University Museum where he challenged Darwin's theory of evolution (see box, page 134). Though Wilberforce did not live here, the diocesan registry was in a building at the back of the house. In the 1970s and 1980s no. 39 was home to Richard Ellman, biographer of James Joyce and Oscar Wilde.

The only house set back from the road, **no. 40** dates from around 1600. From 1772 until he retired to **no. 37**, it was home to Shortland; it is now part of Linacre College, established in 1962 as the first graduate society for both sexes and all subjects. At the northern end of the front garden of **no. 42** is an ancient boundary stone that reads 'Here endeth North Gate Hundred', an area first recorded in the mid-12th century, when it extended over most of Oxford, but by the 16th century referring only to the parish of St Mary Magdalen, of which this was the northernmost point. The quiet house at **no. 43**, dated 1600 on the front, has been since 1947 a Quaker meeting house; the elegant early 19th-century houses with the iron balconies at **nos 45–54 St Giles'** have both been home to several Church of England clergy. For two decades from 1846, no. 46 was occupied by the Reverend Stephen Reay, keeper of the Bodleian's oriental books, and his wife Eleanor, whose joint grave you can see in St Sepulchre's cemetery (see page 275). From 1876, no. 45 was home to Frederick Metcalfe, for 35 years the controversial and unpopular vicar of St Michael at the Northgate, described as an 'irascible egotist' who referred to his dwindling congregation as 'pushing tradesmen and dissenters'.

The ❹ **Eagle and Child** has been a pub since 1650, mostly under the ownership of University College until it was bought by St John's in 2004, its profits used to fund student bursaries. Also

known locally as the Bird and Baby, its name is said to derive from a popular medieval story of an eagle snatching a noble-born infant. The 'Rabbit Room' at the back was from the 1930s a favourite haunt of the Inklings, a group of Christian academics and fantasy writers – including C. S. Lewis and Tolkien – who met regularly to critique each other's work. At the back of the bar are mementoes of the group including a signed letter to the landlord; after the pub was modernised in 1962, the now elderly gentlemen moved their custom to the Lamb & Flag opposite (see below). Greens Café at **no. 50** also makes a good pitstop, with seating in the time-warped 17th-century rooms upstairs.

The more imposing late-18th-century building at **no. 55** was from the 1860s until 1927 the home of the Reverend Joseph Dodd and his son John Theodore, who used it as the headquarters of the Christian Social Union, a society established in 1889 to study the application of Christian principles to contemporary social and economic problems. Since 1928 it has been part of Regent's Park College (whose crest features prominently above the door), formed initially in East London to offer an education to Baptists and other dissenters barred from attending Oxford and Cambridge. The Oxfam bookshop at **no. 56**, opened in 1987, was the first of the charity's specialist bookshops.

St Giles'

On the other side of Pusey Street is the gothic revivalist ❺ **Pusey House**, built in 1912–18 by appropriately named church architect Temple Moore. Pusey House was founded in 1884 in memory of Edward Pusey (1800–82), a leading member of the Oxford Movement (see box, page 84), which sought to reintroduce Catholic traditions to the Anglican Church. Though a plaque on the side of the chapel – below the glorious east window – claims it as Church of England (in parenthesis), it is tempting to add 'only just' since even the organisation's website calls it 'a centre for Catholic life', charged with 'doing something to arrest the further decay of faith in Oxford'. In his 1960 autobiography *Summoned by Bells*, John Betjeman describes something of the sensual and transgressive pleasures of emerging from his 'lavender-scented bath' to worship here: 'Those were the days when that divine baroque / Transformed our English altars and our ways. / Fiddle-back chasuble in mid-Lent pink / Scandalized Rome and Protestants alike'. Since 1981 the southern portion of Pusey House has been home to St Cross College, a graduate college founded in 1965.

If Pusey House conducts its rituals largely behind closed doors (with women refused admittance until the 1950s), the openly Catholic ❻ **Blackfriars** next door seems more welcoming. Founded in 1216 and established in Oxford less than a decade later, the Dominican order still observes the rules of poverty, chastity and obedience, though today women can become members and married lay people associates. The priory in St Giles' was established in 1921 and is now a hall of the University where both friars and lay members can study for degrees. It's worth visiting the chapel – designed by ecclesiastical architect E. Doran Webb – for its austere but beautiful interior, with a modern take on a vaulted ceiling, plain glass and low-relief Stations of the Cross that avoid the usual graphic depictions of suffering, requiring the onlooker to use his or her imagination.

Now the University Ioannou Centre for Classical and Byzantine Studies, **nos 66** and **67** – still with their original shopfronts – were built by ironmonger George Wyatt in 1869. The neighbouring Taylorian Institution is described more fully on page 242: built in the 1840s together with the adjacent Ashmolean, its aim was 'teaching and improving the European languages' and its giant columns are topped by statues representing Spain, Germany, Italy and France.

At the south end of St Giles', in the central island on **Magdalen Street**, is the ❼ **Martyrs' Memorial**, funded by public subscription in 1841 to remind Oxford of the gruesome fate inflicted on Thomas Cranmer, Hugh Latimer and Nicholas Ridley by Catholic queen Mary I in 1555–56 in punishment for their support of Protestantism (see box, page 123). In the mid-19th century the Anglican Church was threatened by the growth of both Nonconformism and the pro-Catholic Oxford Movement (see box, page 84) – though ironically the style chosen for the memorial was the gothic which Oxford Movement followers promoted as the true

121

style for religious architecture. Specifically invoking the Eleanor crosses erected by Edward I in the 1290s to mark the resting place of his wife's body on its journey from Lincoln to London, the elaborately crocketed and pinnacled monument was designed by George Gilbert Scott (who was to refurbish many Oxford college chapels) following a competition. Six niches with pointed gothic arches sit below statues of the trinity of martyrs, topped by a soaring spire; the inscription on the base recalls their bravery in maintaining 'sacred truths... against the errors of the Church of Rome'.

Scott used leftover funds to add a gothic aisle to the north of **❽ St Mary Magdalen** (open daily, 11–16), beyond the memorial. Though the church dates from the late 12th century, the oldest part visible today is the early 14th-century south chapel (Lady Chapel) with its three tracery windows (the exterior statues were added in 1914). Despite financial support from 19th-century Protestants, the church is avowedly Anglo-Catholic: in addition to a 14th-century font, its interior includes incense holders and in the south aisle a portrait of martyr Charles I, a confessional and a statue of Our Lady of Joy carved in Bruges.

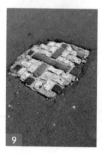

Return up Magdalen Street and turn right into **Broad Street**: just past the first arched doorway into Balliol College, set in a circle of cobbles in the middle of the road, is the **❾ martyrs' cross** marking the site where Cranmer, Latimer and Ridley were burned at the stake, commemorated by a plaque on the Balliol wall. It was this 'gloomy and inauspicious place' that Jude chose to meet Sue Bridehead in Thomas Hardy's 1895 novel *Jude the Obscure*. Continue to the main entrance to Balliol.

The Oxford Martyrs

The Oxford Martyrs memorialised in St Giles' – Hugh Latimer, Nicholas Ridley and Thomas Cranmer, all educated at Cambridge – were important actors in Henry VIII's Protestant reform of the Church in England. As a result, they became victims of the so-called Marian persecution that followed the accession of Henry's daughter Mary in 1553. As she attempted to return the country to Catholicism, more than 280 Protestants were executed and several hundred chose exile. Latimer, a famous preacher, had been Bishop of Worcester under Henry VIII but fell from royal favour when he opposed the king's 'Six Articles' affirming aspects of traditional Catholic doctrine – Henry was insufficiently Protestant for Latimer. Ridley was Bishop of London and Westminster and a member of the committee that assembled the first English Book of Common Prayer in 1548–49 under Cranmer. And Cranmer himself, Archbishop of Canterbury under Henry and his successor Edward VI, was a prime mover of the Reformation.

Latimer, Ridley and Cranmer were accused of heresy and tried at the University Church of St Mary on 12 September 1555 before being held at the Bocardo Prison, in a watchtower by the North Gate. Latimer and Ridley were burnt at the stake just outside Balliol on Broad Street on 26 October 1555. the terrible execution perhaps witnessed by Cranmer.

Cranmer then made several recantations, finally on 21 March 1556 publicly submitting to the to the Pope and accepting Catholic doctrine from a platform specially erected in St Mary's. However, he ended his speech by renouncing his recantations and declaring that he would thrust the right hand with which he had written them into the flames first. He was taken from the church to Broad Street, placed his hand into the fire, and died with great courage.

Balliol College
Broad Street, OX1 3BJ
www.balliol.ox.ac.uk
Open daily, 10–17

Balliol's imposing Broad Street frontage – with no castellation but typical Oxford dormers – was designed in 1867 by gothic revivalist Alfred Waterhouse (best known for London's Natural History Museum) after a scheme by Palace of Westminster co-designer Augustus Pugin was rejected on the grounds that he was a Catholic. Future Balliol master Benjamin Jowett described the new building as 'the best thing that has been done in Oxford in this way', adding disparagingly that 'an old lady has given us about £15,000 towards the completion of it'. He was referring to Yorkshire philanthropist and railway heiress Hannah Brackenbury, who funded the work because she believed her ancestors included college founder John de Balliol: her crest sits above the entrance.

Founders John de Balliol and his wife Dervorguilla of Galloway, parents of John I of Scotland, established the college in 1263 as an act of penitence following land disputes with the Bishop of Durham that saw de Balliol publicly whipped outside the doors of Durham Cathedral. The college's formidable academic reputation was cemented in the 19th century by masters including Jowett ('the Jowler'), an inspiring teacher, renowned theologian, translator of Plato and eminent Victorian prude who largely succeeded in his desire to 'innoculate England' with Balliol alumni. His mix of arrogance and erudition were satirised in the verse: 'Here come I, my name is Jowett; / There's no knowledge but I know it. / I am the Master of this College. / What I know not isn't knowledge.' Subsequent notable alumni and college members include British politicians H. H. Asquith, William Beveridge, Yvette Cooper, Edward Heath, Roy Jenkins, Boris Johnson,

Harold Macmillan and Chris Patten; first president of Botswana Seretse Khama; royals Olav V and Harald V of Norway, Tuanku Jaafar of Malaysia and Empress Masako of Japan; writers Hilaire Belloc, Robert Browning, Graham Greene, Gerard Manley Hopkins, Aldous Huxley and Nevil Shute; and scientists Richard Dawkins, Anthony Leggett and Oliver Smithies.

Waterhouse's Broad Street ranges tower over the ⑩ **Front Quadrangle**, which also includes to your left (west) the 15th-century old hall with its large arched windows (converted to a library by Jowett) and the master's lodgings (marked by an oriel), and straight ahead the old library. The polychrome building next to the old library – also designed to dominate – is the ⑪ **chapel**, built in 1857 by Oxford Movement favourite William Butterfield (see Keble College, below). Following the route outlined in the leaflet included with the modest entry fee, walk through the pinnacled archway to the chapel entrance: the passage is lined with war memorials, with the World War II list on the right ending with five Germans including Adam von Trott, executed in 1944 for his part in a plot to assassinate Hitler.

Butterfield's chapel was much reviled and his decorative scheme for the interior was plastered over in the 1930s. Today, the main adornment is stained glass from previous chapels that had been dismantled by Butterfield but was restored in 1912 with money raised by a group who wished to have the whole building torn down. The luminous windows on either side of the antechapel and to the left of the unusual silver-gilt altar of 1927 are the work of Abraham van Linge, completed in 1637; the east window and the St Catherine window on the south wall date from the 1520s. To the left of the altar is a memorial to Jowett designed in 1894 by Onslow Ford, creator of the Shelley Memorial in University College: the once formidable master is depicted as a fragile figure lying beneath a scallop shell against a backdrop of gold mosaic.

Return to the Front Quadrangle and take the passage at the far side of the old library: the ⑫ **gates** at the end allegedly bear the scorch marks of the pyre of the Protestant martyrs, condemned to death by judges including Balliol master James Brookes. Formerly at the college entrance and sold for firewood during Waterhouse's reconstruction, they were saved by an alumnus and returned in 1926.

The main feature of the Garden Quadrangle beyond is Waterhouse's ⑬ **hall** at its far end, an accurate if overscaled imitation of its medieval antecedents. Accessed by a stone staircase, the interior includes medievalist features such as a beamed roof, stone fireplaces and panelled walls hung with portraits of masters and alumni. You can buy drinks in the buttery below. On either side of the hall are an unashamedly 1960s accommodation block (left) and senior common room by Oxford Architects Partnership.

Return along Broad Street and turn right, back into St Giles' The blue-painted falafel stand on the right was put up as a ⑭ **cabmen's shelter** in 1896, replacing a previous shelter on wheels

and providing seating, tables, lockers and running water. It originally stood next to the underground gentlemen's toilets in the central reservation, which were completed at about the same time. Closed in 2008, these have now received planning permission to be turned into short-let accommodation. Further south in Magdalen Street, built in 1909 and still in operation, were some of the first ladies' public toilets in the UK.

Moving north, most of the buildings on the east (right) of St Giles' from this point on belong to St John's College.

14

St John's College
St Giles', OX1 3JP
www.sjc.ox.ac.uk
Open daily, 13–17

St John's College was founded on the site of the medieval St Bernard's College in 1555 – during the counter-Reformation of Mary I – by Catholic Thomas White to 'strengthen the orthodox faith'. A Lord Mayor of London and wealthy clothier, White was a member of the Merchant Taylors' guild, which had adopted St John as its patron saint. Early college members include Catholic martyr Edmund Campion (1540–81); Archbishop of Canterbury and adviser to Charles I William Laud (1573–1645), executed on charges of treason for his persecution of Puritans; and Bishop of London William Juxon (1582–1663), who ministered to Charles I on the scaffold. More recent alumni include writers Kingsley Amis, Robert Graves, A. E. Housman, Philip Larkin and Timothy Mo; and politician Tony Blair.

The oldest part of the frontage, incorporating the main entrance, is formed from the 15th-century buildings of St Bernard's topped by 16th-century dormers. Above the entrance is a statue of St Bernard flanked by Archbishop of Canterbury and All Souls founder Henry Chichele, who had founded St Bernard's in 1437, and Thomas White, holding a model of the tower. The northern range, with its expressive gargoyles, lion masks and carved animals and a castellated gatetower bearing a single statue of John the Baptist, was built in 1880 by George Gilbert Scott Jr (son of the designer of the Martyrs' Memorial).

The inner face of the gatetower in the ⑮ **Front Quadrangle** has an emaciated St John the Baptist added in 1936 by Eric Gill. The ⑯ **chapel** to the left (north) dates from 1530 but was remodelled in 1843. The chancel has a soaring hammer-beam roof with carved angels and an impressive east window; to the left of the altar is the Baylie chapel of 1642 with a fan-vaulted ceiling and stained glass commemorating Laud and Juxon, both of whom are buried here, as well as former president Richard Baylie (1585–1667), entombed in a lavish monument that depicts him reclining on a pile of books with his thumb as a bookmark.

Return to the Front Quadrangle and walk through the fan-vaulted passage opposite the gatetower to the ⑰ **Canterbury Quadrangle**, its buildings and decoration creating a single satisfying composition that unites conventional ranges to north (left) and south with frontages influenced by newly fashionable Renaissance classicism to east and west. The library to the south had been built in 1601 with stone from the ruins of

Beaumont Palace (see page 244) in what was then the college garden. Three decades later Laud decided to incorporate it into a quadrangle, adding a matching building opposite containing the president's lodgings and west and east ranges fronted by arcades of Tuscan columns – the first structural classical columns in Oxford – with glorious central frontispieces. Set in scalloped niches topped by a sleeping lion and unicorn, bronze statues of Charles I and Queen Henrietta Maria by French sculptor Hubert le Sueur are surrounded by cornucopia and swags framing coats of arms, crowns and mitres: the compositions proclaim the unity of Church and state for which both Charles I and Laud were to lose their lives. In the spandrels of the arcades are naively carved busts of the virtues and liberal arts with their attributes; above them is a frieze of masks, mitres, angels and fabulous beasts. Laud is said to have celebrated the quadrangle's completion with two banquets that together cost half as much as the buildings.

Continue through the arch in the east range to the extensive **18** **gardens**, laid out in the 1770s and praised by reigning monarch George III with the claim that his 'dominions did not afford another example of gardening skill to match it'.

Continue north up St Giles' to the elegantly classical ⓳ **St Giles' House** (recognisable by the sturdy piers topped by impressive urns that flank the entrance), owned by St John's since the 1960s. Described by Nikolaus Pevsner as 'the best house of its date in Oxford', it was built in 1702 for MP Thomas Rowney Sr by master-mason Bartholomew Peisley, who was soon to work at nearby Blenheim Palace. From the 1850s until it was taken over by St John's, the house was mandatorily commissioned as lodgings for assize judges on their visits to the city – no doubt to the annoyance of its more permanent residents.

Return to the ⓴ **Lamb & Flag** pub, opened as a tavern by St John's in 1695 and named for a symbol – associated with St John the Baptist – of Christ as the Lamb of God carrying a banner with a cross. It is in this 'obscure and low-ceiled tavern up a court' that Jude gets drunk and recites the Nicene Creed in Latin to prove his academic prowess in Thomas Hardy's 1895 novel. Like the Eagle and Child across the street, the Lamb & Flag was once a haunt of Tolkien, C. S. Lewis and the Inklings, and profits today are used to fund St John's bursaries. Like many Oxford pubs, it features in episodes of *Inspector Morse*, as well as in the pilot episode of spin-off *Endeavour*.

If you need refreshments, St Giles' and Little Clarendon Street have several options; the only café in the next stretch of the walk is in the University Museum gallery, which provides pleasant surroundings but little more than drinks, cakes and sandwiches.

Turn left down **Lamb and Flag Passage**, the alley that runs alongside the pub. On the right, with a concrete frame that steps confidently over the old college wall encasing a regular arrangement of glazed student cells, is the Sir Thomas White Building, designed for St John's by Arup Associates in 1975. Continue to **Museum Road**, noting on the corner of Blackwall Road another modernist building – this time a curved, corrugated blank wall of brick that forms the street façade of the De Breyne and Hayward Buildings you will encounter at Keble (see below).

Lamb and Flag Passage

The Oxford Evolution Debate

In November 1859 Charles Darwin published *On the Origin of Species*, setting out the theoretical basis for evolution through natural selection. Just over six months later, on 30 June 1860, this revolutionary theory was debated at a meeting of the British Association for the Advancement of Science at the Oxford University Museum (then still under construction), a debate that was to attain the status of myth.

The popular version of the encounter centres on a confrontation between Samuel Wilberforce, Bishop of Oxford, and Thomas Huxley, a biologist and early advocate for Darwin's theory – the Christian establishment versus scientific rigour. When Wilberforce allegedly challenged Huxley to say whether it was through his grandfather or grandmother that he claimed descent from monkeys, Huxley was said to have replied that he would rather have a monkey for his grandfather than a man who distorted the truth – delivering a knock-out blow for science.

Sadly, this account has been discredited by historians, who point out that contemporary journalistic records don't mention the confrontation. Wilberforce was in fact a subtle thinker who believed he was able to demonstrate that Darwin's theory was scientifically flawed because, for example, there was no fossil record showing the development from one species to another – evidence being provided, of course, by subsequent discoveries.

The legend of the debate – a victory of reason over superstition, science over clericalism – developed as the 19th century wore on. This was a period when natural science at the University became the province of professionals, often from middle-class backgrounds, who valued empiricism above all, rather than men with a privileged Anglican background, who saw the study of nature as ultimately leading to a closer understanding of God. That transition produced Oxford University's longstanding and ongoing eminence in science and medicine.

On the opposite side of **Parks Road** is the ㉑ **University Museum of Natural History** (open daily, 10–17), founded in 1860 at the instigation of Regius Professor of Medicine Henry Acland to consolidate knowledge and teaching of science within the University. Funding came largely from profits generated by Oxford University Press' sales of Bibles. Created a decade after the classical Ashmolean, the building was unapologetically gothic, with Acland much influenced by Oxford tutor and critic John Ruskin, who argued that gothic – more 'natural' and less rule-bound than classicism – was more appropriate to celebrate the natural world, especially if all the decoration was 'informative, conveying truthful statements about actual facts'. In line with Ruskin's principle that ornament should be designed by the craftsmen who execute it, Irish architect Benjamin Woodward engaged stonemasons James and John O'Shea, who added cats, dogs, rabbits, parrots, owls, flowers and foliage to window surrounds, arches and capitals. Unfortunately money ran out and the O'Sheas – despite offering to work for free – were dismissed after decorating the porch with caricatures (since destroyed) of some of their least favourite dons.

The overall impression is of a grand town hall, with the roofs of the central tower and stair turrets recalling a French château. Only a few of the exterior windows have carvings, but the gothic arch of the doorway has Adam and Eve supporting fruit and foliage, below an angel with a book in one hand and a dividing cell in the other. Outside the entrance is a stone commemorating the 150th anniversary of the event at which Bishop of Oxford Samuel Wilberforce and biologist Thomas Huxley debated Charles Darwin's theory of evolution (see box, page 134). The roof of the tower is a nesting site for a long-established colony of swifts.

It is worth going inside, if only to see the grid of slender cast-iron columns that terminate in appropriately skeletal ribs supporting a glazed roof. The perimeter gallery is carried on sturdier columns of polished minerals from around Britain – all meticulously labelled – fronted by statues of eminent male scientists (a bust of chemist Dorothy Hodgkin, see below, at the entrance to the Pitt Rivers Museum is a recent addition). From the gallery (where you will find the café) you can appreciate the individually moulded capitals of the iron columns with their filigree of foliage stretching to the roof as well as capitals and bases carved by the O'Sheas from plant specimens supplied by the Botanic Garden. Among the many impressive dinosaur skeletons is a cast of the remains of the dodo immortalised in Lewis Carroll's *Alice in Wonderland* and by Hilaire Belloc in the lines: 'The voice which used to squawk and squeak / Is now for ever dumb – / Yet you may see his bones and beak / All in the Mu-se-um'.

21

Continue to the rear of the University Museum to visit the shadowy hall that houses the **22 Pitt Rivers Museum**, designed in 1885 by Thomas Deane, who had succeeded Woodward after his death in 1861. Each level of the galleried space is crammed with cases and drawers, each in turn packed with exhibits from around the world arranged by type rather than age or region to highlight cross-cultural connections.

Created for the collection of General Augustus Pitt Rivers (1827–1900), who amassed firearms and weaponry before expanding his acquisitions into other areas, the museum now holds 500,000 items – though a process of 'cultural decolonisation' may lead to the return of some of these to the peoples from whom they were taken. Still, you could easily spend several years peering into cases and drawers filled with pottery and tools, masks and statues. To add to the confusion, items are displayed with their original labels to give an insight into the thinking of the first curators.

The University Museum became the nucleus for Oxford's Science Area, developed over the 20th century and beyond as numbers of science students expanded from 5 per cent in 1887 to around one-third of undergraduates and nearly half of postgraduates today.

The small building to the south of the complex is the first **②③ chemistry laboratory**, created at around the same time as the museum and still part of the University's Department of Chemistry. With its four tall chimneys and a steeply pitched roof, it was bizarrely (or perhaps appropriately?) modelled on the 14th-century Abbot's Kitchen at Glastonbury.

In 1897 Thomas Graham Jackson designed the neighbouring **②④ Radcliffe Science Library** in an eclectic mix of gothic and Renaissance. It is connected by an elegant glass link to the fortress-like extension on Parks Road, built in the 1930s in a similar style to the contemporary Weston Library (see below) by Hubert Worthington, designer of several other buildings in the Science Area.

Return to Parks Road and turn left along **South Parks Road**. The ㉕ **Inorganic Chemistry Laboratory** by architects Lanchester & Lodge – similarly moderne in style to Worthington's library extension, its entrance flanked by elegant obelisks bearing twin lamps – was built in the 1950s based on plans dating from 1935. No concessions were made to nearly two decades of progress (for instance, the front arch is too small for delivery vehicles, which have to use a tortuous route around the back) but despite deficiencies in both the layout and fittings of the laboratories, the building has been home to many important discoveries – see the plaques beside the gateway detailing the development of the blood-glucose sensor used by diabetics and the now ubiquitous rechargeable lithium-ion battery.

Recognition for female scientists has been hard won: when Dorothy Crowfoot Hodgkin 1910–84; (see page 336) was awarded the Nobel Prize in Chemistry in 1964 for developing the technique of X-ray crystallography that enabled her to establish the structures of compounds such as vitamin B12 and penicillin, her achievement was diminished with crass headlines such as 'Oxford housewife wins Nobel' (*Daily Mail*) and '£18,750 prize to mother of three' (*Telegraph*).

Opposite the Inorganic Chemistry Building is ㉖ **Rhodes House**, built in the late 1920s by Herbert Baker – who had worked extensively with colonialist Cecil Rhodes (see page 98) in South Africa – as the headquarters of the Rhodes Trust and a centre for studies of the British Empire, Commonwealth, Africa and America. The design combines elements from English and South African country mansions with an entrance whose dome and portico echo the Pantheon in Rome – a tribute to the power of empire.

Above the door is a low relief of the *Goede Hoop*, the ship in which Jan van Riebeeck sailed to South Africa to found Cape Town in 1652, opening the area to white settlers. The bronze bird on the dome is based on the Zimbabwean national emblem, itself based on carved stone birds found in the ruined city of Great Zimbabwe, one of which was removed by a European speculator in 1889 and sold to Rhodes.

Cross the road and continue to walk east. Next door to the Inorganic Chemistry Laboratory is the **㉗ Earth Sciences Building**, designed by WilkinsonEyre (who also redeveloped the Weston Library, see below) in 2010. Behind the fairly conventional west frontage, topped by ventilators like ships' funnels, is a dramatic 'narrative wall' of Jurassic stones suggested by the department's academics.

Beyond this is the former **28** **Dyson Perrins Organic Chemistry Laboratory**, designed by Paul Waterhouse, son of the architect of the redevelopment of Balliol (see above), with funding from Charles Dyson Perrins, manufacturer of Worcestershire Sauce. A puzzling Oxford inscription behind the railings at the western end translates as 'I, Waterhouse [Hydatoecus], a Balliol man, made this. Oh that it were better': extracting the capitals and reordering them allegedly gives the year of the building's opening (1915). Another inscription combines the surnames Perrins and Perkin (William Jr, Professor of Chemistry from 1912 to 1929) with all duplicate letters omitted.

Cross the road to look at the steel and glass **29** **Chemistry Research Laboratory** (CRL), built in 2004 by RMJM to replace the outmoded Dyson Perrins facilities: the block on the street, with 48 eight-person laboratory modules and workspaces, is linked by a spacious atrium to a building behind containing meeting spaces and seminar rooms. It's worth peering in the windows to watch the scientists at work – either at their computers on the street side or donning their white coats to move into the narrow labs behind. Retrace your steps down South Parks Road and turn

left along the alley between the two brick houses, signposted to the **30** **Rothermere American Institute** (RAI). To your left is the atrium and back of the CRL; at the far end to your right is the RAI, founded in 2001 for the study of the history, culture and politics of the United States.

Continue walking along the back of the CRL and turn right on to **Mansfield Road**. On your left is the boat-like University sports and social club and on your right the entrance to Mansfield College.

Mansfield College
Mansfield Road, OX1 3TF
www.mansfield.ox.ac.uk
Open Monday to Friday, 9–17

Mansfield was founded in 1838 in Birmingham by George Mansfield and his sisters Elizabeth Mansfield and Sarah Glover to train Nonconformist ministers, in particular Congregationalists, who advocated the separation of Church and state and the replacement of the Anglican establishment with self-government by local churches. The college moved to Oxford in 1886 at the instigation of prime minister William Gladstone to provide a focus within the University for Protestant dissenters, who had been allowed to study here since an 1871 Act of Parliament forbade the use of religious criteria to control admission. Alumni and college members include politician Chris Bryant; filmmaker Adam Curtis; and anarchist Uri Gordon.

Designed by Basil Champneys, architect of the Rhodes Building at Oriel, in a Tudor-gothic style, the campus is refreshingly open. The chapel is on the street side of the **31 Main Quadrangle**, making it accessible to the public, with the library opposite; the northern range contains the hall and lecture rooms. Behind the functionally redundant gateway with its oriel, turret and statue of John Milton you can see the shiny and functionally necessary ventilators of the CRL. Though decoration is sparse, the fine masonry of Champneys' buildings is beautiful in its own right.

It's worth asking the porter if you can visit the **32 chapel**, which unusually doubles as a dining hall. On the far (north) side – in defiance of conventions of church orientation – are finely carved choir stalls and a pulpit with a soaring gothic hood; to the south is the kitchen. The arcades to east and west are fronted by statues of dissenters – from John Wycliffe, who attacked the veneration of saints, monasticism, the authority of the pope and the privilege of the clergy in the 14th century, through Luther, Calvin and Knox to John Wesley four centuries later. Each of the windows above commemorates a facet of religious history from the New Testament, through the medieval church of Bede and Roger Bacon, Anselm and Dante, to the Puritans (Cromwell and Milton) and Nonconformists: Elizabeth Fry, probably the only woman, looks down from the west wall above the kitchen. A helpful key to the figures is usually available on a shelf in the aisle beside the entrance.

At the west side of the campus is a striking statue of **33 Eleanor Roosevelt** in quiet contemplation of the state of the world, unveiled by Hillary Clinton in 2018 to celebrate the role of her predecessor at the White House in drafting the 1948 Universal Declaration of Human Rights. Beyond the statue is the Bonavero Institute of Human Rights, opened by UN secretary-general Kofi Annan in the same year.

34

Continue down Mansfield Road. On your right is New College's elegantly minimalist Clore Music Studios, designed in 2019 by John McAslan. On the path beside it is a **34** **Civil War plaque** commemorating the site of the earthworks built in 1643–44 to defend the territory appropriated as his headquarters by Charles I during the conflict (see box, page 168): this first set of fortifications ran from Worcester College in the west, across northern Oxford and St Giles', to Mansfield Road and on to the grounds of Magdalen. Continue down Mansfield Road to Harris Manchester College.

Harris Manchester College
Mansfield Road, OX1 3TD
www.hmc.ox.ac.uk
Chapel open Monday to Friday, 10–17.30; Saturday, 9–12

Harris Manchester was founded in Warrington in 1757 as a Nonconformist training college for Unitarians before moving to Manchester in 1786. Established in Oxford in 1893 and now admitting only mature students (over 21s), its alumni and college members include Joseph Priestley, the discoverer of oxygen; Frances Newman, the dissenting brother of the sainted John Henry (see box, page 84); athlete Roger Bannister; and trade unionist and Britain's first female train driver Karen Harrison.

The college buildings were designed by Manchester-based Unitarian architect Thomas Worthington (father of Hubert, see above): the street front has the usual Oxford castellated gatetower with the library marked by an oriel to the right and the chapel by a large gothic window to the left. The chapel is worth visiting for fans of Pre-Raphaelite art: a complete set of stained-glass windows designed by Edward Burne-Jones and manufactured by William Morris in the last decade of the 19th century features a frieze of inert knights, angels, saints and maidens with rampant, life-filled Morris foliage above and below.

At the corner of Mansfield Road and Holywell Street is the **35** **Siew-Sngiem Clock Tower** and **Sukum Navapan Gate**, completed in 2014 by Yiangou Architects. Pastiche classical, the gateway includes a carving of an Asian elephant, symbol of Thailand, on its keystone in tribute to its founders, Thai sisters Maevadi Navapan and Dr Darnitha Karnchanachari. The eccentric clocktower bears the inscription 'It's later than you think... But it's never too late' – a quote from Dorothy L. Sayers used to reference the college's intake of mature students; the chimes of the bells have been set at two minutes past the hour.

28 Holywell Street

Music Room

36

Turn right into **Holywell Street**. The houses on the right, from the corner to no. 30, all belong to Harris Manchester: most date from the mid-17th century but were remodelled with fashionable flat fronts a century later.

The crests on **nos 28** and **29** include those of pottery manufacturers Josiah Wedgwood and Thomas Bentley, benefactors of the college in its Warrington days. Most of the rest of this side of the street is owned by Wadham (see below): the Holywell Music Room, a beautifully simple white building resembling a Nonconformist chapel, was built in 1748 as the first room in England solely for public performances of music (for more on Holywell Street and the Music Room, see page 22).

At the corner of **Parks Road** is the **36 King's Arms**, established in 1606 and the oldest pub in Oxford. Novelist Graham Greene is said to have drunk here with spy Kim Philby in the 1940s; the Don's Bar at the back maintained its ban on women until 1973, one of the last Oxford pubs to do so.

Opposite is the Weston Library, built by Giles Gilbert Scott (grandson of George Gilbert Scott) in the 1930s as an extension to the Bodleian Library, to which it is connected by a tunnel running under Broad Street (see page 52). The café in the entrance hall, recently remodelled by WilkinsonEyre, is a pleasant place to take a break. Walk north up Parks Road. On your right is the entrance to Wadham College.

Wadham College
Parks Road, OX1 3PN
www.wadham.ox.ac.uk
Open daily, 13–16.15

Wadham College was founded in 1610 by Dorothy Wadham, recent widow of Nicholas, a west-country landowner. A remarkable woman, in the four years after her husband's death Dorothy negotiated the college's charter and statutes with James I and the Archbishop of Canterbury, instructed workmen (employing a master-mason from Somerset and advising that the library be built above the kitchen to keep the books dry) and appointed fellows and staff – all without ever visiting Oxford. Alumni and college members include architects Christopher Wren and Thomas Graham Jackson; conductor Thomas Beecham; writers Monica Ali, Alan Coren, Cecil Day-Lewis and Michael Rosen; actors Felicity Jones and Rosamund Pike; broadcaster Melvyn Bragg; politician Michael Foot; and Archbishop of Canterbury Rowan Williams.

The most complete example of an early 17th-century college, Wadham presents a somewhat forbidding three-storey frontage to the street, with a central tower, gabled end blocks, and castellation punctuated by tall slabs of chimney. In the 1650s the warden's rooms above the entrance were the meeting place for the Oxford Philosophical Club, the precursor to the Royal Society, with members including Wren and scientists Robert Boyle and Robert Hooke.

Opposite the gatetower in the ㊲ **Front Quadrangle** is an understated Tower of Orders, with Doric, Ionic, Corinthian and Composite columns flanking (respectively) the doorway to the hall, naive statues of the founders (Nicholas in armour and Dorothy in a floor-length dress), James I under an elaborate canopy and the royal arms. The hall, accessed via a stone staircase, is one of the largest in Oxford, with a spectacular hammer-beam roof and carved wooden screen. To the north (left) of the Tower of Orders is a clock designed by Wren.

Take the passageway beside the clock and enter the ㊳ **chapel** via a door on your right. Designed to the traditional Oxford T-plan, it has a superb Jacobean screen with strapwork ornament and much original stained or painted glass. The major monument in the antechapel (opposite the doorway) depicts the young, ruffed John Portman, an undergraduate who died in 1624 aged 19, reclining on a pile of books, topped by pediments with a pair of putti, statues of the four virtues and a figure representing time. Beside it is a monument made up of piles of books commemorating Thomas Harris, a fellow who died aged 20 in 1614. The richly coloured east window in the chancel is the work of Bernard van Linge: among the finely drawn, fluid compositions depicting believable characters from the Old Testament is Jonah and a whale (top right) imagined with fishy scales. On hearing critical reports of the images of the prophets in the windows on the left of the chancel, Dorothy Wadham fired the glazier and found a successor to craft the much more accomplished glass on the other side.

Behind the chapel is the ㊴ **Fellows' Garden** – like the rest of the college formerly part of an Augustan priory and a pleasant place to sit or stroll. In the far (north-west) corner is one of the original 'Emperor Heads', commissioned by Christopher Wren in the 1660s to stand outside the Sheldonian Theatre (see page 51) and donated to the college by the family of sculptor Michael Black, who carved new versions in the 1970s.

Continue up Parks Road. On your left are the gardens of Trinity, which you can look at through ornate iron gates set between massive stone piers with impressive ball finials.

Further up on the right is a gateway to Rhodes House (see above) from which you can see the Cotswold-style mansion that makes up the bulk of the building.

Further still (almost at the junction with South Parks Road) on the left is the former ④ **University Department of Agriculture**, built in 1907: above the arched doorway is an oriel decorated with swags and a broken pediment topped by what looks like an ostrich. No. 9 (next door) appears to be a perfect early Georgian country house but was in fact built in the 19th century and remodelled in its current form in the 1920s. Continue beyond Museum Road to the entrance to Keble College.

Keble College

Parks Road, OX1 3PG
www.keble.ox.ac.uk
Open daily, 14–17

Keble is the first new Oxford college for 250 years after Wadham and Pembroke. Founded in 1870 in memory of poet and Oxford Movement leader John Keble (1792–1866) (see box, page 84) to take advantage of the relaxation in rules governing students' religion, the college aspired to make an Oxford education available to 'persons willing to live economically... wherein sober living and high culture of the mind may be combined with Christian training'.

Alumni and college members include writers Frank Cottrell-Boyce, Giles Coren and Edward St Aubyn; musician Peter Pears; broadcasters Tony Hall, Katy Brand and Chris Hollins; journalist Andreas Whittam Smith; and politicians Andrew Adonis, Ed Balls and Imran Khan.

The founding committee, which included Edward Pusey (see above), chose as their architect William Butterfield, designer of the chapel at Balliol and numerous gothic revival churches. Butterfield's mission to 'give dignity to brick' through polychromatic decoration has been derided as the 'holy zebra style': certainly Ruskin, recently involved in the University Museum opposite, loathed it, giving up his walks in the University Parks to avoid Keble's offending frontage. Funds for the large and impressive chapel, hall and library came from Tractarian

sympathiser William Gibbs, who had a monopoly in importing guano (bird droppings) from the Galapagos Islands for use as fertiliser. Butterfield's full palette of stripes, zig-zags, diamonds and chequerboard in red, white and blue – as well as his buildings' gothic windows and Tudor chimneys – can be appreciated from the quieter Museum Road as well as on the main Parks Road frontage.

The vast **41 Liddon Quadrangle** illustrates the shortcomings of Butterfield's vision: the buildings are certainly powerful, but the effect is more that of an asylum or hospital than a place of learning, with the polychromy appearing merely fussy and repetitive, like applied embroidery or cross-stitch. There are residential blocks to the east and west (rooms are arranged economically along corridors rather than around the traditional staircases), with the hall and library to the south facing the towering **42 chapel** to the north. At twice the height of the surrounding ranges, its size is emphasised by the sunken lawn, tall gothic windows surrounded by chequerboard polychromy and a roofline topped by pinnacles. Inside, despite the soaring vaulting, the first impression is of gloom, with dark walls of polychromatic brick and tiles, carved stone and marble punctuated by a band of cartoonish mosaics of Bible scenes. Unlike in most college chapels, the pews face the raised altar.

In a side chapel is William Holman Hunt's 1853 painting *The Light of the World*, presented by the widow of Oxford University Press Printer Thomas Combe (see page 259) but perhaps understandably rejected by Butterfield.

Exit the quadrangle via the north-western corner to the **43 Newman Quadrangle**: both the residential Arco Building (1995), its curving brick frontage raised on pilotis, and Sloane Robinson Building (2002) were designed by Rick Mather. Return to the Liddon Quadrangle and walk through a passage at the western end of the hall to the **44 Hayward Quadrangle**, dominated by the astonishing snaking glass De Breyne and Hayward Buildings, designed by Ahrends, Burton and Koralek in the mid-1970s. A mix of student residences and fellows' rooms with an underground bar you can peer into, the structures have a transparency and sinuous form that contrast with the closed rigidity of Butterfield's façades (though the street side on Museum Road, you may remember, has the blank walls of a fortress).

Walk south to the far end of the quadrangle and turn left through a service space to the Pusey Quadrangle: smaller and open-ended, with a detached warden's lodging to the south and clock tower to the west, this is more differentiated and so less oppressive than the Liddon Quadrangle.

Almost opposite the entrance to Keble is the University Department of Physics, dominated by the **45** **Clarendon Laboratory's Townsend Building**, designed by Thomas Graham Jackson in 1910 with a grand neoclassical frontispiece. A plaque to the left of the entrance states that – surprisingly – it was financed by the Worshipful Company of Drapers.

There is also a blue plaque to Harry Moseley, whose work helped reveal the structure of the atom and whose early death at Gallipoli in 1915 led governments to consider the need to protect scientists from conscription.

To the north is the **46** **Beecroft Building**, designed by Hawkins\Brown and opened by internet pioneer Tim Berners-Lee in 2018. While the upper storeys have large areas of glazing revealing circulation and informal meeting areas designed to encourage encounters that might spark ideas, below ground are two floors of 'black box' labs buffered by monolithic concrete slabs that protect sensitive nano-scale experiments from vibrations.

The University Parks to the north of the building is a pleasant area for a stroll or to return to the start of the walk, turn left along **Keble Road**. At no. 3 (on the right) is a blue plaque to **47** **James Legge** (1815–97), a Congregationalist missionary who spent more than 30 years in Hong Kong before settling in Oxford. Here he was the first occupant of the Chair of Chinese and the first Nonconformist to be made a professor, working to open the University to women, to promote religious tolerance and to liberalise the curriculum and examinations system. ●

University Parks

Visit...

Pitt Rivers Museum
South Parks Road, OX1 3PP
www.prm.ox.ac.uk

**University Museum of
Natural History**
Parks Road, OX1 3PW
www.oumnh.ox.ac.uk

Eat/Drink...

G&D Café
55 Little Clarendon Street, OX1 2HS
www.gdcafe.com

Greens Cafe
50 St Giles', OX1 3LU

Najar's Place
Cabmen's Shelter
St Giles, OX1 3JP

Taylors Deli Co.
31 St Giles, OX1 3LD
www.taylorsoxford.co.uk

Christ Church College

4
Four Colleges & a Cathedral

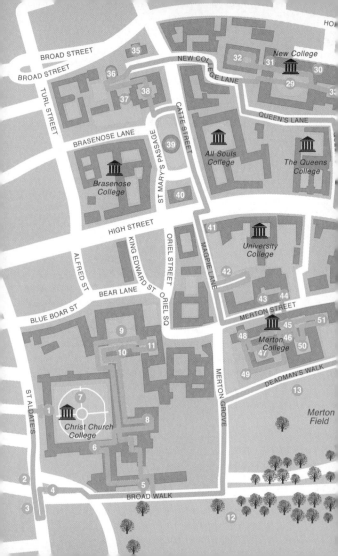

Four Colleges & a Cathedral

1. Tom Tower
2. Old Palace
3. Alice's Shop
4. Memorial Garden

Christ Church College
5. Meadow Building
6. Hall
7. Tom Quad

8. Cathedral
9. Peckwater Quadrangle
10. Library
11. Canterbury Quadrangle
12. Christ Church Meadow
13. Deadman's Walk
14. James Sadler

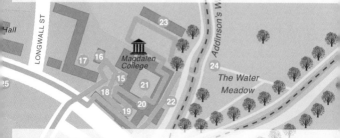

Magdalen College
15. Founder's Tower
16. Grammar Hall
17. St Swithun's Quadrangle
18. Outdoor Pulpit
19. Chaplain's Quadrangle
20. Chapel
21. Great Quadrangle
22. Old Kitchen and Riverside Terrace café
23. New Building
24. Addison's Walk

25. Eastgate Hotel
26. Ruskin College of Art
27. Examination Schools
28. St Edmund Hall

New College
29. Front Quadrangle
30. Hall
31. Chapel

32. Cloister
33. Garden Quadrangle
34. City wall

35. Clarendon Building
36. Sheldonian Theatre
37. Divinity School
38. Bodleian Library
39. Radcliffe Camera
40. University Church of St Mary
41. Old Bank Hotel
42. Almshouses
43. Beam Hall
44. Postmaster's Hall

Merton College
45. Front Quadrangle
46. Hall
47. Mob Quad
48. Chapel
49. Grove Building
50. Fellows' Quadrangle
51. St Alban's Quadrangle

College information

Christ Church
Entry via Meadow Gate, Broad Walk, off St Aldate's
Opening times Monday to Saturday, 10–17; Sunday, 14–17. Closures of the whole college or parts of it posted two weeks in advance on www.chch.ox.ac.uk/plan-your-visit/opening-times
Price (January 2021) £15/£14 including multimedia guide. Tickets can be booked online to save queuing

Picture Gallery and Canterbury Quadrangle
Entrance from Merton Street
Opening times October to May, Monday and Wednesday to Saturday, 10.30–13 and 14–16.30; June same times but open until 17; July to September, Monday to Saturday, 10.30–17, Sunday, 14–17
Price £4/£2

Magdalen
High Street (Magdalen Bridge end)
Opening times January to late June and October to December, 13–18 or dusk if this is earlier; late June to early October, 10–17 or dusk if this is earlier. Closures posted on www.magd.ox.ac.uk/discover-magdalen/visiting-magdalen/ or call 01865 276000
Price £7/£6

New College
Entry via New College Lane
Opening times mid-October to mid-March, Tuesday to Saturday 13.30–16.30; mid-March to mid-October, daily 10.30–17. Closures posted on www.new.ox.ac.uk/planned-closures or call 01865 279562
Price winter £5/£4; summer £7/£6

Merton
Merton Street
Opening times Monday to Friday, 14–17 or dusk if this is earlier; Saturday and Sunday, 10–17 or dusk if this is earlier. Closures posted on www.merton.ox.ac.uk/visitor-information or call 01865 276310
Price £3/£2

Four Colleges & a Cathedral

Start: Tom Tower
Finish: Merton College
Distance: 3 miles

This walk focuses on four Oxford colleges – Christ Church, Magdalen (pronounced Maudlin), New College and Merton – that together offer a history of college architecture and of the development of the University. The route also takes in several of the University's most important institutions, as well as waterside meadows and medieval lanes. You could choose to do the walk visiting only one or two colleges, visit the colleges independently (especially if you have covered the stretches between them as part of other routes) or incorporate college visits into other walks. Be warned that all charge an entry fee and you should check they are open before you set out by consulting their websites or phoning the porter's lodge. To complete the walk within a day (allowing time for lunch and a tea break), you should probably begin at about 10.30.

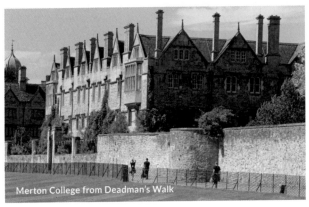

Merton College from Deadman's Walk

Begin the walk at ① **Tom Tower** on **St Aldate's**, the entrance to Christ Church for college members and an Oxford landmark since 1680, when Christopher Wren added the tower and bell chamber to a gateway built when the college was established in 1525.

Perhaps the most magnificent of Oxford's colleges, Christ Church was founded as Cardinal College by Thomas Wolsey (1473–1530), a cardinal, Archbishop of York and chancellor to Henry VIII. The site included the former Priory of St Frideswide, which Wolsey closed down, as well as several neighbouring streets, which he demolished. Only the lower part of what is now Tom Tower and the hall were completed before his downfall and death, and the college was refounded twice by Henry VIII, first in 1532 and again in 1546 under its present name. At this point the priory church was rebuilt to take on the dual role of college chapel and cathedral of the new diocese of Oxford, with the dean as head of both college and cathedral chapter – an arrangement that survives today.

Charles I made Christ Church his headquarters in the 1640s when Oxford became his Civil War capital (see box, page 168). But it was not until the 1660s that Dean John Fell – a disciplinarian and reformer who turfed students out of pubs and even expected them to attend lectures – launched a campaign of works to complete the campus. At this point the north side of the main quadrangle and some of the St Aldate's frontage were still open to the street and Tom Tower was no more than an archway flanked by two turrets embellished by elaborate panelling, their polygonal bases topped by octagonal piers.

Fell called in Wren, whom he had used earlier for the Sheldonian Theatre (see below): busy building St Paul's in London, the architect agreed to complete the tower as a favour, with a design that would be 'Gothick to agree with the Founder's work' but not 'as busy as he began'. Ignoring Fell's request to make the structure an observatory, he added a square-based tower topped by a tall octagonal lantern with an ogee dome, and finished the turrets with ogee caps. The pedestal provided for a statue was left empty until Dean Henry Liddell (father of Alice of *Alice in Wonderland* fame, see below) installed one of Wolsey in 1870. The tower takes its name from Great Tom, a bell dedicated to Thomas Becket that was rescued from Osney Abbey and brought to Christ Church, initially to hang in the cathedral. It rings 101 times at 21.05 each evening: the number represents the 100 students of Henry VIII's foundation plus an additional place funded through a later bequest; 21.05 signals the student curfew according to Oxford time, which is five minutes behind Greenwich Mean Time.

As well as Charles Dodgson (aka Lewis Carroll, 1832–98), who lived at Christ Church for 47 years as a student then mathematics don, alumni and college members include writers W. H. Auden, Richard Curtis, Marina Hyde, Adrian Mitchell, Jan Morris and Sir Philip Sidney; politicians Jonathan Aitken, George Canning, Tom Driberg, Alec Douglas-Home, Anthony Eden, William Gladstone, Nigel Lawson and Robert Peel as well as William Penn (the Quaker founder of Pennsylvania) and Zulifkir Ali Bhutto (prime minister of Pakistan); theologians Edward Pusey, John Wesley and Rowan Williams; critic John Ruskin; scientists Albert Einstein and Robert Hooke; philosophers A. J. Ayer and John Locke; musicians Adrian Bolt, John Taverner and William Walton; TV presenters David Dimbleby and Ludovic Kennedy; and Edward VII.

Walk south down the street towards the pedestrian crossing. The timber-framed building with elaborate plasterwork on the right, on the corner of Rose Place, is the ❷ **Old Palace**, its name surviving from an earlier house said to have belonged to Robert King, first Bishop of Oxford. Note the strange figures – including un-ecclesiastical cloven-hoofed hybrids – that support the oriel windows.

Further down on the same side, at no. 83, is ❸ **Alice's Shop**, formerly the grocer's where Alice Liddell would buy her favourite barley sugars and the inspiration for the Old Sheep Shop in Carroll's *Through the Looking Glass* (1871), when Alice finds herself: 'in a little dark shop, leaning with her elbows on the counter, and opposite to her was an old Sheep, sitting in an arm-chair knitting'. John Tenniel used the interior as a model for his illustration of the episode, producing its mirror image for the looking-glass world. The boat trip upstream to Godstow, during which 30-year-old Dodgson invented the Alice stories to entertain ten-year-old Alice and her two younger sisters, began just south of Christ Church at Folly Bridge.

Cross the road and enter the gate to Broad Walk, just to the north, to access the tourist entrance to the college. The ❹ **Memorial Garden** along Broad Walk was established in the 1920s after pleas for funds for a monument to college members killed in World War I failed to raise enough money. The quotation inscribed on the path at the entrance is from John Bunyan's *Pilgrim's Progress* (1678).

Oxford in the Civil War, 1642–46

'The colleges were used as barracks or warehouses. Magdalen became an artillery park, the Great Quad at Christ Church was a cattle pen. In the music and astronomy schools tailors stitched uniforms... the Schools of Law and Logic were granaries, that of Rhetoric a workshop for portable bridges... All over town printing presses churned out propaganda that carters smuggled throughout the land... The Commons sat in the Great Convocation House and the Lords in the Upper Schools.' Charles Carlton, *Going to the Wars*.

Though Parliamentarian forces, with the support of some townspeople and both MPs, occupied Oxford from September 1642, on 29 October – less than a week after the first pitched battle of the Civil War, at Edgehill, about 40 miles to the north – Charles I entered the city, intending at first to continue to London.

While members of the University were overwhelmingly High Church and Royalist, occupation of the city by an unruly army was unpopular. Nevertheless, Charles set up his court at Christ Church while his queen, Henrietta Maria, lodged at neighbouring Merton, the only college to support the Parliamentarian side. The area became a massive entrenched camp for the Royalist army and new earthwork fortifications were begun, probably running from the gardens of Worcester College, crossing what is now Mansfield Road and ending in the grounds of Magdalen; the south of the city was protected by the Cherwell and Thames. The height of the garden mound at New College – originally purely ornamental – was greatly increased to make it an observation platform. A regiment of townsmen was raised and in spring 1644 a regiment of scholars was formed.

Until its surrender to Parliamentary forces in 1646, Oxford was effectively the Royalist capital of England, the seat of the Court, the Privy Council (at Oriel), the central law courts and the Oxford Parliament. (Cambridge, symmetrically, became a Parliamentarian stronghold.) College silver plate was transformed at the Royal Mint in New Inn Hall Street into coins and medals to reward troops and the mill at Osney was requisitioned to grind gunpowder. Typically for the time, soldiers were expected to extract much of their living from the civilian population, which they did by extortion and violence, unchecked as the king was not convinced that the citizenry was loyal.

Towards the end of May 1644 a Parliamentarian army commanded by the Earl of Essex crossed the Thames and marched to Woodstock to the north; another marched towards Eynsham, west of the city. Threatened with encirclement, Charles escaped to safety in Worcester on 3 June.

The following year, Parliamentary forces in the area came under the command of the great general Thomas Fairfax. Siege works were built to the east of the Cherwell and a Royalist outpost to the west of the city was taken before this first siege was lifted. The Royalists, having already flooded meadows and burnt down houses in the suburbs, decided to demolish all dwellings within within 3 miles of the city to deny Parliamentarian troops billets. The king returned to Oxford in November and a further line of fortifications was added.

In April 1646 Fairfax returned with the main Parliamentary army and orders to besiege the city. Charles slipped away again on 27 April, ordering those who remained to resist but, confusingly, to avoid further bloodshed. Oxford surrendered to Parliamentary forces on 25 June.

Christ Church

Entry via Meadow Gate, Broad Walk, off St Aldate's, OX1 1DP

www.chch.ox.ac.uk

To buy tickets and/or pick up a multimedia guide for **Christ Church** go to the visitor centre to your right – a sensitive conversion and extension of a thatched barn. If you have bought tickets online and can make do with a map and booklet (plus the information below), go straight into the college through the gateway to your left. If you wish to visit only the Christ Church Picture Gallery – a significant collection of old masters housed in a bold modern building designed by Powell & Moya in the late 1960s – you can use the entrance on Merton Street and pay a much lower admission fee: you will also see James Wyatt's Canterbury Quadrangle, designed in the 1770s and incorporating the monumental college library built earlier in the century. You can attend evensong in the cathedral, which is free and begins 5 minutes later than the advertised time as the cathedral, like Great Tom, runs on Oxford time.

The **❺ Meadow Building**, through which you enter the campus, was built in the 1860s by Thomas Deane, who was later to design the Pitt Rivers Museum. With fashionable Venetian windows and now faded polychromatic decoration, it provided accommodation for 57 students in suites consisting of a sitting room, bedroom and study, accessed from generous staircases.

Cross the irregular quadrangle and go up the steps, following signs, to the spectacular ceremonial staircase that leads to the hall. The tall arched windows and fan-vaulting, appearing to swirl out from a single slender central column, were installed in the still unroofed tower in the 1630s, possibly following a now lost design from Wolsey's time. The present stairs were designed in 1805 by Wyatt, who had already built the Canterbury Quadrangle (see below): it is on this staircase that Professor McGonagall welcomes Harry and his classmates to Hogwarts in the first Harry Potter film, while the hall beyond was recreated in the studio for the series.

Wolsey was famed for his appetite, and prioritised the provision of a ❻ **hall** – with kitchens below – before a library. A demonstration of the ambition that perhaps contributed to his downfall, the Christ Church hall is still the largest in Oxford apart from Keble. The magnificent hammer-beam roof was created by Humphrey Coke, chief carpenter to Henry VIII: its gilded central bosses bear the arms of the see of Winchester, where Wolsey was bishop. Most of the stained glass dates from the 1880s and

Ceremonial staircase

171

commemorates members of the college, with Charles Dodgson depicted with Alice and several of his animal characters in the window above the fireplace on the left as you enter and Wolsey standing next to Dutch scholar Erasmus in the fan-vaulted bay beyond. Among the many fine portraits of hatted, wigged and gowned worthies are William Pitt and George Canning on the left wall and Anthony Eden, William Gladstone, John Locke and a rare triple portrait by Peter Lely of Dean Fell with two churchmen on the right. Above the high table is Henry VIII, flanked by Elizabeth I and Fell on one side and Wolsey on the other, behind a bust of Elizabeth II as a reminder that the college is a royal foundation with the reigning monarch as the founder's representative. The only other woman featured is geographer Judith Pallot, whose portrait hangs to the right of the entrance, opposite W. H. Auden and Dodgson. The hall is still used (and closed to the public) for breakfast, lunch and dinner, with the choice of an informal sitting or a later formal meal at which gowns are worn and grace said in Latin.

Leave the hall by the other side of the staircase: at its foot is a door studded with the words 'No Peel' in protest at the home secretary's 1829 proposals to grant more freedom to Catholics. To your right is **7 Tom Quad**, the largest quadrangle in Oxford, left unfinished by Wolsey but enclosed completely under Dean Fell in the 1660s with housing for the canons of the cathedral built to the north in exact imitation of the earlier ranges. Across the sunken courtyard, its spoil used to make

Broad Walk, is Tom Tower: the statue of Queen Anne was added during her brief reign in the early 1700s, soon after the tower's completion.

Wolsey had intended his quadrangle to have a cloister (as at Magdalen, see below, where he was a fellow) and you can still see the bases and springing for its arches, replicated on later ranges even though the plan had been abandoned. The castellated parapets, hall pinnacles and the tower above the hall staircase were added by George Bodley and Thomas Garner in the 1870s: the statues in ornate niches above the entrance to the staircase represent Wolsey flanked by two angels. Rising from the central pool – dug on the orders of Fell as a reservoir after a fire in one of the canon's houses – is a statue of Mercury that replaces an original destroyed in 1817 in an undergraduate prank involving the 14th Earl of Derby (later to serve three terms as British prime minister). The pool features in Evelyn Waugh's *Brideshead Revisited* (1945) when aesthete Anthony Blanche feigns nonchalance by clowning around after being 'put in the Mercury' by a group of 'hearties'.

Enter the ❽ **cathedral**, the smallest in England though the mother church of the largest diocese, developed from the 12th-century church of the Priory of St Frideswide. The massive piers that line the nave – alternately round and octagonal – date from the late 12th century, with the north transept and chapels added in the 13th and 14th centuries, the spectacular vault of the choir installed *c.* 1500, the east end remodelled in the 1870s by George Gilbert Scott and the entrance provided by George Bodley at around the same time. Scott was also responsible for the seating, which faces inwards as in a college chapel. Crammed with monuments, the space also contains some remarkable stained glass.

The north aisle – which retains its 12th-century rib vault – has at its west end a window of *c.* 1630 by Abraham van

Linge depicting Jonah contemplating the city of Nineveh. The 14th-century Latin Chapel at the east end contains the carved shrine of St Frideswide, destroyed on the orders of Henry VIII and reconstructed in 2002 from fragments found down a well. Beside it is an oak 'watching loft' built to guard the saint's relics as well as three 14th-century tomb chests, one still with its original colouring – if not its figures' heads. The luminous window contains glass designed by 25-year-old Edward Burne-Jones in 1858. The Lady Chapel, next to the Latin Chapel and dating from the mid-12th century with fragments of early decoration on its ceiling, as well as the north choir aisle and south choir aisle, also have glass by Burne-Jones – this time created in the 1870s in a more insipid Pre-Raphaelite mode. The north choir window commemorates Frederic Vyner, murdered in 1870 at the age of 23 by Greek brigands in an incident that sparked an international crisis, and the south choir window Edith Liddell, sister of Alice, who died in 1870 at the age of 22.

The window in the south transept showing the martyrdom of Thomas Becket dates from *c.* 1320. Among the monuments here are several to Royalists who died during the Civil War. Exit the cathedral via the south aisle to the cloister, with its tablets to bellringers and college staff. The 12th-century Romanesque door with chevron decoration leads to the chapter house: even if closed, you can glimpse the magnificent original rib-vaulted roof.

Return to Tom Quad and exit via Fell's Tower (opposite the hall), completed by Bodley during the long rule of Dean Liddell (1855–91), with a statue of Fell on the quadrangle face and Liddell on the other side. The draughty passage between is known as Kill Canon Passage. The ❾ **Peckwater Quadrangle** beyond, named after the family that ran the inn over which it was built, was designed by Henry Aldrich, dean from 1689. A friend of Nicholas Hawksmoor, Aldrich had travelled in Italy and his three ranges follow classical principles, with a rusticated base below giant Ionic pilasters, alternating triangular and

arched pediments over the first-floor windows and a central pediment supported by Ionic columns. After Aldrich's death in 1710, the work was completed by George Clarke, who was later to design the glorious entrance range at Worcester. Instead of the fourth residential building envisaged by his predecessor, Clarke provided a monumental ⑩ **library**, given drama by colossal Corinthian columns and a deep entablature in contrasting white stone. The original arcade at ground level was enclosed in the 1760s, soon after the interior was finally completed. The Serlianas (triple windows) on the short sides were the first in Oxford.

Continue beyond the library to the ⑪ **Canterbury Quadrangle**, designed in the 1770s as the first Oxford project by James Wyatt, who was also to work on the library at Oriel and the Radcliffe Observatory. From here you can access the Picture Gallery with its collection of old masters. Return to Tom Quad and exit through the hall staircase to the cloister and Meadow Quadrangle.

To get to Magdalen, you can go directly along Deadman's Walk or take a tour around **12 Christ Church Meadow** (about 15 minutes longer), a triangle of flood-prone pasture bounded to west and east by the Thames and the Cherwell. To follow the scenic route, walk past the visitor centre, turn left at the towpath along the Thames and follow the meandering path, keeping left around the back of the college boathouses to the banks of the Cherwell, then bear right at Broad Walk to skirt the back of the Botanic Garden before emerging at the gates to Rose Lane.

To take the more direct route, walk east along the front of the Meadow Building and turn left, with the college gardens on your left. Turn right again and follow the path leading east alongside the 13th-century wall and back of Merton: known as **13 Deadman's Walk**, this was the route that linked the synagogue that stood to the north of where Tom Quad is now with the Jewish burial ground (see page 15) opposite Madgalen.

Near the end of the path is a plaque to aeronaut **14 James Sadler**, an Oxford pastry chef who on 4 October 1784 became the first Englishman to make a hot-air balloon flight, taking off from Christ Church Meadow and landing 30 minutes later some 6 miles to the north in Woodeaton.

Turn left along **Rose Lane** to the **High Street**, where turning left gives you a wide choice of cafés and restaurants (you can also buy refreshments in Magdalen's Old Kitchen Bar and Riverside Terrace).

Magdalen College
High Street (Magdalen Bridge end), OX1 4AU
www.magd.ox.ac.uk

Magdalen College was founded in 1458 by William Waynflete, another Bishop of Winchester and Lord Chancellor (this time to Henry VI). The extensive site, just outside the city's East Gate, had been the Hospital of St John. Magdalen supported the Royalists in the Civil War, surrendering most of its silver to the king and allowing its Great Tower to become a look-out post. Following the royal defeat, Oliver Cromwell and Thomas Fairfax were both given honorary degrees. Most eccentric of the college's longserving heads was Martin Routh, president from 1791 until his death at 99 in 1854: bewigged and dressed in Georgian knee-britches, he encouraged his younger wife Eliza to travel the city in a chaise drawn by a donkey, regularly ending lunch with the words: 'Woman, the ass is at the door'.

Among many notable Magdalen alumni and college members are politicians Malcolm Fraser (Australia), Lord Denning, Dominic Grieve, William Hague, Jeremy Hunt, Keith Joseph and George Osborne; film director Terrence Malick; scientists Howard Florey, Anthony Leggett, Desmond Morris and Erwin Schrödinger; journalists Ian Hislop, John Sergeant and Louis Theroux; comedian Dudley Moore; writers Julian Barnes, John Betjeman, Seamus Heaney, Alan Hollinghurst, C. S. Lewis, Robert Macfarlane, T. E. Lawrence and Oscar Wilde; musician Andrew Lloyd Webber; business people Martha Lane Fox and J. Paul Getty; library founder Thomas Bodley; cardinal Thomas Wolsey; King Jigme Wangchuck of Bhutan and Edward VIII.

The Great Tower

Magdalen's High Street frontage is dominated by the Great Tower, completed in 1509 with a plain base capped by an elaborately carved and crocketed superstructure. The tallest building in Oxford, it proclaimed the importance of the University to those arriving in the city. The gateway beside the porter's lodge, with its statues of Waynflete (left), St Swithun (patron saint of Winchester cathedral, right) and Mary Magdalene (top), dates from the 1880s, along with the ranges to its west.

Porter's lodge

Enter the college into St John's Quadrangle. On your right is the long wall of the antechapel, with an impressive west window and castellated and pinnacled roofline, adjoining the Muniment Tower. To the north is the **15 Founder's Tower**, once the ceremonial entrance to the Great Quadrangle, its intricate panelling and bay windows fronting what was originally the president's lodgings. The statues are of Edward IV and Waynflete below Mary Magdalene and St John the Baptist.

To your left, in the north-western corner of the quadrangle, is **16 Grammar Hall**, dating from 1614: this is all that remains of a complex made up of Magdalen College School, founded by Waynflete to teach choristers and local children and now on a site at the east end

of Cowley Road, and the college's predecessor Magdalen Hall, which was to move to Catte Street and merge with Hertford.

Demolished to allow the college to expand, both institutions were replaced in the 1880s by **⑰ St Swithun's Quadrangle**, designed together with the new president's lodgings next to Grammar Hall by George Bodley and Thomas Garner – as with their work on Tom Quad at Christ Church, in conformity with existing buildings.

Return to the porter's lodge. On the chapel side is a 15th-century **⑱ outdoor pulpit** from which a sermon is still preached on the Sunday nearest to St John the Baptist's Day (24 June): traditionally the courtyard would be strewn with bullrushes to create the illusion of the wilderness and river where John performed his baptisms. Continue through a diminutive doorway beyond the pulpit to the irregular **⑲ Chaplain's Quadrangle**. Here you can see the back of the chapel and Great Tower: in front of the chapel is a 1964 bronze of Christ showing his wounds to Mary Madgalene by David Wynne, who in the same year sculpted The Beatles and was subsequently to introduce them to Maharishi Mahesh Yogi.

Return to St John's Quadrangle and enter the Muniment Tower: the vault has bosses carved with angels, arms, foliage and human faces while in the window are fragments of 15th-century glass. Enter the **⑳ chapel** by the door to your right. On the wall inside the entrance are misericords saved from the original building after a wholesale refurbishment in the 1830s. The unusual grisaille west window – a *Last Judgment* with baroque swirls of figures – and the smaller windows with their portraits of saints date from the 1630s: the former was dismantled for safekeeping at the start of World War II and languished in a cellar before being restored in the 1990s. Below the paired windows on the north wall is the tomb of Waynflete's merchant father, brought from a dilapidated Lincolnshire

church during the Magdalen chapel's 19th-century refurbishment. The stone organ screen with its castellated and panelled parapet above a frieze of angels was installed at the same time: to see beyond it, you can attend choral evensong (without charge), Tuesday to Sunday during term time at 18.00.

Exit the chapel to the magnificent **21** **Great Quadrangle**, built in the 1470s and enclosed by a cloister that is unique in either Oxford or Cambridge. On the buttresses are grotesque statues of human figures, animals and hybrid monsters known as 'heiroglyphics'. Added in 1508, these are believed to symbolise the virtues (for instance a lion for courage and pelican for parental love) and vices (a pair of boxers for contention); they may also have inspired the creatures in *The Chronicles of Narnia*, begun in the 1950s towards the end of C. S. Lewis' 30-year stint as a Magdalen fellow.

Leave the cloister to the north. Loop round to the right to find the **22** **Old Kitchen and Riverside Terrace café**, occupying the only remaining part of St John's Hospital, dating from 1300.

Across the lawn is the arcaded **23** **New Building**, 27 bays long and with the strength and austerity of a neoclassical barracks. Dating from the 1730s, it was envisaged by its designer George Clarke (see above) as the northern flank of a grand quadrangle, with its end bays, intended to abut other ranges, left unfinished for a century until the plan was abandoned – though only after the college hired builder Daniel Evans (see

page 115) to demolish the northern side of the cloister and then immediately rebuild it following protests. To your left (west) is the 200-year-old Magdalen plane tree.

To see more of Magdalen's extensive grounds (a circuit of about 20 minutes), take the path to the east through the elaborate wrought-iron gateway, cross the bridge and then turn left along 24 **Addison's Walk**, named after poet, essayist and politician Joseph Addison (1672–1719), who took daily exercise here and whose essays on landscape were to influence English garden design. Part of the path follows the eastern edge of the Royalist earthworks built to defend the city from Parliamentarian forces during the Civil War. Soon you will pass the back of New Building on your left and on your right the water meadow, an island between the River Cherwell and Holywell millstream. Deer graze here in summer, after the protected snake-head fritillaries have bloomed: formerly the deer were limited to 40 (bizarrely to match the number of Magdalen scholars) by shooting them from the windows of New Building but more recently the herd has been allowed to increase and culling has been forbidden during term time – to the relief of students if not deer. Continue walking: on the wall to your left where the millstream widens and the path turns right is a plaque with a poem by C. S. Lewis inspired by birdsong heard here.

Just before the end of this stretch of path, on the right, are iron gates to the meadow, brought from Joseph Addison's home at Bilton, and bearing his initials, JA, and those of his wife, CW. Soon you come to a wooden bridge leading to the fellows' garden, which surprisingly you are free to explore. To the right of the bridge is a sculpture, Y, by Mark Wallinger that resembles a tree with antler-like branches. Commissioned in 2008 to celebrate the college's 550th anniversary, it apparently references the Greek letter upsilon, which has a numerical value of 400, as well as the medieval additional Roman numeral of Y, with a value of 150. Continue the circuit back towards the college.

Exit through the porter's lodge and turn right into the High Street. On your right is the southern range of Magdalen's late

'Y' by Mark Wallinger

19th-century St Swithun's Quadrangle, with a pair of ornate castellated and gabled oriels at its eastern end, followed by the Longwall Library, built in 1850 by local architect John Chessell Buckler to house Magdalen College School when the college wanted to expand into its site. Look right up **Longwall Street**: the wall on the eastern side was built in 1467 to lay claim to Magdalen's territory before any of its buildings were realised.

Continue along the High Street (for a more detailed description of this stretch of the walk, see page 34). The ㉕ **Eastgate Hotel** on your left, a 1900 imitation of a 17th-century coaching inn, stands on the site of Oxford's East Gate, demolished in 1771 and depicted in the cartouche between the first-floor windows. Across Merton Street are the ㉖ **Ruskin College of Art** and ㉗ **Examination Schools**, designed by Thomas Graham Jackson in 1880 and 1875 respectively. The Ruskin building originally housed the Delegacy for Non-Collegiate Students, established to make an Oxford education accessible to those who could not afford to live in college. The Examination Schools were built when the University introduced written papers to replace oral exams whose rigour was increasingly called into question. In compulsory costume of academic gowns and sub fusc (black and white including socks, which must cover the ankles with no flesh exposed), students still sit exams in the two halls on the first floor. The panels on either side of the central arch show a *viva*, with a nervous candidate and three stern dons, and successful students at their graduation ceremony, where even today they kneel in front of the vice-chancellor to be hit on the head with a Bible.

Turn right up **Queen's Lane**. On your right is the modest door to ㉘ **St Edmund Hall** (see page 30), the sole survivor of the medieval halls established to house and educate undergraduates before the formation of the college system. Named after Edmund

Queen's Lane

of Abingdon (*c* 1174–1240), an Archbishop of Canterbury and devout ascetic as well as an expert in mathematics, dialectics and theology, it is mentioned in documents from 1317 but is thought to have been founded up to a century earlier. You can see a 2007 statue of Edmund's emaciated form through the railings to the churchyard of St Peter-in-the-East, now the St Edmund Hall library. The church itself was founded possibly in Saxon times as a place of prayer or thanksgiving for travellers departing or entering the city via the East Gate. The current building was begun in the 1130s, with the tower added in the 1300s.

Follow the road around to the left. The rough stone building on your right is the 14th-century latrine block of **New College**, still used in part for that purpose today. Ahead of you are the many crocketed pinnacles of All Souls, with the two tall towers of Nicholas Hawksmoor's eccentric North Quadrangle (see page 42) to the left. Follow the road under the arch and turn right to New College's fortress-like entrance.

New College

Entry via New College Lane, OX1 3BN
www.ox.ac.uk

New College was founded in 1379 by William of Wykeham – like Wolsey at Christ Church and Waynflete at Magdalen a Bishop of Winchester and Lord Chancellor, in this case to Edward III and Richard II. Its original name was 'The Warden and Scholars of St Mary's College of Winchester in Oxford' but it became known as New College to distinguish it from Oriel, founded as the House of the Blessed Mary in 1324.

Building on land formerly occupied by the city dunghill, Wykeham set up his college to train clergy to replenish the ranks following the Black Death. Until the 19th century entry was restricted to pupils of Winchester College, with students awarded degrees purely on the recommendation of the warden. Subsequent – and more rigorously tested – alumni and college members include writers John Fowles, Patrick Gale, John Galsworthy, Sophie Kinsella, Kate Mosse, Dennis Potter, A. N. Wilson and Naomi Wolfe; publisher Victor Gollanz; politicians Tony Benn and Hugh Gaitskell; actors, TV personalities and filmmakers Kate Beckinsale, Angus Deayton, Hugh Grant, Sally Phillips, Mel Smith, Florian Henckel von Donnersmarck and Lucy Worsley; chef Rick Stein; art historian Neil MacGregor; and rabbi Jonathan Sacks.

With the warden's lodgings on the first floor and statues of the Virgin Mary flanked by the founder and the angel of the Annunciation, the New College entrance was the earliest of the University's many gatetowers. Architecturally influential, the college also contains the first of Oxford's enclosed quadrangles and the first chapel with a T-shaped plan. You can attend choral evensong (for no charge) during term time at 17.45 on Sunday or 18.15 any other evening except Wednesday: the acclaimed choir, made up of fourteen men and sixteen boy choristers, is one of the only remaining all-male Oxford ensembles.

Enter the gateway to the **㉙ Front Quadrangle**, until the 1670s only two storeys high – as you can tell from the contrast between the rough stone of the lower floors and the dressed stone above. The south and east ranges contained rooms for college members, with the library on the upper floor of the east range (facing the entrance); more imposing buildings with large tracery windows and rooflines embellished with crocketed pinnacles were provided to the north for the hall and chapel, with the antechapel projecting into the courtyard to the left of the entrance. This is mirrored by the Muniment Tower in the north-eastern corner, which contains the entrance to the hall, with the college treasury on its top floor.

Climb the vaulted staircase to Oxford's oldest **㉚ hall**, designed in imitation of the hall of a country house, with a platform for a 'high table' at one end, a gallery above a screen at the other and a central fire whose smoke would escape through the lantern above. The linenfold panelling, now hung with portraits of past wardens as well as a surprising number of female college members, was added in the 1530s: both panelling and roof were restored to something approximating their original form in the 1860s by George Gilbert Scott, who was also to provide new ranges of college accommodation along Holywell Street (see page 21).

Return to the Front Quadrangle and enter the **㉛ chapel** via a passage to the north of the gatetower. The T-shaped plan that was soon to become standard within Oxford colleges may in fact have developed by accident, with the antechapel intended

as the west end of a nave that was truncated to build a cloister. With its twin pairs of soaring gothic arches, the lofty space still contains much of its original stained glass depicting saints in elaborate niches. The extraordinary west window was designed in the 1770s by Joshua Reynolds: the row of society beauties in floating gowns masquerading as the seven virtues were described by diarist John Byng, visiting soon after its completion, as 'half-dressed languishing Harlots'.

In front of the window is *Lazarus Rising from the Dead*, a powerful sculpture by Jacob Epstein installed in 1947 presumably as a poignant tribute to the dead of World War II. On the entrance wall is a memorial by typographer and sculptor Eric Gill to college members who lost their lives in World War I: an amazing feat of lettering, it gains potency from being a simple list of 263 names, running without interruption across a length of 9 metres in a visual representation of the seemingly endless death toll. On the floor on the opposite side of the space are 14th- and 15th-century brasses including several that feature the Grim Reaper. The memorial to four German college members who died in World War I, also designed by Gill, was commissioned by William Spooner, warden from 1903 to 1925 and best remembered for 'Spoonerisms' such as 'Kinquering Congs' for 'Conquering Kings'. His memorial – in Latin and presumably Spoonerism-free – hangs on the wall to the left of the entrance.

The chancel provided a template many Oxford colleges would follow: an aisle lined with pews, in which the college community would gather to pray for the soul of the founder, terminated by a dramatic reredos made up of tiers of saints (and sometimes college members) in place of a church's east window. The roof and reredos here, both plastered over by James Wyatt in the mid-17th century, were remodelled in the late 1870s by Scott. Some of the medieval misericords can still be seen in the back rows and the ends of the pews have beautifully carved figures.

31

31

Leave the chapel and turn right into the low ❷ **cloister**, created in the 1390s to enclose a graveyard for college members after the plan for a larger church was abandoned. Still conveying a strong sense of the atmosphere of the medieval institution, it contains 14th-century statues removed from the tower of the University Church of St Mary (see below) following a restoration at the end of the 19th century. The massive holm oak in the north-western corner features in the scene from *Harry Potter and the Goblet of Fire* (2005) where Draco Malfoy is turned into a white ferret.

Return to the Front Quadrangle and take the passage opposite the gatetower to the ❸ **Garden Quadrangle**, the University's first open courtyard space, its three ranges built mostly at the end of the 17th century. Beyond the beautiful gilded screen, wrought around the college motto 'Manners Mayketh Man' (unusually proclaiming the importance of behaviour above birthright and in English rather than Latin), are the gardens themselves, laid out in 1530 on the site of the kitchen garden.

A magnificent stretch of 12th-century ❹ **city wall**, with battlemented ramparts and bastions, runs along the northern edge: Wykeham accepted responsibility for maintaining it and it is still inspected every three years by the mayor and his retinue. The central mound was begun at the end of the 16th century and vastly enlarged to become a look-out post during the Civil War: New College also allowed its cloister to become a munitions store and to be used for musketry training. Through a gap in the back (east) wall you can see the courtyard of the Sacher Building, designed by David Roberts in the 1960s (see page 18), with the 1958 Barbara Hepworth bronze *Garden Sculpture (Model for Meridian)* at its centre; over the southern wall rise the brutalist concrete tower and jagged gables of St Edmund Hall's Kelly and Emden student accommodation (see page 32), built at around the same time by architects Kenneth Stevens Associates.

Bridge of Sighs

35

Emerge on to **New College Lane**, its high windowless walls giving a strong sense of how the medieval city may have looked, with narrow lanes lined by college buildings designed to protect privacy and privilege. The wall on your right is the back of the New College cloister and on your left is the warden's barn, built in 1400 to store produce from the college estates and linked to the warden's lodgings by a bridge in the 1670s.

The so-called Bridge of Sighs at the end of the street was created in 1913–14 by Thomas Graham Jackson to link new residential buildings for Hertford College to the existing campus.

Cross **Catte Street** and walk up the steps towards the Sheldonian Theatre (for more detailed information on this stretch of the walk, see pages 44 to 52). On the right is the ㉟ **Clarendon Building**, designed by Nicholas Hawksmoor in 1712–13 as offices and a very grand print works for Oxford University Press. The building takes its name from the 1st Earl of Clarendon, whose successful *History of the Great Rebellion* (1702–04) financed its creation. The statues on the roof, some by James Thornhill, who decorated the hall at nearby Blenheim Palace, represent the muses.

Directly in front of you is the  **Sheldonian Theatre**, initiated by Dean Fell of Christ Church (who was also vice-chancellor of the University) as a secular space to stage ceremonies that had previously been held in the University Church of St Mary. Created from 1664 by Christopher Wren and based loosely on the Theatre of Marcellus in Rome, it was Oxford's first classical building and the architect's first major work. Skirt the theatre to the left to see its main entrance, designed to resemble the doorway to a Palladian church, though decorated with an un-Palladian fussiness.

The  **Divinity School** opposite – a masterpiece of late gothic, with pinnacles, castellation and a façade made up almost entirely of glazing set into delicate tracery – was begun in the 1420s as a single-storey building where theology was taught and examined, with an upper floor added soon afterwards to house the library of Humfrey, Duke of Gloucester, the precursor to the Bodleian (see below). Wren provided the central doorway in 1669 (you can see his initials above it) to create a ceremonial route to the Sheldonian Theatre for use during graduation ceremonies.

Enter the doorway opposite the Clarendon Building into the Schools Quadrangle of the  **Bodleian Library**, established in 1602 by Thomas Bodley, a diplomat at the court of Elizabeth I. The range to your right (with the entrance to the library at its centre) is the Proscholium, built as an extension to the

Divinity School and borrowing its flamboyant roofline and delicate network of blind arcading. The other ranges were conceived by Bodley to provide 'better built scholes... than those ruinous little rooms' that had previously served for lectures and examinations, with the names of the disciplines taught given in Latin above their doorways. The third storey was originally intended for the display of the Bodleian's many portraits, making it the first public art gallery in Britain.

In front of the Proscholium stands a swaggering statue of the third Earl of Pembroke, one of the library's chief benefactors; the gatetower opposite, its upper storeys built to safeguard the University's financial deposits, features a statue of James I presenting a copy of his collected writings to a woman representing the University (where, of course, women were still unable to study) with an allegory of Fame blowing his (own) trumpet. Known as the Tower of the Five Orders, it has columns rising through the orders of Tuscan, Doric, Ionic and Corinthian to Composite, offering an easily digestible lesson in architectural history.

Exit through the gateway opposite the one by which you entered to a stunning view of the **39** **Radcliffe Camera** or Radcliffe Library, conceived by Hawksmoor as the centrepiece of a new academic area he referred to as the Forum Universitatis. Completed after his death in 1736 by his assistant James Gibbs, the circular structure had an open colonnade at ground level, topped by a reading room (the *camera*) with a high domed ceiling and an arcade running around its perimeter with bookshelves on the outer face. Drawing on his training in Italy (whose architecture Hawksmoor knew only from books), Gibbs embellished the original design, making it lighter, more sculpturally expressive and more playfully baroque. The ground-floor colonnade was enclosed in 1862.

To see more of Hawksmoor's work, peer through the iron grille on the eastern side of the Radcliffe Camera into the spectacular North Quadrangle of All Souls, built in 1716–34 and oriented to offer views of the library the architect was unable to complete.

39

Magpie Lane

At the junction with the **High Street** is the **40** **University Church of St Mary**, used for University examinations, debates and degree ceremonies until the completion of the Sheldonian. At its rear (on Catte Street) is a vaulted chamber dating from the 1320s where meetings of the University's academics (known as the Congregation) were held; it now houses the excellent Vaults & Garden café. The exterior with its large windows was remodelled to unify the rear of the church during a 15th-century rebuilding campaign. The magnificent tower dates from *c.* 1280, with the spire – a glorious ensemble of ornate pinnacles and statues of saints – added about 50 years later.

Cross the High Street. The Quod restaurant of the **41** **Old Bank Hotel** – with the arms of Elizabeth I on its upper storey – is in fact a 1900s reconstruction of a 16th-century house that stood on the site. The four bays on the right of the main hotel date from 1775 with the more confident section to the left added in 1798: both were initially occupied by drapers John Parsons and Thomas Fletcher, who together set up a private bank that survived for a century before being taken over by Barclays in 1900.

Walk down **Magpie Lane**, its name derived from a local inn. No. 2 on the left, with two overhangs, dates from 1588 (the date is carved above the window), with no. 5 slightly later. The wall on the other side of the lane marks the boundary of Oriel. Turn left into **Kybald Street**: on the left are **42** **almshouses** established in 1816 with a bequest from banker John Parsons; after the building was taken over in 1959 by University College, American donors funded an extension to almshouses in St Clement's to compensate. The modest modern building on the corner of Kybald Street and Magpie Lane is residential accommodation built for Corpus Christi by Powell & Moya in 1968. Return to Magpie Lane and at the bottom turn right into **Merton Street** to see Wyatt's imposing gateway to Christ Church's Canterbury Quadrangle (see above), designed as a triumphal arch: from here you access the Christ Church Picture Gallery.

Gateway to Christ Church

Return along Merton Street and opposite Magpie Lane is the chapel of **Merton College**, begun in the 1290s to double as the new parish church of St John the Baptist – hence the public entrance on the street side, below a large tracery window flanked by statues of the dedicatee and the Virgin Mary. The street front of the choir (the oldest part of the building) has sturdy buttresses topped by thrusting gargoyles, some with doubled heads. The transepts were added between 1365 and 1425 and the low tower between them, with its eight pinnacles and castellated parapet, dates from c. 1450.

Merton Street

On the opposite side of the road is a pink building with four gables built in the 1580s: according to a plaque at its far end, it was the birthplace of Berkshire MP Henry Marten (1602–80), an ardent Republican and one of the signatories to the death warrant of Charles I. Next door is **43** **Beam Hall**, a medieval academic hall named after its founder Gilbert de Biham that was converted into a house in the 15th century: a plaque commemorates anatomist and neurologist Thomas Willis (1621–75), a former resident whose major discovery was the 'Circle of Willis', a group of arteries at the base of the brain. The adjacent stone building with the twin gables is **44** **Postmaster's Hall**, originally part of Merton (a postmaster, from the Latin *portionista*, meaning a student receiving a portion of food and drink, is the college's term for a senior undergraduate). A plaque identifies the building as the birthplace and lifelong home of curmudgeonly Oxford historian Anthony (à) Wood (1632–95).

The flamboyant house just along the street was built in 1908 by Basil Champneys (architect of the Rhodes Building) as lodgings for the warden of Merton. Opposite, flanked by double Doric columns, is the beautifully simple 1599 doorway to St Alban's Hall, incorporated into the quadrangle Champneys added to the site in the early 1900s (see below).

Return along the street to the entrance to the college, a gatehouse built in the 1460s by master-mason Robert Janyns (who also added the tower to the chapel).

Merton College
Merton Street, OX1 4JD
www.merton.ox.ac.uk

Merton was founded in 1264 by William de Merton, Lord Chancellor to Henry III, regent while Edward I returned from the Crusades to take the throne following his father's death and subsequently Bishop of Rochester. The oldest college in Oxford, its statutes and to some extent its architecture served as a model for the many institutions that followed. Above the doorway on Merton Street – between statues of Edward I and the founder – is a relief of a book, with the Lamb of God opposite de Merton kneeling in prayer, flanked by John the Baptist and a unicorn. Alumni and college members include Thomas Bodley, founder of the library; historian Anthony Wood; anatomist William Harvey; cultural theorists Theodor Adorno and Stuart Hall; writers Max Beerbohm, T. S. Eliot, Louis Macneice and J. R. R. Tolkien; and Emperor Naruhito of Japan.

In the absence of any fixed idea of how a college might be organised, Merton's **45 Front Quadrangle** developed piecemeal. To the left of the gatetower on the street side were the original warden's lodgings, extended in 1300 from houses bought by de Merton from St Frideswides's Priory, politician Robert de Flixthorpe and 'Jacob the Jew' (presumably soon to be driven out of Oxford, see page 89): the rest of the quadrangle occupies what were once their gardens. To the right is the chapel with

its elaborate tracery east window and opposite the gatetower is the **46 hall**, where lectures were given and founding fellows (numbering between 30 and 40) could dine together. Rebuilt by George Gilbert Scott in 1874, it retains its original door with iron hoops and curlicues, which you can see if you walk up the steps.

Take the passage between hall and chapel and follow signs to **47 Mob Quad**, the first of Oxford's enclosed college quadrangles, built over a century from 1288 on the site of the former church of St John the Baptist. The treasury in the (north-east) corner beside the entrance – a fortified tower with a steeply pitched roof – is the oldest element; on either side of it are residential ranges dating from the early 1300s. As became traditional, these consisted of pairs of chambers – each made up of a large room with beds for three or four fellows and individual study cubicles – located on either side of a central staircase, accessed through the small doorways with their pointed arches. The south and west ranges, with chambers below and the oldest library in Oxford above, were built in the 1370s; the large dormers were added in the 1620s.

Leave the quadrangle via the low vaulted passage in the north-west corner and enter the **48 chapel** through its south transept, added to the choir in the 1360s, with the north transept completed some 50 years later. As at New College, plans for a full-scale church – with a nave stretching from the position of the present organ west across the land

where Corpus Christi now stands – were abandoned. On the west wall of the south transept is a monument to Henry Savile (1549–1622), translator of the Bible from Greek to English and founder of the Savilian chairs of astronomy and geometry as well as the warden who instigated Merton's expansion with the construction of the Fellows' Quadrangle (see below). On the west wall of the north transept is a monument to library founder Thomas Bodley (1545–1613), his image – fittingly framed by columns of stacked books – surrounded by nubile maidens said to represent the teaching faculties.

The choir is entered through a 17th-century screen designed by Christopher Wren but only recently restored following its removal by William Butterfield during a radical 19th-century refurbishment that involved replacing the floor and stalls and painting the roof in Pre-Raphaelite style. Thankfully, much of the original stained glass survived, including the Annunciation scene in the spectacular tracery east window and a number of triple windows in the side walls. Featuring the Apostles flanked by scholars kneeling in prayer, these were presented in 1310 by fellow Henry Mansfield, later to become chancellor of the University: his name is inscribed within each.

49

Fitzjames Gateway

Exit the chapel into an informal garden: in front of you is the ㊾ **Grove Building**, designed by Butterfield in 1864 with a polychrome façade but refaced in sandstone in the 1920s following criticisms that it was 'glaring, ugly, pretentious [and] may justly be anathematised'. Cross in front of the library and turn left to return to the Front Quadrangle via the tiny Patey's Quadrangle, named after a 19th-century college butler who sold jam and muffins from a room here. Go through the Fitzjames Gateway (to the west of the hall), built c. 1500 by warden Richard Fitzjames as an extension to his accommodation. His new lodgings were used as an apartment for visiting queens of England including Henrietta Maria, who made Merton her headquarters when Charles I occupied Christ Church during the Civil War, with the two sites linked by a connecting door. On the Front Quadrangle face of the arch are the arms of the see of Rochester, where Fitzjames was bishop, flanked by two angels; the vaulting beneath has bosses carved with the signs of the zodiac, with the royal arms in the centre.

The ⑤ **Fellows' Quadrangle** beyond was built in the early 1600s by masons Savile imported for economy's sake from his native Yorkshire. Though traditional in layout and decoration, it was the first Oxford quadrangle designed with three storeys. The Tower of the Orders – with columns rising through Doric, Ionic and Corinthian to Composite interspersed with pagan decoration including many-breasted goddesses – was a precursor to the one at the Bodleian and may have used the same masons: Savile and Bodley were both fellows at Merton from 1565 and Savile is known to have acted as Bodley's architectural advisor. The rooms occupied by J. R. R. Tolkien as a fellow from 1945 to 1959 were in this range, overlooking the meadow beyond.

Return to the Front Quadrangle and go under the archway to your right to the ⑤ **St Alban's Quadrangle**, built by Champneys in the early 1900s on the site of St Alban's Hall, which had been incorporated into Merton in 1882. An ornate metal screen on the southern side offers views of the garden, which extends to the line of the former city wall.

Return to Merton Street. To return to St Aldate's, take the path alongside the west of the chapel to Christ Church Meadow and turn right along Broad Walk.

Visit...

Bodleian Library
Broad Street, OX1 3BG
www.bodleian.ox.ac.uk

Sheldonian Theatre
Broad Street, OX1 3AZ
www.sheldonian.ox.ac.uk/visit

University Church of St Mary
High Street, OX1 4BJ
www.universitychurch.ox.ac.uk

Eat/Drink...

Bodleian Café
Weston Library,
Broad Street, OX1 3BG
www.benugo.com

Cafe Loco
The Old Palace,
85/87 St Aldate's, OX1 1RA
www.goingloco.com

Grand Café
84 High Street, OX1 4BG
www.thegrandcafe.co.uk

Head of the River
Folly Bridge, St Aldate's, OX1 4LB
www.headoftheriveroxford.co.uk

Queen's Lane Coffee House
40 High Street, OX1 4AP
www.qlcoffeehouse.com

Quod Restaurant and Bar
92–94 High Street, OX1 4BJ
www.quod.co.uk

Vaults & Garden Café
1 Radcliffe Square, OX1 4AH
www.thevaultsandgarden.com

The White Horse
52 Broad Street, OX1 3BB
www.whitehorseoxford.co.uk

5
West of Carfax:
industry & reform

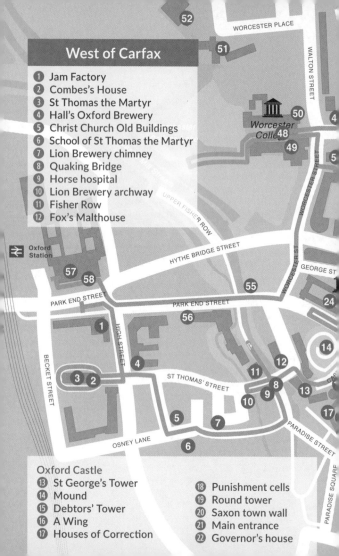

West of Carfax

1. Jam Factory
2. Combes's House
3. St Thomas the Martyr
4. Hall's Oxford Brewery
5. Christ Church Old Buildings
6. School of St Thomas the Martyr
7. Lion Brewery chimney
8. Quaking Bridge
9. Horse hospital
10. Lion Brewery archway
11. Fisher Row
12. Fox's Malthouse

Oxford Castle

13. St George's Tower
14. Mound
15. Debtors' Tower
16. A Wing
17. Houses of Correction
18. Punishment cells
19. Round tower
20. Saxon town wall
21. Main entrance
22. Governor's house

WORCESTER PLACE

WALTON STREET

Worcester College

UPPER FISHER ROW

Oxford Station

HYTHE BRIDGE STREET

WORCESTER ST

GEORGE ST

PARK END STREET

PARK END STREET

HIGH STREET

BECKET STREET

ST THOMAS' STREET

PARADISE STREET

OSNEY LANE

PARADISE SQUARE

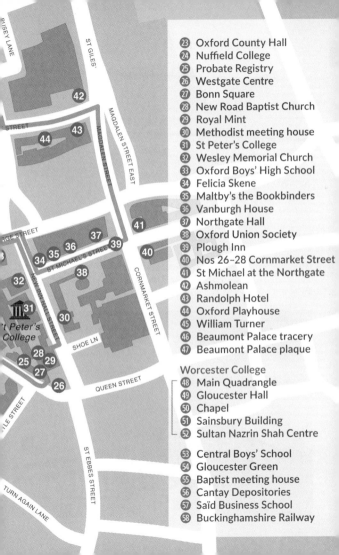

23 Oxford County Hall
24 Nuffield College
25 Probate Registry
26 Westgate Centre
27 Bonn Square
28 New Road Baptist Church
29 Royal Mint
30 Methodist meeting house
31 St Peter's College
32 Wesley Memorial Church
33 Oxford Boys' High School
34 Felicia Skene
35 Maltby's the Bookbinders
36 Vanburgh House
37 Northgate Hall
38 Oxford Union Society
39 Plough Inn
40 Nos 26–28 Cornmarket Street
41 St Michael at the Northgate
42 Ashmolean
43 Randolph Hotel
44 Oxford Playhouse
45 William Turner
46 Beaumont Palace tracery
47 Beaumont Palace plaque

Worcester College
48 Main Quadrangle
49 Gloucester Hall
50 Chapel
51 Sainsbury Building
52 Sultan Nazrin Shah Centre

53 Central Boys' School
54 Gloucester Green
55 Baptist meeting house
56 Cantay Depositories
57 Saïd Business School
58 Buckinghamshire Railway

West of Carfax: industry & reform

Start: Jam Factory
Finish: Oxford Station
Distance: 2.4 miles

This walk begins and ends in an area formerly filled with slums and light industry. It takes in two of Oxford's oldest buildings – the castle and the tower of St Michael at the Northgate, both connected to the prison system – as well as the first middle-class housing on the fringes of the 19th-century suburb of North Oxford. In terms of religion (a seemingly inescapable part of the city's history), it runs from the High Anglicanism of St Thomas the Martyr to the site of Baptist rituals and Oxford's first Methodist meeting house. Only two colleges are covered, and it is worth trying to time the walk so you reach Worcester (near the end) between 14.00 and 16.00 to allow for a visit to one of Oxford's most charming combinations of buildings and gardens.

The start and end point is Oxford station, an undistinguished gateway to the city built in the 1970s and with a major redevelopment planned. From the forecourt, cross **Park End Street** (taking care at the crossings, where it is unclear whether pedestrians or traffic have right of way) and walk east (left). On the corner of Hollybush Row is the ❶ **Jam Factory**, built in 1903 to conform to the recent Factories and Workshops Act after Frank Cooper's Oxford Marmalade company outgrew its High Street home (see page 34). The imposing four-storey frontage on Park End Street, with oranges carved in stone between the first-floor windows, embodies the confidence of a firm whose products featured in college breakfasts and then travelled the world with alumni craving a taste of home. The building had a workers' canteen on the top floor, well-lit rooms where a female workforce cut up fruit and bottled marmalade on the floors below, and grocery shops at street level. The single-storey extension to the east and south, with its handsome curved corner, was added in 1925: walk down **Hollybush Row** to see the tall chimney of the boilerhouse that heated the copper vats in which the fruit was cooked. This part of the complex, including rooms originally for storage and despatch, now houses the Jam Factory, a café and arts venue with a small, well-chosen menu.

Continue down Hollybush Row and take the first right to the church of St Thomas the Martyr: to your left before you enter the churchyard is a brick arch with a large crucifix that once formed the gateway to the attached convent, founded in the mid-19th century to minister to the area's slumdwellers. At the front of the churchyard is ❷ **Combes's House**, built in 1702, according to the inscription on the wall, 'at the charge of Mr John Coombes, Cityzen and Plaisterer of London, for the Benefit of as many Poor children as the rent of this house will Pay for their teaching to read and write'. Though born in Oxford, Combes made his fortune in London, where

he let out several properties: his schoolhouse is said to be unique in its arrangement of a schoolroom on the ground floor, alongside two rooms to house the schoolmaster, with rented accommodation to fund its running costs above. The role of schoolmaster was to be filled by the parish clerk: Combes specified that he should be 'duely qualified' (unlike in today's Free Schools) or another teacher be chosen by churchwardens.

❸ St Thomas the Martyr itself was founded in 1190, with the chancel at the east end (in front of you as you enter the churchyard) a remnant of the original building: walk round to the south side where nestling between two buttresses is a diminutive door with ironwork scrolls claimed by Jan Morris to be the oldest door in Oxford. The church's tower and nave date from the early 16th century and much of the rest from the 19th century. For 50 years from 1842, the vicar of St Thomas was Thomas Chamberlain, a High Church sympathiser who not only established a convent but also introduced frowned-on paraphernalia such as altar candles, wore forbidden

Eucharistic vestments and invited Oxford Movement leaders including Edward Pusey to preach (see box, page 84). His grave is marked by the large granite cross at the south-western corner of the churchyard.

Take a tour around the churchyard – a wildlife oasis within an otherwise built-up area – and return to the entrance: in front of the chancel are the graves of many of the sisters from the convent while among the first row of tombstones to the north is a memorial to Olive Gibbs (1918–95), chair of CND in the 1960s and twice mayor of Oxford, who is also commemorated on plaques on Christ Church Dwellings and in Bonn Square (see below). St Thomas the Martyr is now affiliated with St Barnabas in Jericho and hosts services for the Romanian community.

Cross Hollybush Row. On the building on the corner of St Thomas' Street – until 2011 the Chequers pub – you can still see the tiled logo of **❹ Hall's Oxford Brewery**, one of several brewing firms attracted to the area by its many waterways. Founded in 1646 as the Swan Brewery before being acquired by William Hall in 1795, Hall's operated until 1926 from nearby Swan's Nest Island.

Alongside the breweries came factories and light industry, taking advantage of cheap land and the transport links of the Oxford Canal – opened in 1790 to connect the coalfields of the Midlands with London via the River Thames – and the Great Western Railway, which arrived half a century later. And alongside industry came workers' housing – often shoddily built, overcrowded and lacking in sanitation. Walk west along **St Thomas' Street** and take the first right down **Woodbine Place**: on your left are ❺ **Christ Church Old Buildings**, designed in 1866 by local church architect Edward George Bruton to provide decent accommodation following slum clearances ordered by the Dean and Chapter of Christ Church, which was responsible for the running of the parish. The only surviving housing of its kind in Oxford, the model dwellings are similar in style to those pioneered by the Peabody and Guinness trusts in London – a three-storey brick block arranged around a courtyard, with 30 flats (each with three bedrooms, a sitting room, scullery and WC) accessed from the street via staircases within arched openings. Turn left along **Osney Lane** at the bottom of Woodbine Place to find the plaque to longtime resident Olive Gibbs (see above).

Opposite the flats on Osney Lane is the ❻ **School of St Thomas the Martyr**, built in 1904 through public subscription after the vicar of St Thomas begged Christ Church for a site because there was currently no school within the parish. The building, with separate entrances for boys and girls and a surprisingly baroque brick gable above a big triple window that presumably lit a communal hall, is now occupied by Broken Spoke, a not-for-profit social enterprise offering cycle training, repairs and courses in mechanics.

Continue along Osney Lane and walk through the alley in front of you (**Woodins Way**). On the left is the **7** **Morrell's Lion Brewery chimney**, with the date 1901 – when water power was replaced by coal – inscribed on a plaque on its side. The brewery was founded in 1743 by Richard and Edward Tawney (see below), who sold it half a century later to father and son Mark and James Morrell: by 1824, the family had made enough money to build the grand Headington Hill Hall to the east of Oxford, subsequently the home of villainous publisher Robert Maxwell and now part of Oxford Brookes University.

As wages – and consequently demand for beer – increased and brewing became mechanised, the St Thomas' Street site was redeveloped in the 1880s by the inappropriately named architect Harry Drinkwater. After an acrimonious family dispute, the operation closed in 1998 and the site was turned into housing. Stop at the bridge and look to your left to see the brewery's red-painted waterwheel, with behind it the weir that formed a millstream to power production before the move to coal.

Continue to the junction with **Paradise Street**, then turn left and walk alongside Castle Mill Stream to ❽ **Quaking Bridge**. The blue plaque of 2014 commemorating the buddleia was one of five installed around the city by artist Imogen Rigden to celebrate the plant's 'courage in persistently growing in inhospitable urban dust'. The single-storey red-brick building on the left of the bridge was built by Drinkwater as a ❾ **horse hospital**, with the chimney ventilating the blacksmith's forge. Continue left along St Thomas' Street to the impressive wrought-iron ❿ **archway to the Lion Brewery**, flanked by gilded lions apparently holding sprigs of clover. The converted apartment blocks retain Drinkwater's late 19th-century façades: the brewhouse was to the left of the entrance, the offices to the right and the stone building in the centre, dating from the mid-1700s, was the office of the head brewer.

Retrace your steps to Quaking Bridge and look left along ⓫ **Fisher Row**. The fine flat-fronted three-storey house at no. 1 was built in the 1790s by Edward Tawney, owner of the malthouse opposite, perhaps using his share of the proceeds from the sale of the Lion Brewery to the Morrells. Three times mayor of Oxford, Tawney supplied debtors in Oxford prison (see below) with food and also built an almshouse next door to his own home (if in somewhat less grand style). A plaque on the gable gives the date (1799) and name of the founder. Continue across the bridge and look to your left up **Tidmarsh**

11

12

Lane to see Tawney's vast ⓬ **Fox's Malthouse**: as malting required a large floor area to spread the grain but little light and no machinery, the building has small windows and just enough floor-to-ceiling height for a man to stand to shovel and turn the grain.

Turn right opposite Tidmarsh Lane and walk uphill through a gate that leads to the remains of **Oxford Castle**, built in 1071 by Robert d'Oilly, the Norman governor of Oxford, as a defensive enclosure with a moat formed by diverting Castle Mill Stream. Until 1997 the site was Oxford's prison and it now houses restaurants, a hotel and a museum. If you do not wish to walk round the site, go straight to the exit on New Road and turn right to look at Oxford County Hall.

Oxford Castle

44-46 Oxford Castle, OX1 1AY

www.oxfordcastleandprison.co.uk

Open daily, 10.00-16.30

Little of Oxford's 11th-century castle survives: the massive ⑬ **St George's Tower**, later appropriated as a tower for St George's chapel (built for the monastic community installed by D'Oilly), was originally part of the defensive walls and the 20-metre-high motte or ⑭ **mound** with its central well was intended as a defensible point if all else failed. These defences were reinforced by Parliamentarians (using the enforced labour of the townspeople) in 1649, after the defeat of Charles I, before being dismantled a couple of years later when the military authorities decided Oxford was 'not tenable' (see box, page 168).

By this point the castle functioned as a prison, with its owners – Christ Church College – renting premises to gaolers who made a living from charging prisoners for board and lodging. New wings were built from the 1780s, after the complex was brought under the control of the county administration, and the site was further expanded from the 1840s by architect Henry Jones Underwood (also the architect of St Paul's in Jericho), who committed suicide before the job was complete. The prison closed in 1997 and amazingly the complex now houses a Malmaison Hotel catering to those who can sleep untroubled by history.

To the right of the entrance is the long, low range of D Wing, dating from the 1790s and still with its barred windows, and the four-storey crenellated ⑮ **Debtors' Tower**, where prisoners were held often for years until they could pay off what they owed. In a gruesome reminder of the penal system of the past, the area you are walking on is designated 'burial garden' in old maps of the site. Skirt the tower to the right to reach the exercise yard: the less rugged four-storey building to your left, with a tall arched single window on its side, is ⑯ **A Wing**, part of Underwood's 19th-century expansion, originally with 150 cells each designed for a single prisoner, though they regularly held three by the time the prison closed. On the other side of the exercise yard are the smaller ⑰ **Houses of Correction** for petty criminals, dating from the first expansion and later converted into kitchens. Dungeon-like ⑱ **punishment cells** lay behind a small door to their left.

Continue past this door to the edge of the site where you can still find the base of a ⑲ **round tower**, built c. 1235, that formed part of the castle walls. Walk around it to re-enter the site and behind bars are some fragments of the ⑳ **Saxon town wall** that predates even the castle. Walk up the ramp to the other side of A Wing, where the disconcertingly beautiful window offers an unsettling glimpse into what remains of the prison interior: modelled on Pentonville in London, it had tiers of cells linked by metal walkways flanking a central full-height well from which every prisoner could be observed.

Continue to the small service yard and walk through the arch to the ㉑ **main entrance** – to both prison and hotel. From 1790 until public execution was abolished in 1868, some 20 people were hanged from a gallows mounted on a platform supported by the heavy corbels you can still see above the doorway, attracting crowds of up to 10,000 onlookers. Between 1732 and 1952 there were 100 executions at the gaol, many for crimes as trivial as sheep theft or housebreaking. Cross in front of the entrance to look at the elegant ㉒ **governor's house** of 1848 with its gothic windows, fine gothic front door and crenellated roofline.

Exit the site via the main gate and turn right along **New Road**. Next to the castle and borrowing its aesthetic is ㉓ **Oxford County Hall**, a battlemented confection resembling a child's fortress, with twin turrets, arrow slits and a sturdy arched doorway. Described in a 1926 history as 'quite the most abominable pseudo-gothic Assize Court in all England', it was built in the 1840s by John Plowman to house the county courts, with a tunnel giving direct access to the prison. The council's offices were moved into the adjacent modern building in the 1970s and the courts to St Aldate's in 1986 but the County Council still meets in the council chamber. On the far side of the building is a milestone marker from 1755 and a signpost from the early 20th century that 'symbolises the role of Oxfordshire County Council in providing and maintaining a countywide network of services'.

To visit ㉔ **Nuffield College** (open Monday to Friday, 9–17), retrace your steps past the castle and enter through the gateway beyond the incongruously tall tower on the other side of New Road. The University's first graduate-only college and the first to admit both male and female students, Nuffield was founded in 1937 by car manufacturer William Morris (1877–1963, Lord Nuffield from 1934, see box, page 228) – though in later life he was to deride it as 'that bloody Kremlin... where left-wingers study at my expense'. Alumni and college members include politicians Manmohan Singh (India), Kofi Abrefa Busia (Ghana) and Patricia Hewitt and Austin Mitchell (UK); and banker Mark Carney.

Nuffield stands on the site of the coal wharf and basin that once terminated the Oxford Canal, which its patron bought and had filled in: originally it was to extend across the goods wharf too, now a carpark on the other side of Worcester Street (see below). Building work was delayed until 1949, by which point Morris had persuaded Austen Harrison, a former government architect in Palestine, to replace his modernist plans with 'something on the lines of Cotswold domestic architecture'. The end result is a 'quadrangle' with rectangular pools of water – recalling Islamic garden design – surrounded by ranges that might indeed have been airlifted from an English village green, except for the discordant library tower with its copper-coated spike. If you have the opportunity, it is worth trying to visit the chapel (rarely open), which has wonderful stained glass by John Piper.

Turn left from the exit to return along New Road. The building with the impressive portico that you can see on raised ground to your left is Canal House, built in the 1820s as a statement headquarters for the Oxford Canal Company: it is now the residence of the master of St Peter's (see below). Also on the left just before the pedestrian crossing is the former Crown Court and then ㉕ **Probate Registry**, a gothic revival survival from 1863 with the royal crest above the door.

Continue towards Bonn Square. The Art Café on the corner makes a good stopping point for brunch or lunch: although the food queue moves swiftly, it's a good idea to find a table upstairs before you order. The ㉖ **Westgate Centre** opposite was redeveloped following much controversy in 2017: the curved Bonn Square front with its massive oculus was designed by Dixon Jones, architects of the Saïd Business School (see below). A large roof terrace provides a wide range of chain interpretations of world cuisine, and even if you are not hungry it might be worth taking the escalators to enjoy the free views of Tom Tower, Christ Church Cathedral and the roofs of Oxford's modest housing stretching to the hills beyond.

227

William Morris and Morris Motors

Originally a bicycle repairman, then a maker of cycles, motorcycles and cars, William Morris (1877–1963) became one of the UK's leading industrialists and a philanthropist on a heroic scale.

He set up his first business, mending cycles, in the garden shed of his parents' modest home at 16 James Street, between Iffley Road and Cowley Road. This was followed by a shop at 48 High Street (see page 37) and by 1902 Morris was assembling motorcycles from bought-in parts in a disused livery stable on Longwall Street. After a false start in the automobile business (as a partner in a firm set up by a wealthy undergraduate that soon went bankrupt), he rebuilt the Longwall workshop in a palatial neo-Georgian style (see page 18) and began repairing and selling cars. In 1913 the first Morris Oxford car was designed in Longwall Street and large-scale manufacturing started in the former Oxford Military College in Cowley. After World War I production rapidly increased and by 1925 more than 50,000 vehicles were being turned out annually.

Morris Motors grew, factories opened around the country and then overseas, competitors and suppliers were acquired, and production diversified to include trucks, buses and tractors. Post-war successes included the Morris Minor (launched in 1948 and manufactured until 1972). In 1952 Morris Motors merged with an old rival, Austin, to form the British Motor Corporation, with Morris, briefly, as chairman – he retired at the end of the year.

By the early 1970s more than 20,000 workers were employed at the Cowley plant. However, industrial relations were a recurrent problem, compounded by poor management and outdated designs – an exception being the original Mini, in production across the world from 1959 until 2000.

A series of mergers, demergers and sales effectively ended the British-owned mass-production of cars, with the Cowley plant ('Plant Oxford') – where, at the time of writing, most of the MINI range is still assembled – now owned by German giant BMW.

Morris had married Elizabeth Anstey in 1903: the couple were childless and lived modestly. In 1933 they bought Merrow Mount, a house in the village of Nuffield, some 15 miles south-east of Oxford, renaming it Nuffield Place (it is now a 1930s time capsule owned by the National Trust).

Five years later Morris was ennobled as Viscount Nuffield. He gave much of his vast wealth to charitable causes, particularly those associated with education and medicine. Among his many major benefactions were the Nuffield Foundation, set up in 1943 'to advance educational opportunity and social well-being across the United Kingdom', and Nuffield College (see page 226), a graduate college specialising in the social sciences.

From the 12th century until 1870 **27** **Bonn Square** was the churchyard of St Peter-le-Bailey, which stood facing the site of the present Westgate mall before being rebuilt in New Inn Hall Street (it now serves as the chapel for St Peter's College, see below). Records from 1585 until the cemetery's closure list 6,800 burials, and this mass of bones accounts for the raised ground level. When the Tirah Memorial, Oxford's first war memorial, was erected at its centre in 1900, its foundations had to be sunk 7 metres (almost the extent to which it is high) to reach solid ground. Commemorating those who died during the Tirah expedition of 1897–98 to secure British dominion over the Indian North-West Frontier and Khyber Pass, the memorial lists three buglers along with a vast majority of privates, a contrast to the tributes to officers found in most college chapels.

Bonn Square was named in 1974 to celebrate Oxford's twinning with what was then the West German capital during the mayoralty of Olive Gibbs (see above) – as a plaque on the corner of New Inn Hall Street indicates. The nearby sculpture by Diana Bell of two stacks of books with the words 'knowledge', 'trust', 'understanding' and 'friendship' in English and German was installed in 2009. On the wall of the **28** **New Road Baptist Church** behind the sculpture is a further multilingual plea for international harmony in the form of a plaque with the word 'peace' in English, Arabic, Hebrew and Sanskrit:

this was unveiled in 2010 by Bruce Kent, like Olive Gibbs a prominent CND campaigner. The chapel itself dates from 1798, though its elegant temple front – an exercise in academic classicism with a generous porch supported on Doric columns topped by a semi-circular window flanked by Ionic columns and blank niches – was added in 1819 by John Hudson, surveyor of Oxford's bridges.

Cross the square to **New Inn Hall Street**: the house with the double gable at no. 1, on the left, was established as a ㉙ **Royal Mint** by Charles I, who requisitioned most of the University's silver plate to be melted down into 'Oxford Crowns' when he made Oxford his capital during the Civil War (see box, page 168). Further down the street on the opposite side, at nos 32–34, is a modest stone building that was Oxford's first ㉚ **Methodist meeting house**, founded in 1783 and described by father of Methodism John Wesley (1703-91) after his inaugural sermon as a 'lightsome, cheerful place, and well filled with rich and poor, scholars as well as townsmen'. Wesley's sermon was his first public address in Oxford since he was effectively booed from the pulpit after spending almost two hours castigating the University for spiritual apathy in a sermon in the University Church in 1744. The arched gateway and gatehouse next door belong to Frewin Hall, founded in 1421 as St Mary's College and now an annexe of Brasenose: it was here that Dutch scholar Erasmus stayed in the 1490s while preparing his Greek translation of the New Testament.

Most of the buildings on the other side of the street are part of ㉛ **St Peter's College**, founded in 1928 to provide education for men of 'limited means' by Francis James Chavasse (1846-1928), Bishop of Liverpool, and his son Christopher Maude Chavasse (1884-1962), later Bishop of Rochester. On the paving outside the main gate is a plaque commemorating Christopher's twin brother Noel, the only participant in World War I to be awarded two Victoria Crosses: a doctor (and Olympic athlete), Noel died two days after he had repeatedly ventured into no-man's land at Passchendaele to retrieve wounded soldiers while wounded himself, winning him the second award. St Peter's ran into financial difficulties in the 1930s and was saved by a large injection of cash from car

manufacturer William Morris (see above); it was granted full college status in 1961. Alumni and college members include filmmakers Simon Beaufoy and Ken Loach; chef Hugh Fearnely-Whittingstall; and *Thomas the Tank Engine* author Reverend Wilbert Vere Awdry.

St Peter's occupies a disparate collection of buildings on the site of the medieval New Inn Hall: while there is no public access, unusually for an Oxford College these are mostly visible from the street. At the southern (Bonn Square) end is the former Central Girls' School, built in 1901 by architect Leonard Stokes to accommodate 300 pupils: the central block with its tall ground-floor windows contained the main schoolrooms, with a pupil-teacher centre with separate facilities for male and female trainee teachers on the upper floors of the two wings. Looking through the college's iron gates you can see the red-brick ranges built in the 1930s to house the first students and to the left glimpse the dramatic glazed stairtower of a residential block added by Chamberlin Powell Bon and Woods in the mid-1980s. The former church of St Peter-le-Bailey, its high tower adorned with a statue of St Peter below dramatic winged gargoyles, was designed by Basil Champneys (also employed at Mansfield, Merton and Oriel) in 1874 and and is now the college chapel. The main entrance to the site is through the elegantly proportioned Linton House, built as impressive offices for the recently formed Oxford Canal Company in 1797 and used as a rectory after the company moved to new headquarters in the 1820s – a building that is now a residence for the master of the college (see above).

Continue along the street to the **32 Wesley Memorial Church** (open Monday to Saturday, 10–17), built in 1878 to provide larger premises for the community's worship in recognition of legislation permitting the admission of Nonconformists to the University. With its soaring spire, massive stained-glass window and porches with elaborately pierced and sculpted gables, the church seems from the outside to have sold out, rejecting Nonconformist simplicity in favour of High Anglican gothic. Inside, the traditional chapel arrangement of a single main floor below a substantial gallery is accommodated uncomfortably within the Anglican plan. The building opposite was formerly Saint Edward's School, founded in 1863 by St Thomas the Martyr vicar Thomas Chamberlain (see above).

Walk along the alley just beyond the Wesley Memorial Church and either look through the railings or if the gates are open enter the garden of the University Faculty of History to see the remains of a bastion from the old town wall discovered by workmen digging the church's foundations. Either walk through the gardens to **George Street** or continue to the end of New Inn Hall Street and turn left: the University Faculty of History on the corner was formerly **33 Oxford Boys' High School**, a playfully eclectic building with a relatively sober ground floor surmounted by scalloped niches, scrolls and swags, an elaborately carved gable embellished with the ox and ford from the city's coat of arms and a pretty bell turret. Designed in 1879–81 by Thomas Graham Jackson, architect of the Examination Schools on the High Street as well as numerous college buildings, the school was established thanks to the efforts of Thomas Hill Green (1836–82; see page 304), a moral philosopher who promoted women's admission to the University and was the first University member elected to Oxford City Council. The mottos of University (left) and town suspended from swags at either side of the large central window indicate that the school was a joint town-and-gown initiative. Alumni include T. E. Lawrence (Lawrence of Arabia) and comedian Ronnie Barker.

Return to New Inn Hall Street and take the first left down **St Michael's Street**. Oxford's oldest Indian restaurant, Chutneys, is on the corner, serving reasonably priced lunches beneath the benevolent gaze of US president Bill Clinton, photographed towering over smiling staff. One of the first houses on the left has a blue plaque to ㉞ **Felicia Skene** (1821–99), who in 1869 was the first woman in England to be appointed by the Home Office as a prison visitor: agitating for gaols to be places of reform and advocating counselling rather than punishment, she played the harmonium in the prison chapel, offered food and shelter to the newly released and kept open house for the destitute. The building next door, now home to the Bike Zone cycle shop and Handle Bar Café and Kitchen, was until 2010 the premises of ㉟ **Maltby's the Bookbinders**, processing tens or even hundreds of thousands of student theses in the well-lit first-floor workshop.

A few doors along on the same side of this wonderfully eclectic street is no. 24, a 17th-century house with a pedimented doorcase and two Dutch gables. Next door is ❸❻ **Vanburgh House** (both buildings are now occupied by the Vanburgh Hotel), also dating from the 17th century but refaced in 1721 by Bartholomew Peisley, a master-mason who worked with architect John Vanburgh on nearby Blenheim Palace and then embellished his own home with overscaled elements from its design – heavy keystones, massive Doric pilasters rising through two storeys and a projecting cornice. Peisley also built the magnificent St Giles House (see page 132).

A few doors further along is ❸❼ **Northgate Hall**, a Primitive Methodist church built in 1870 but rendered redundant when the movement merged with Wesleyan Methodism in 1932: the contrast between its simple pedimented frontage and the much grander, almost contemporary Wesleyan Memorial Church at the end of the street (see above) perhaps reveals why the two branches of Methodism had initially grown apart. For the rest of the 20th century Northgate Hall was home to the Oxford Inter-Collegiate Christian Union, the Oxford Lesbian and Gay Community Centre and a refuge for the homeless: in a sign of the times, it is now occupied by a branch of Bill's restaurant chain.

Stretching along the opposite side of the street and railed off from public access is the ❸❽ **Oxford Union Society**, founded almost 200 years ago and host to weekly termtime debates featuring often controversial speakers from the worlds of politics (Colonel Gaddafi, Richard Nixon, Malcolm X) and entertainment (Kermit the Frog, Martin Scorsese, ASAP Rocky) as well as literature and science. Newsworthy incidents range from the passing of the motion 'This House would under no circumstances fight for its King and country' in 1933 to the unjustifiable ejection of blind Ghanaian student Ebenezer Azamati in 2019.

The members' club boasts similarly arcane traditions to the Palace of Westminster, and indeed many MPs honed their skills in Oxford, with Gordon Brown the only university-educated post-World War II prime minister not to have studied here.

The original purpose-built debating chamber – a neo-medievalist fantasy with a steeply pitched conical roof – was designed in 1857 by Benjamin Woodward, architect of the University Museum; soon afterwards a team that included Dante Gabriel Rossetti, Edward Burne-Jones and William Morris decorated the ceiling with scenes from Arthurian legend, though ignorance of the technicalities of fresco painting meant the images quickly faded. The wing nearest the street was built in 1910 to accommodate the bar, dining room and snooker room.

On the corner of St Michael's Street and **Cornmarket Street** is the ㊟ **Plough Inn**, in service from 1656 to 1924 and a tailor's shop until its reinvention as The Plough at 38 in 2018. The first-floor window and three gables facing Cornmarket Street have survived from the original building. An even more remarkable survivor is ㊵ **nos 26–28 Cornmarket Street**, almost opposite. Reliably claimed to be the oldest surviving house of more than two storeys in Oxford, its upper floors on Ship Street tilt alarmingly over the ancient woodworm-scarred column that supports the first-floor jetty. It seems likely it was built in 1386 by vintner and mayor of Oxford John Gibbes as the New Inn ('Neweyn within the Northgate'), with a three-gabled frontage on Cornmarket Street and two wings extending backwards around an open courtyard with shops at ground level and rooms above. Slight differences in the appearance of no. 28 and the rest of the building are the result of different bouts of 20th-century restoration, with the simpler frontage of nos 26–27 probably nearer to the way the original might have looked.

'On this site in 1279 were two tenements gifted to Oseney Abbey by Walter Grant in 1195. Robert Mills rebuilt & registered an Inn here on the 2nd September 1656. This local hostelry served thirsty travellers, town & gowns people until 1924. Renovated and opened in 2018 this famous building & one of Oxford's oldest watering holes is now serving fantastic food & real ales after nearly a century as a tailor's shop.'

40

The rugged tower of ㊶ **St Michael at the Northgate** (open winter, 10.30–16; summer, 10.30–17) on the other side of Ship Street – its double-arched windows supported by extraordinary bulging columns with deep capitals – is Oxford's oldest surviving structure, built c. 1050 as part of the town's fortifications. The church's chancel dates from the 13th century, the Lady Chapel from the 14th and the nave from the 15th. It is worth looking inside to see the four small panels of 13th-century stained glass in the chancel, made up of simple shapes set against luminous blue backgrounds, and the 14th-century panel in the Lady Chapel showing Christ crucified on a lily, a rare survival of a common medieval motif largely obliterated as offensive to Puritan sensibilities.

A visit to the tower enables you to see the marriage certificate of artist and socialist William Morris and Jane Burden (see page 23) and the door of the cell from the Bocardo Prison, above the town's North Gate, where Oxford Martyrs Hugh Latimer, Nicholas Ridley and Thomas Cranmer were held before being burned at the stake in 1555 and 1556 for their refusal to accept the Catholic doctrine introduced by Queen Mary (see page 123) – as well as panoramic views over the city.

Walk north along Cornmarket Street and then **Magdalen Street**: on the right at the junction with Beaumont Street is the Martyrs' Memorial (see page 121) commemorating the Oxford Martyrs. On the far side of Beaumont Street are the Taylorian Institution and ㊷

41

240

42

Ashmolean (open daily, 10–17), probably Europe's first public museum and today one of the most important UK galleries outside London. The Ashmolean originated when astronomer and alchemist Elias Ashmole (1617–92) acquired (possibly fraudulently) the collection of John Tradescant, gardener to Charles I, which was housed from 1683 in what is now the History of Science Museum on Broad Street (see page 62). The current building, together with the Taylorian, was designed in the 1840s by Charles Robert Cockerell to accommodate subsequent substantial bequests of statuary and paintings. Raised on a massive plinth above street level, it has an E-shaped plan that gives equal space to the two institutions housed within its wings and offers the Ashmolean's galleries maximum natural light. The baroque exuberance of Cockerell's interpretation of classicism is apparent in the amalgam of elements from the Greek, Roman and Renaissance past, with abundant decoration in white Portland stone standing out against the Bath stone backdrop.

To appreciate the architecture, first look at the Beaumont Street elevation: blank walls decorated with a row of impressive wreaths flank a glorious central portico with soaring fluted Ionic columns (their unusual capitals taken from the Temple of Apollo at Bassae in Greece which Cockerell had helped to excavate some 30 years previously) supporting an elaborately carved pediment topped by a statue of the seated Apollo, patron of the arts. The short elevations of the wings each has a pair of similarly tall columns surmounted by urns flanked by panels depicting griffins, and the whole complex is unified by a frieze probably inspired by the Temple of Apollo at Didyma. Walk up **St Giles'** to the main entrance to the Taylorian (marked Insitutio Tayloriana, in typical Oxford fashion), named after classical architect Robert Taylor (1714–88), who left a bequest to establish a foundation for 'teaching and improving the European languages'. Here the giant columns are topped by statues representing France, Italy, Germany and Spain. Enter the relatively modest doorway and walk up steps within a narrow vaulted passageway to emerge to the splendour of the museum portico. Inside to the left is the main gallery, screened at each end by arches supported on Doric columns and lit by a clerestory in conformity with the latest German ideas on displaying art. To the right is a cantilevered staircase with a cast of the frieze from the Temple at Bassae at ceiling level. Completed in 2009, a six-storey extension at the rear by Rick Mather Architects doubles the gallery space and provides an education centre, conservation studios and other facilities.

Opposite the Ashmolean is the dispiritingly ugly **43** **Randolph Hotel**, the height of luxury and modernity when it opened in 1866, with an American elevator and 68 rooms to cater for an influx of travellers arriving by rail (according to its brochure, a hotel omnibus met 'all the most important trains'). Inspector Morse frequently drank in the bar (now called the Morse Bar) – as did his creator Colin Dexter – and in *The Remorseful Day*, looking out at the Ashmolean, reflected that it was unlikely there was 'a bar anywhere

in Britain with a better view'. The hotel featured prominently in *The Jewel That Was Ours* (televised as *The Wolvercote Tongue*) when an American tourist was found dead in one of its rooms. The Randolph was designed by William Wilkinson (1819–1901), who also laid out the Norham Manor estate (see page 310) and lived and worked next door at 5 Beaumont Street (marked by a blue plaque) from 1860 to 1886 before taking up residence in the hotel towards the end of his life.

A few doors along is the **44** **Oxford Playhouse**, designed in 1938 by Edward Maufe for the Oxford Players, who had outgrown their home on Woodstock Road (see page 297): the last theatre to be built before the war, the discreet addition to the Georgian street

fully respects its profile, with just a hint of art deco around the entrance. The theatre has witnessed performances by Oxford students Rowan Atkinson, Alan Bennett, Dudley Moore and Michael Palin (and future politicians Nigel Lawson and Shirley Williams), as well as eminent professionals including Judi Dench, John Gielgud, Ian McKellen and Sybil Thorndike. In 1966 Richard Burton (an alumnus of Exeter) and Elizabeth Taylor appeared for free in a student production of *Dr Faustus*, with Taylor taking the non-speaking role of Helen of Troy.

Beaumont Street

Sackler Library

45

Beaumont Street itself, described by architectural historian Nikolaus Pevsner as 'the finest street ensemble in Oxford', was laid out in the 1820s on the site of Beaumont Palace, begun by Henry I in 1130 and a Carmelite monastery from 1318 until its destruction during the Reformation two centuries later. The first development of middle-class housing in Oxford, the area was the precursor to the suburb of North Oxford – also built on land belonging to St John's College – which would creep northwards over the second half of the century. A beautiful curve of flat-fronted terraces, many with columned and pedimented doorcases and with covered iron balconies on the south-facing side and open ones facing north, Beaumont Street was planned to appeal to financiers, builders and prominent tradesmen and by the second half of the century was home largely to professionals such as doctors, dentists, solicitors and architects.

Turn right up **St John Street**: near the corner on the right, a rotunda marks the entrance to the Sackler Library, a neoclassical oddity completed in 2001 by Robert Adam. The full-size rotunda of the main building is visible behind it or by looking along **Pusey Lane**. St John Street's homes were intended for lesser tradespeople and others for whom Beaumont Street was unaffordable: an early resident was Oxford artist **45** **William Turner** (1789–1862), who lived at no. 16 (marked by a blue plaque) for 30 years. Turn left along **Beaumont Place** and left again into

Beaumont Buildings

Beaumont Buildings, a charming terrace of chequerboard brick houses built for college servants and those working in Beaumont Street's grander houses.

Continue past the double-fronted house where the road narrows and turn left into **Beaumont Lane**: mounted on the first brick wall on the right are fragments of stone window tracery said to be from ㊻ **Beaumont Palace**, most of the rest of which was carted away to build the library of St John's College. Turn right along Beaumont Street and on the right near the end is a further reference to the palace in the form of a ㊼ **plaque** marking the birthplace of Richard I (1157-99), who reigned for ten years from 1189, and his younger brother King John (1166-1216).

At the end of Beaumont Street is Worcester College.

Worcester College
1 Walton Street, OX1 2HB
www.worc.ox.ac.uk
Open daily, 14–16

Worcester College was founded in 1714 by wealthy Worcestershire landowner Thomas Cookes (1648–1701), aided by substantial donations from amateur architect and University MP George Clarke (1661–1736). The site was the former Gloucester Hall, established in 1283 to house Benedictine monks studying at the University. Clarke himself designed the entrance range – probably assisted by Nicholas Hawksmoor, who was working at All Souls (see page 41) where Clarke was a fellow – as well as much of the ㊽ **Main Quadrangle**, built over a period of 70 years from 1720. Unusually for an Oxford college, the classical frontage resembles a grand town house, with a central pedimented recessed block flanked by oversized projecting wings embellished with Serlian windows topped by swags. Alumni and college members include writers Richard Adams and Thomas de Quincey; film and TV creatives Alex Cox and Russell T. Davies; actor Emma Watson; tycoons Rupert Murdoch and John Sainsbury; and longserving Thai prime minister Seni Pramoj.

The central block of the entrance was built first, followed by the hall (in the wing to the left) and chapel (to the right). Unexpectedly, on the quadrangle side is a generous loggia running the full width of the frontage, its open colonnade surmounted by an elegant arrangement of windows and a central pediment that together constitute one of Oxford's finest classical façades. To the left (south) of the eclectic Main Quadrangle are the picturesque 15th-century cottages left over from ㊾ **Gloucester Hall** when money to complete the quadrangle ran out: the differences between them indicate they were probably built incrementally by individual Benedictine abbeys for their students, with the coat of arms of each above its door.

The hall and chapel were built by the 1780s, with neoclassical interiors designed by James Wyatt, but the **50** **chapel** (its entrance to the north of the colonnade) was given a riotous makeover in the 1860s by medievalist William Burges, who transformed it into one of Oxford's most extraordinary interiors – more like an elaborate drawing room for an eccentric animal lover than a place of worship. The classical structure Wyatt provided (which Burges dismissed as 'the vilest Renaissance of George III's time') can still be discerned, but now heavily camouflaged by wall and ceiling decoration including a gilded frieze of Pre-Raphaelite angels, knights and disciples set within fake marble below vertical panels with images of animals surrounded by patterns of stylised flowers. The ends of the pews feature carved animals including a tortoise, camel, elephant, crocodile, walrus and even a dodo (on the second pew to the right of the altar).

Exit the quadrangle via an opening in the south-west corner (diagonally opposite the chapel) that leads to a vast open lawn with mature trees. Turn right and take the path to a lake, fringed by weeping willows. Keep walking round the lake until you come to the sports fields: looking back towards the college, you get a view of two of Worcester's fine recent buildings, each displaying a radically different approach to contemporary architecture. The neo-vernacular **51** **Sainsbury Building**, a hall of residence designed in 1982 by MacCormac Jamieson and Pritchard, uses different heights (from single to four storeys) and orientations, as well as open terraces, to evoke the picturesque quality of an Italian hill town. Beside it is the restrained and graceful **52** **Sultan Nazrin Shah Centre**, designed by Niall McLaughlin Architects in 2018 in a contemporary take on classicism, with a deep entrance portico set within a rectangular podium topped by the segment of a drum, the whole made up of expansive glazing interspersed with slender fins of stone.

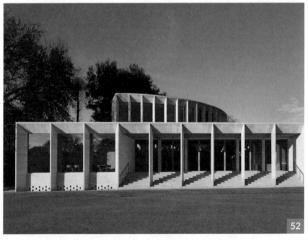

At the end of Beaumont Street, turn left down **Worcester Street** then take the second left towards Gloucester Green.

The former ㊾ **Central Boys' School** (now a Chinese restaurant) is on the left, built at the same time and by the same architect as the Central Girls' School in New Inn Hall Street (see above) but in a very different style that pays homage to the picturesque cottages it replaced. Offices were sited on the noisier street side, lit by bay windows, with classrooms clustered around a circular

top-lit hall behind. Though the intake was boys-only, the carvings above the door show St Anne reading to a group of girls on the left and King Alfred addressing a group of boys on the right. For fans of markets, continue to ㊾ **Gloucester Green**, formerly the site of a city gaol, cattle market and bus station before being redeveloped in the 1980s with buildings clad in red brick with kitsch detailing. Some 100 stalls offer hot food, deli items and vintage clothing and furniture, as well as cheap deals on just about everything.

Return to Worcester Street and continue walking past the junction with **George Street**: on your left you pass the gates to Nuffield College (see above) through which you can see the main

quadrangle if you did not visit it earlier. Turn right along **Park End Street** at the far end of the carpark: intended to form part of Nuffield before money ran out, this was until the 1940s the goods wharf for the Oxford Canal, which terminated in a basin where the college now stands. On your right beside the Lighthouse pub is a tall pillar built of Staffordshire Blue engineering bricks – both hard and water resistant – that once was a gatepost to the wharf. The pub itself stands on the site of a ㊾ **Baptist meeting**

Wharf gatepost

251

house dating from 1661 but destroyed by rioters during the Jacobite Rising of 1715: a plaque on Pacey's Bridge (named after James Pacey, the pub landlord from 1830) claims that baptisms took place in Castle Mill Stream below.

Continue along Park End Street, built in the 1790s to provide an alternative route for traffic using the canal wharves and named after Parkend in the Forest of Dean, the source of much of the coal arriving in Oxford. On the left at nos 37–39 are the vast **56 Cantay Depositories** (the name is inscribed on the twin gables that bookend the building), completed in 1901 for Arthur Cowley & Co., a specialist in shipping and storing furniture at a time of increased mobility both within the UK and around the Empire. Steelframed yet clad in brick, the building had display windows at ground level with the storage space above divided into discrete fireproof sections. Several other buildings along the street were showrooms for the motor trade.

At the end of the street turn right in front of the Royal Oxford Hotel and then left towards the station: the dominant new building on the right is the **57 Saïd Business School**, created through donations of some £70 million from Syrian-Saudi businessman, political fixer and arms dealer Wafic Saïd, a major supporter of Margaret Thatcher, after whom part of the complex is named. Opened in 2001, the building by Dixon Jones, architects of Westgate (see above), has a deeply recessed entrance within a stone-

clad frontage, subsidiary walls that use huge quantities of hand-made bricks, and a copper-clad ziggurat on the roof. On the pavement at the eastern end of the entrance is a plaque commemorating the former terminus of the 58 **Buckinghamshire Railway**, built in 1851 with the same cast-iron technology used for the Crystal Palace at the Great Exhibition and now re-erected as a museum in Quainton, Buckinghamshire. ●

58

Visit...

Ashmolean Museum
Beaumont Street, OX1 2PH
www.ashmolean.org

Oxford Castle
44-46 Oxford Castle, OX1 1AY
www.oxfordcastleandprison.co.uk

St Michael at the North Gate
Cornmarket Street, OX1 3EY
www.smng.org.uk

Eat/Drink...

Art Café
14 Bonn Street, OX1 1LQ
www.artcafeoxford.co.uk

Chutneys Indian Brasserie
36 St Michael's Street, OX1 2EB
www.chutneysoxford.co.uk

Handle Bar Café and Kitchen
28-32 St Michael's Street, OX1 2EB
www.handlebaroxford.co.uk

Jam Factory
4 Hollybush Row, OX1 1HU
www.thejamfactoryoxford.com

Plough Inn
38 Cornmarket, OX1 3HA
www. ploughat38.com

MOUN

Mount Place

6
Jericho:
work & welfare

Jericho

1. Radcliffe Infirmary former outpatients
2. Fountain of Triton
3. Radcliffe Infirmary main block
4. Chapel of St Luke
5. Mathematical Building
6. Alchemical Tree
7. Radcliffe Observatory
8. Blavatnik School of Government
9. Oxford University Press
10. St Paul's (now Freud)
11. Jericho Health Centre
12. Jude the Obscure
13. Jericho Tavern
14. Phoenix Picturehouse
15. St Sepulchre's Cemetery (see page 275)
16. Holyfield House
17. W. Lucy & Co
18. Drinking fountain
19. Oxford Canal
20. No. 27 Cranham Street
21. Old Bookbinders
22. Combe Road
23. Jericho Community Centre
24. St Barnabas
25. St Barnabas Boys' School
26. Oxford Baptist Chapel
27. Oxford Synagogue and Jewish Centre
28. Margaret Thatcher
29. Ruskin College
30. Clarendon Institute

WALTON WELL R

Fidler's Island

ROGER

Stream

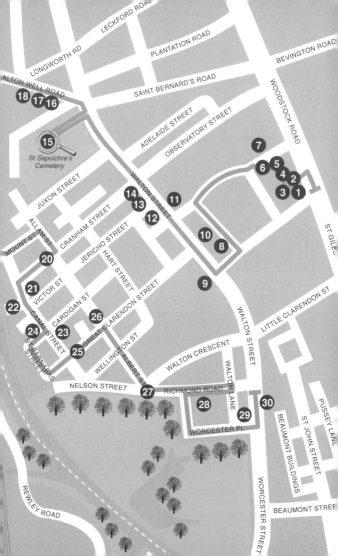

Jericho: work & welfare

Start: Former Radcliffe Infirmary
Finish: Clarendon Institute
Distance: 2.1 miles

With its narrow streets of workers' housing, remnants of industry and philanthropic institutions established by employers to improve the health and spiritual welfare of their employees, Jericho reveals a completely different side of Oxford from the grand academic foundations of the city centre. The area – probably named after Jericho House, a 17th-century coaching inn which in turn may have been named because in the Bible Jericho signifies a remote place – was developed from the 1820s to accommodate workers from the ironworks that arrived in 1825 and from Oxford University Press (OUP), established in Walton Street a year later. Expansion was rapid – by 1833 Jericho's population numbered more than 1,500 and by 1850 it had doubled – but many of the houses were poorly built, with little sanitation beyond communal privies and wash-houses. A severe outbreak of cholera in 1832 was followed by two more in 1849 and 1854: a survey of 1848 cited Jericho as a centre of disease thanks to lack of hygiene, the prevalence of slaughter-houses, pigsties and cowsheds and its proximity to the waterlogged and sewage-drenched land beside the Oxford Canal. Some say the area got its name because its dwellings were so badly constructed that if you blew a trumpet at them they would surely fall down.

Synonymous with poverty from the late 19th century, Jericho faced a major crisis in the 1960s when proposals to flatten its dilapidated housing stock – largely rented from landlords including St John's and Worcester colleges, OUP and the Lucy & Co. ironworks – were successfully resisted by a strong Residents' Association. Today, though the many pubs and restaurants along Walton Street are thriving and houses attract high prices, as of 2011 only one-fifth of households were owner-occupied, with about half rented from private landlords and a further one-fifth social housing.

This walk begins with the Radcliffe Infirmary, founded as a charitable institution with wards and a chapel funded by OUP Printer Thomas Combe (1796–1872), before weaving through the narrow streets between Walton Street and the canal.

At the southern end of **Woodstock Road** and now part of the new Radcliffe Observatory Quarter – the University's most ambitious development for over a century – the **Radcliffe Infirmary** was established in 1770 to treat those unable to afford medical care. The 2-hectare site, then open fields, was donated by longserving Oxford MP Thomas Rowney Jr (1693–1759), with money for the building drawn from the estate of Dr John Radcliffe (1650–1714), physician to Queen Anne. Though junior doctors were paid, physicians and surgeons gave their services for free; funds for day-to-day running were raised by donors, who until as late as 1920 had the right to impose their own lists of patients. A strict code of conduct required patients to behave with decorum, attend chapel, refrain from swearing or playing cards and read only newspapers and magazines approved by the chaplain. The Radcliffe was equally fastidious about the illnesses it treated, and until various points in the 19th century would not admit patients with infectious diseases,

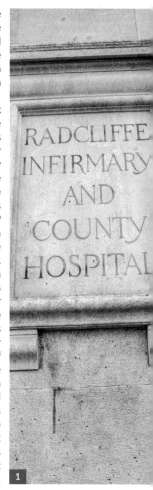

epilepsy, ulcers, inoperable cancers or dropsy, along with pregnant women, children under seven and the mentally ill.

The southernmost building on Woodstock Road, next to Somerville College, is the ❶ **former outpatients department** – a neoclassical block with an impressive doorcase designed in 1911 by Edward Warren, brother of the president of Magdalen College and architect of the fountain and clock on the far side of Magdalen Bridge. On the wall beside the name plaque is a reminder of pre-NHS medicine – a money box soliciting contributions. This was the site of the first use of penicillin, when in February 1941 local police constable Albert Alexander was treated for a badly infected wound caused by a scratch from a rose thorn: initially he made a rapid recovery but died when stocks of the medicine ran out. The Radcliffe moved to a site in Headington in 2007 and the former outpatients department now houses the University's primary-care research team.

Walk north and enter the main courtyard through Gate 1. From here you can see the heavily glazed infill designed by Niall McLaughlin Architects in 2016 to replace the originally U-shaped outpatients building's empty core – a strategy typical of the mix of conservation and intervention within the plans for the Radcliffe Observatory Quarter site. A replica of an 1858 copy of Bernini's ❷ **Fountain of Triton** from the Piazza Barberini in Rome sits incongruously in front of the hospital's restrained ❸ **main block**: designed by Stiff Leadbetter in the 1760s, this was initially given a dramatic flourish by a double staircase leading to the first-floor entrance.

To the right is the similarly restrained, neo-gothic ❹ **chapel of St Luke** – with a charming carving of Christ the Good Shepherd above the doorway – designed in 1865 by Arthur Blomfield, architect of the much less conventional church of St Barnabas (see below). Both chapel and church were financed by OUP Printer Thomas Combe, who as a major donor to the infirmary, funding the establishment of two children's wards in the 1870s, was able to secure treatment for OUP workers.

Spilling out in front of the glazed atrium of the ⑤ **Mathematical Building** is paving designed by Oxford mathematician Roger Penrose in 2012, based on his 1974 discovery that just two shapes can be combined in an infinite number of patterns, a concept complicated further here by the addition of stainless-steel arcs to the rhomboid granite tiles. The building itself was completed in 2013 by superstar architect Rafael Viñoly, masterplanner for the Radcliffe Observatory Quarter site.

Walk through the Mathematical Building atrium (or, if it is closed, return to Woodstock Road and re-enter the site by the next gate). To your left is the ⑥ **Alchemical Tree**, designed in 2015 by artist Simon Periton and referring to Salomon Trismosin's 1582 alchemical treatise *Splendor Solis*, which shows the alchemical birth and death of the king. If the tree, placed within a grove of silver birch, could act as a metaphor for the importance to scientific discovery of examining what is hiding in plain sight, slogans including Myanmar politician

Aung San Suu Kyi's 'democracy is when people keep a government in check' highlight the frailty of political integrity and offer an ironic nod to the shiny Blavatnik School of Government (see below) on the far side of the campus.

Immediately in front of you is the ⑦ **Radcliffe Observatory**, generally recognised as one of the major monuments of English neoclassicism and at the time of its construction one of the most important scientific buildings in Europe. Begun in 1772 by architect Henry Keene and completed after his death by James Wyatt (both of whom also worked at Oxford colleges), its domestic-scale lower floors are topped by an extraordinary, elongated octagonal tower modelled on the Tower of the Winds in Athens of c. 50 BCE. The four expansive windows, divided by columns and topped by pediments, once accommodated the Observatory's telescopes – Oxford's increased light and pollution prompted the facility to move to South Africa in 1939. The globe at the top, by sculptor John Bacon, depicts Hercules and Atlas supporting the world. Above the stringcourse is a frieze of the eight winds and at the top of the first floor, set between Ionic pilasters, are panels depicting the signs of the zodiac: both are made in Coade stone, a material newly pioneered by Eleanor Coade, who employed Bacon in her London factory.

The domed rotunda in front of the Observatory, built in the mid-19th century to house a refracting telescope, is now a reading room. A weather station, originally in the building but now in a white-painted wooden box at the back, holds the record for the longest continuous series of rainfall and temperature readings in the UK, with notes dating back more than 200 years.

8

Take the path around to the ❽ **Blavatnik School of Government**, founded in 2010 with a £75 million donation from Ukrainian-born oil magnate and Donald Trump supporter Leonard Blavatnik, the richest person in the UK as of January 2018. The spaceship-like building, designed by Tate Modern architects Herzog & de Meuron in 2015, consists of a rectilinear glazed plinth topped by stacked glazed drums of diminishing size – referencing famous circular Oxford buildings such as the Radcliffe Camera (see page 44) and, perhaps, the Observatory itself.

According to the architects, the design's central 'courtyard' or Forum, ringed with walkways to encourage interaction between floors, echoes the school's mission to 'teach governance in a way that strengthens communities and fosters collaboration'. Outsiders looking in might find the exterior's promise of transparency to be skin deep, with views restricted largely to a foyer with sofas cunningly curved so no two people can sit next to one another.

Continue to **Walton Street** and cross the road. Opposite the Blavatnik is the headquarters of ❾ **Oxford University Press**– surely the grandest premises ever built for a publisher, let alone a printing works. With its senior staff – the Printers to the University – living on site and many of its workers (known as 'press boys and girls') housed in Jericho, OUP was to dominate the area, financing many of its landmarks through institutional or personal donations, promoting the value of education, sobriety and godliness and eventually filling its cemetery.

The largest university press in the world, and the second oldest after Cambridge, OUP was founded in around 1480 to print Bibles, prayer books and scholarly works. It expanded into more general publishing in the late 19th century, in part to defray the mounting costs of producing the *Oxford English Dictionary*, which overran by several years and several volumes (see information on James Murray, the first editor, page 332). Though its dedicated printing press was closed in 1989 and its paper mill at Wolvercote in 2004, OUP continues to publish some 6,000 titles a year and employ some 6,000 people worldwide. Officially a department of the University, it

has since the 17th century been governed by a group of fifteen academics (known as Delegates), who still approve all new titles.

The OUP premises were built in 1826, when demand for Bibles and prayer books, fuelled by the spread of British influence across the colonies, caused the company to outgrow its previous home, the Clarendon Building in Broad Street (see page 51). Walton Street at the time was little more than a track for driving cattle, so the site was presumably chosen because of its proximity to the Oxford Canal, used to deliver coal to power OUP's steam-driven presses. This made it all the more remarkable that architect Daniel Robertson should envisage the central entrance as a triumphal arch set behind giant Corinthian columns, linked by single-storey ranges to taller end pavilions, also with Corinthian columns. The western and northern wings of the quadrangle behind, which included houses for the supervisors of the print works, were completed by Edward Blore, who also worked on Buckingham Palace. To the south on Woodstock Road is an equally confident brutalist extension designed in 1969 by John Fryman of Architects Design Partnership.

Almost opposite OUP to the north is the formerly resplendent church of ⑩ **St Paul's**, built in 1836 and since 1987 home to Freud's bar (open from 15.00). The first new parish church in Oxford for more than 300 years, it was financed through public subscription supplemented by a generous endowment from OUP. Once the finest Grecian church in Oxford, its portico fronted by four lofty fluted Ionic columns inspired by the Erechtheum in Athens of *c.* 400 BCE, it was designed by Henry Jones Underwood (who also greatly expanded Oxford's prison, see page 223) with an apse added two decades later by Edward George Bruton. Inside, the stained glass – some of it featuring local characters such as OUP Printer Thomas Combe – is still visible and a shabby Christ stares down from the vault, amazed at the quantities of bread and wine consumed below. During its heyday, with Combe as churchwarden, St Paul's was a bastion of the Anglo-Catholic Oxford Movement (see box, page 84), its services renowned for their incense and candles, elaboration and pomp. The church closed in 1969 when the parish was amalgamated with St Barnabas.

45 Walton Street

Continue north up Walton Street, Jericho's main shopping street and its eastern boundary. Before development began, most of the land north of Jericho Street and south of Walton Crescent was owned by St John's College, with that in the middle belonging to the Reverend Peter Wellington Furse, inherited from an ancestor who had bought it in the 1570s. The first wave of building from 1820 to 1850, stretching in a strip down most of Walton Street and east from OUP as far as Albert Street, was largely of cheap rented houses on land Wellington Furse sold to developers. Over the second half of the century, land along the canal – sold by the Wellington Furses to wharf owner Henry Ward – was drained and developed similarly cheaply, along with the St John's estate, which leased rather than sold plots and exercised tighter control over building standards.

Belonging to the first phase of construction, the unusually elegant, flat-fronted Georgian houses at nos 44 and 45 Walton Street (on the left) have the chequerboard polychromatic brickwork found on many of the area's terraces. The new **⓫**

Jericho Health Centre opposite, designed in 2012 by architects Hawkins\Brown for the University, which leases the ground floor to local medical practices, gives the motif a modern spin in undulating bands of basketweave bricks.

The ⓬ **Jude the Obscure** pub (on the left), opened in 1871 as the Prince of Wales, it was renamed in 1995 to exploit Jericho's Thomas Hardy connections. On arriving at 'Christminster' (Oxford), *Jude the Obscure*'s eponymous hero lodges 'on inexpensive terms in... a room in a suburb nicknamed Beersheba' – a deeply impoverished neighbourhood generally thought to be modelled on Jericho. Hardy trained initially as an architect, and Beersheba's church of 'St Silas' is almost certainly St Barnabas, designed by the author's one-time employer Arthur Blomfield. The 'obscure and low-ceilinged tavern up a court', where Jude gets drunk and recites the Nicene Creed, is probably the Lamb & Flag, off St Giles' (see page 132).

Dating from 1920, the ⓭ **Jericho Tavern** next door was built on the site of Jericho House, the inn thought to have given the area its name. It hosted the first official gig by On A Friday (recent graduates from Abingdon public school who were to become better known as Radiohead) in 1987 as well as a subsequent gig at which they met their manager. 'Young and free', Supergrass secured a record deal after performing at the Jericho in 1994. Other acts who played here early in their careers include Mumford and Sons, Foals and Pulp.

The ⓮ **Phoenix Picturehouse** was built in 1913 as the North Oxford Kinema, with a new, streamlined façade added in 1939. For four decades from 1930 it was owned by the Poyntz family, screening foreign-language films that drew in culture-hungry audiences from the University's modern-languages departments. It is now part of the Picturehouse chain. For more signs of gentrification, glance down Cranham Street, where in 2015 Riach Architects gave a local-authority sheltered-housing scheme a colourful facelift that helped to raise prices to approaching £500,000 per flat, with a penthouse valued at over £1 million.

Continue up Walton Street. If you need to refuel, stop at one of the many pubs or cafés before the next stretch of the walk, which is largely along residential streets. However, you are never more than ten minutes' walk from Walton Street at any point, so it is easy to find your way back here.

On the right, the terrace at nos 96–101, dating from 1829, is an extraordinarily unspoiled example of the modest chequerboard cottages characteristic of the area. Turn down the alley almost opposite, past the cycle shop, to the entrance to ⓯ **St Sepulchre's Cemetery**, described by Jan Morris as 'the gloomiest and most enthralling of the Oxford burial places'. An overflow cemetery to relieve the city's congested graveyards, with no church of its own attached, it was established on farmland in 1848, with its area divided into discrete sections assigned to the parishes of St Giles, St Mary Magdalen and St Michael at the Northgate, as well as St Paul's (see above), which had no burial ground of its own. Seven University colleges were also granted plots. The original area was full by 1855 and the graveyard was extended; the gothic gatehouse and lodge by Bruton (architect of the apse of St Paul's) was added in 1865. St Sepulchre's was closed for burials in 1945 and its romantically rustic, Norman-style chapel by Underwood (architect of St Paul's) was demolished c. 1970.

If you don't wish to take a tour of the cemetery at this point, continue with the walk and return to it at the end or revisit it another time.

96-101 Walton Street

14

15

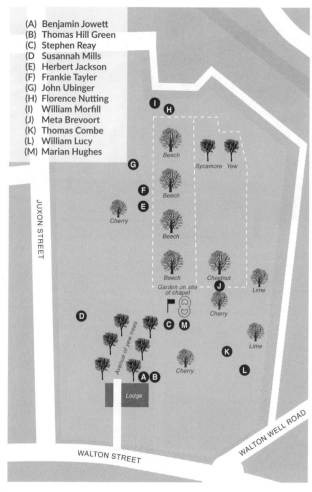

(A) Benjamin Jowett
(B) Thomas Hill Green
(C) Stephen Reay
(D) Susannah Mills
(E) Herbert Jackson
(F) Frankie Tayler
(G) John Ubinger
(H) Florence Nutting
(I) William Morfill
(J) Meta Brevoort
(K) Thomas Combe
(L) William Lucy
(M) Marian Hughes

JUXON STREET

Beech

Beech

Sycamore   Yew

Cherry

Beech

Beech   Chestnut

Lime

Garden on site
of chapel

Cherry

Avenue of yew trees

Cherry

Lime

Lodge

WALTON WELL ROAD

WALTON STREET

Drawing its dead from across the city, St Sepulchre's has a wealth of interesting and eccentric people buried within its walls: this route leads you past the graves of the great and good, as well as taking in unusual headstones of those who are largely forgotten. The burial ground has a well-researched website containing a hand-drawn plan dating from 1988 that with the help of photographs – and a level of perseverance – should enable you to locate any grave. In case you wish to consult the plan, its grave numbers are given in parenthesis here: rows are numbered from the entrance (1) to the boundary wall in front of you at the far end of the site (55); plots within rows are numbered from the wall furthest away from the entrance (1) to the entrance side (71). Letters refer to the different sections of the cemetery assigned to colleges or parishes. Otherwise, follow the map opposite.

Turn right at the entrance. Approximately ten graves along (Row 4, C51), you will find **(A) Benjamin Jowett** (1817–93), master of Balliol (see page 125) from 1870 until his death. The Balliol lion is carved on top of his tomb. Almost next to Jowett (Row 4, C49) lie **(B) Thomas Hill Green** (1836–82), moral philosopher, social reformer and one of the prime movers in establishing the first Oxford women's colleges, and his wife Charlotte, who survived

him by almost half a century (see page 304). Return to the main path: the seating area to your right marks the site of the demolished chapel. In a prestigious plot next to what would have been the door (Row 14, B43) are orientalist **(C) Stephen Reay** (1782–1861) and his wife Eleanor, their grave marked by a chapel-shaped vault they commissioned from sculptor Thomas Grimsley, whose firm was responsible for some of the cemetery's finest headstones.

Cross the path and near the wall is a terracotta cross with an image of the Good Shepherd in its central disc (also the work of Grimsley) that marks the grave of **(D) Susannah Mills** (1792–1874), inscribed 'Well done, good and faithful servant' (Row 14, D67). Mills was employed in the household of Professor of Astronomy Stephen Rigaud and looked after his seven children for more than a decade after his wife died in c. 1827; after a lengthy stint as housekeeper for bachelor professor Charles Daubeney, she lived in Walton Street as companion to one of the Rigaud children until her death.

Continue down the central path and turn left at the second big beech tree. Here you will find the near-recumbent headstone of eccentric private tutor **(E) Herbert Jackson** (1851–1921), whose shabby clothes and fondness for tea gave him the nickname, in snobbish Oxford, of 'the British workman' – rendered in Latin as 'operarius Britannicus' in the inscription (Row 36, L56.5).

Walk forward to a monument in gleaming white marble with a carving of a racing car emerging from a sunburst (Row 41, N55). This is the grave of **(F) Frankie Tayler** (1905–34), a racing-car mechanic from a Jericho family who met his death in a practice run with famed driver Kaye Don just eight months after promising his new wife never to race again. His widow, Phyllis, survived to the age of 95. Behind Tayler's tomb to the left is a monument with a violin (Row 44, N60) that commemorates Jericho residents **(G) John Ubinger** (1880–1917) and his son Eric (1906–29). Born in Bavaria, John (Johann) was a decorator and violinist who was incarcerated as a German alien during World War I and sent back to Germany, where he died: presumably his widow Sarah's fear of anti-German sentiment caused her to omit their surname from the headstone. Also known for his violin playing, Eric was a compositor (a skilled typesetter) at OUP, one of about 30 printers and compositors buried in St Sepulchre's. Sarah was to survive her son by almost 35 years.

Follow the path towards the rear boundary wall and turn right. A distinctive memorial in the form of a felled tree (Row 52, P41) marks the grave of **(H) Florence Nutting** (1855–86), a young woman from Leamington Spa who died after mysteriously falling out of a moving train near Oxford station. Behind it is a memorial to Slavonic specialist **(I) William Morfill** (1834–1909) and his wife Charlotte (see page 325) in the form of a marble cross (Row 53, P42).

Continue along the path and then turn right again, back towards the entrance wall. On the right, under the chestnut tree, is a low plinth (Row 31, J26) dedicated to American **(J) Meta Brevoort** (1825–76), the first woman to scale the Matterhorn and the first female mountaineer to wear trousers. Beside it, a rustic cross marks the grave of her sister Elisabeth (1822–75), who crossed the Atlantic with her children to live with Meta after the death of her husband, Frederic W. Coolidge, in 1855: their son William became a renowned mountaineer in his own right. Further towards the corner, in a sandstone vault with a large cross on top (Row 10, A16), lie **(K) Thomas Combe** (1796–1872), founder of St Barnabas and Printer at OUP, and his wife Martha. Further on (Row 4, A13) is the grave of another formative figure in Jericho's history, **(L) William Lucy** (1837–73), who gave his name to the ironworks that along with OUP was the area's main employer. Only fragments of the inscription are still visible, but records show that William is buried alongside his wife Alice, who survived until 1937, and three children who died as infants between 1864 and 1871.

Finally, in front of the seating area, is a section dedicated to nineteen sisters of the Society of the Undivided and Holy Trinity (Rows 13 and 14, B30–32), whose convent forms the nucleus of St Antony's College (see page 305), along with their Mother Superior, **(M) Marian Hughes** (1817–1912). The headstones are marked by a trefoil and dentillated edge; poignantly, sixteen of the sisters are identified by their first names only, with no dates.

Turn left at the mini-roundabout at the top of Walton Street and walk down **Walton Well Road**, Jericho's northern boundary. On the corner is an unusually large double-fronted house with a scroll of acanthus around its cornice and a set of pineapple finials topping off its roof. This is ⑯ **Holyfield House**, built in 1891 for the master of Lucy's ironworks, its elaborate cast-iron balcony presumably an advertisement for the firm's craftsmanship.

The entrance to the works – known as Eagle Ironworks from 1838 and ⑰ **W. Lucy & Co.** from 1873 – is almost next door. Founded in 1760, the business moved to its Jericho site in 1825, presumably to take advantage of the nearby canal to import coal from the Midlands and export manufactured goods including bespoke ornamental ironwork for balconies, railings and gateways as well as lampposts, manhole covers, grates, ovens and agricultural machinery. The ironworks was taken over by William Lucy – who conveniently married the daughter of George Jennings, a sanitary engineer and designer of public toilets

featuring elaborate iron railings – when he was in his early twenties, and despite his death at the age of only 36 it was to retain his name until its closure in 2005.

Over the course of the 20th century Lucy's expanded into the manufacture of storage equipment, shelving and library stacking (like ornamental ironwork, much in demand by Oxford's colleges) as well as electrical engineering and stainless steel, continuing to grow into the 1960s, when it employed more than 700 workers. Though the site is now redeveloped as blocks of flats with trite names such as Furnace House and Fettler's House, there are remnants of its former life in the arts and crafts office building (now housing) fronting Walton Well Road – still with a brass letterbox inscribed 'W. Lucy & Co. Ltd.' and a factory clock suspended from its side – the two understandably angry-looking stone eagles perched on top of the brick pillars and several sets of handsome wrought-iron gates, some also topped by eagles, along Walton Well Road. Phillip Pullman's 2003 novel

Lyra's Oxford makes reference to Lucy's in the form of 'Randolph Lucy', a fictitious 17th-century alchemist with an eagle-demon and a laboratory on nearby Juxon Street.

Continue down Walton Well Road. The handsome terrace at nos 11–25 is by the same builder as Holyfield: the use of yellow brick indicates it was probably financed through a loan from the Oxford Building and Investment Company, whose borrowers were pressurised into buying materials from company secretary John Galpin's Oxford and Berks Brick Company, accounting for the large amount of yellow-brick housing built in Oxford in the second half of the 19th century. As well as bands of red and blue-glazed brickwork, decorations include finely carved scenes from the life of Elijah on the arches above the first-floor windows, with the prophet being fed by ravens at one end of the terrace and whisked up to heaven in a fiery chariot at the other.

Further down the street on the right, at the junction with Southmoor Road, is a baroque **⓲ drinking fountain**. Erected in 1885 amid concerns about the growing number of local pubs, the fountain – marking the site of the natural spring that gave the street its name and with the words 'Drink and think of Him who is the Fountain of Life' framing its bronze plaque – was funded by Oxford mayor and coalmerchant William Ward (son of Henry, see above), a prominent member of the Oxford Movement who also donated the land for St Barnabas. The design – originally with a water spout in the form of a grotesque head – was by Harry Wilkinson Moore, architect of many of the houses in Longworth Road.

Continue to the bridge and take the ramp on the far side to the towpath of the **⑲ Oxford Canal**. Built from about 1770 to 1790 to link the Midlands coalfields to London via the Thames and running some 80 miles south from Coventry to Oxford, the canal's heyday was brief: in 1805 its usefulness was eclipsed by the completion of the Grand Junction Canal, which provided a quicker and easier route. Continue as far as the first bridge: on your right is Castle Mill Stream, a tributary of the Thames linked to the canal further downstream at Isis lock, and the railway lines; on your left would once have been the brightly lit windows of the Lucy foundry. The canal originally ended at a basin and wharves just beyond Hythe Bridge Street but these were filled in during the 1950s to provide land for Nuffield College (see page 226).

Jericho Footbridge

Leave the towpath at the first bridge (the Jericho Footbridge) and continue into **Mount Place**, its former workshops and the terrace of housing down Canal Street giving a sense of Jericho as it might have been just after the flood-prone and contaminated canalside was drained and developed in the 1860s. Continue along **Mount Street**, which ends with two unusual stone-faced houses. To your left is another entrance to the former Eagle Ironworks, its gates topped by a pair of iron eagles. Turn right into **Allam Street**: on the corner (at no. 7) is a larger house with a gothic portal supported by crouched stone figures. Continue along Allam Street and turn right into **Cranham Street**. **⑳** No. 27,

Mount Place

7 Allam Street

with its large pediment, was built as a Wesleyan chapel in the 1880s before being deconsecrated in the 1920s and used as an architectural workshop, then an ice-cream factory, then a garage (at which point the doors were fitted), then a physics laboratory for Green College. Nos 32–36 and nos 44–45 are unusual in having gothic arches above their openings, with pairs of sash windows separated by a slender column.

Turn left into **Canal Street**, where the tower of St Barnabas dominates the view. Dating back to 1869, when it was founded by Oxford brewery Morrell's (see page 219), the **㉑ Old Bookbinders** pub on the corner of Victor Street is the dispiriting, near-empty dive where Lewis and Morse refresh their brain cells in the televised version of the first Inspector Morse story, *The Dead of Jericho* (1987). Praised for presenting a picture of Oxford that extended beyond the University, the episode used many residents as extras: those involved remember actor John Thaw 'spending a lot of time' in the Bookbinders, while following the first broadcast author Colin Dexter was faced with calls from locals trying to guess which of them had inspired the plot (one man who assumed it was his wife accused Dexter of having an affair with her). Just opposite the pub, the site of the fictional murder, **㉒ Combe Road** (renamed Canal Reach for the episode), offers a rare glimpse of the canal and the Castlemill Boatyard, in operation since the mid-19th century and the subject of an angry dispute between developers and boaters, who with local residents want to retain boat-repair facilities and improve community access to the water. The water-dwelling Gyptians in Philip Pullman's *Northern Lights* (1995) and *Lyra's Oxford* (2007) were based on Jericho boat people and the author – who described Jericho as 'the coastline Oxford shares with Bohemia' – has been a vocal opponent of wholesale redevelopment. The facilities at Combe Road are currently used by College Cruisers, which hires narrowboats to tourists.

On your right is the church of St Barnabas and on your left, on the corner of Cardigan Street, is the **㉓ Jericho Community Centre**, built at the end of the 19th century as St Barnabas' institute.

㉔ St Barnabas itself was financed and founded in 1869 by Thomas Combe, who as OUP Printer for 35 years from 1838 lived with his wife Martha in a house in the OUP quadrangle. Combe became a senior partner in 1851 and by 1855 was wealthy enough to buy the Wolvercote Paper Mill, which he leased and eventually sold to OUP.

A leading member of the Oxford Movement, which looked to the rituals of the pre-Reformation medieval church to counter low-church Nonconformism, he was also a friend and patron to the Pre-Raphaelites, in particular to William Holman Hunt, whom he commissioned to paint *The Light of the World*, created in the garden at OUP in the early 1850s and eventually donated by Martha to Keble College (see page 155). Combe's concern for the spiritual health of his OUP workers led him to teach a Sunday School for his 'press boys' for more than 20 years and eventually to build this church for the community.

Combe instructed his architect Arthur Blomfield – a prolific ecclesiastical designer who was also architect to the Bank of England – to build a church that would accommodate a thousand worshippers, but with 'not a penny to be thrown away in external appearance or decoration'. Blomfield's response was to reject his trademark gothic style, with its reliance on costly carved decoration, and draw instead on early Christian basilicas (inspired in particular by the 11th-century cathedral of Torcello in similarly waterlogged Venice), in accordance with the Oxford Movement's veneration of the early Christian past. Building as cheaply as possible in rubble held together with mortar coated externally in Portland cement, with thin courses of brick and a simple statue as the only exterior decoration, Blomfield was well aware that his design was 'in total disregard of all conventional notions as to fitness and external appearance'. Concerns for safety led the campanile to be reduced in height in 1893, an operation carried out by means of a pulley powered by a donkey who plodded up and down Cardigan Street; the clock ensured OUP workers had no excuse for lateness.

Turn right along **Cardigan Street** and go inside the church porch where a glazed panel offers tantalising views of the richly tiled and painted interior, begun in 1893 and intended to be added to as money allowed, but never fully completed.

Turn left along **St Barnabas Street**, where the austere double-fronted vicarage occupies the corner plot. At the end of the road turn left on to **Great Clarendon Street**. On the left, after the junction with Canal Street, is a long, low stone-faced building with a single, somewhat forbidding doorway, its severity relieved only by three gables with elaborate gothic tracery windows. This was formerly the ㉕ **St Barnabas Boys' School**, built in 1856 for the parish of St Paul's (which can be glimpsed at the end of the road) by George Edmund Street, later to be commissioned for the prestigious new parish church of North Oxford, St Philip and St James (see page 309). When the school finally closed in the 1960s the building was sold to the council on condition it was used to rehouse Jericho residents displaced by redevelopment: it is now a mix of sheltered housing and family homes.

Looking left up **Albert Street** you can see the ㉖ **Oxford Baptist Chapel**, built in 1881 and still in use today. The building opposite, now converted into houses, used to be the back of the Bakers Arms pub: its blank wall is perhaps a nod to its neighbours' abhorrence of alcohol.

Turn right down Albert Street, the westernmost of Jericho's streets to be on high enough ground to form part of the area's first batch of development in the 1830s and 1840s. The vast sheds on the corner of Wellington Street were built in the 1960s to house OUP's expanding printing and binding operations. At the junction of **Richmond Road** is the Alshami Lebanese restaurant, representing one of the many communities now living in Jericho. Opposite is the ㉗ **Oxford Synagogue and Jewish Centre**, its copper roof designed to resemble breaking waves and its porthole window depicting Noah's Ark. Established on this site in a disused lecture hall in 1893, rebuilt in the 1970s and extended in 2004, the centre is unique in catering for Orthodox, Masorti and Progressive forms of prayer with a complicated timetable designed to ensure no one is offended – though a notice on the gateway warns would-be worshippers to phone in advance to check.

Continue past the synagogue along Richmond Road: no. 12 is where former Conservative prime minister ㉘ **Margaret Thatcher** (1925–2013) is alleged to have shared a house with two communists during

Richmond Road

Richmond Road

Cohen Quadrangle

her student days at Somerville in the 1940s, subsisting largely on sausages. It's worth looking at the terrace opposite with its mix of red, yellow and blue-baked polychromatic brickwork.

Turn back and left into **Worcester Place**, where new and old Jericho meet, with the former workshop building at the turn in the road and the two-storey cottages in stark contrast with the expressionist stainless-steel roofscape of the Cohen Quadrangle, completed in 2017 by Alison Brooks Architects for Exeter College. Walton Lane, on the left, provided coachhouses and trade access to houses on Walton Street. The 'Worcester-Place' street sign is one of a number dating from the 1840s and 1850s, recognisable by the hyphen between the two words.

On the corner of **Walton Street** is **㉙ Ruskin College**, established in 1899 by two young Americans, Charles Beard and Walter Vrooman, with financial support from the latter's wife, Amne Grafflin, to allow working-class men who could not afford admission to the University to follow its curriculum, access its libraries and sit some of its exams. Courses in politics, economics and social sciences aimed to empower alumni to act more effectively in promoting working-class interests through trades unions, political parties and cooperative societies; women students were accepted from 1919 and in 1970 the college hosted the first National Women's Liberation Conference. The handsome red-brick building with its stone frontispiece dates from 1912: Vrooman and Grafflin are commemorated on a foundation stone under one of the ground-floor windows. However, appearances are deceptive: the college moved to Headington in 2012 and all but the façade was demolished to be incorporated into Exeter's Cohen Quadrangle, as you can see if you look at the roof.

289

Turn left up Walton Street and on the right is the **30** **Clarendon Institute**, an OUP social club established in 1893 by Horace Hart, Controller of the Press, to provide a gymnasium, theatre, bar, billiard room, library and further-education facilities for employees, who numbered about 550 at the time. The quirky Queen Anne-style red-brick building with its three baroque gables was designed by North Oxford architect Harry Wilkinson Moore (see pages 331 and 335): in what seems a relentless expansion of Oxford's primary industry, it currently houses various departments of the University.

To return to the walk's starting point on Woodstock Road, continue up Walton Street and turn right on Little Clarendon Street. ●

Visit...

St Sepulchre's Cemetery
Walton Street, OX1 2HD
www.stsepulchres.org.uk

Eat/Drink...

Common Ground
37-38 Little Clarendon Street, OX1 2HF
www.commongroundstudy.space

Freud Cafe Bar
119 Walton Street, OX2 6AH
www.freud.eu

The Jericho Café
112 Walton Street, OX2 6AJ
www.thejerichocafe.co.uk

Jericho Tavern
56 Walton Street, OX2 6AE
www.thejerichooxford.co.uk

Jude the Obscure
54 Walton Street, OX2 6AE

Old Bookbinders
17-18 Victor Street, OX2 6BT
www.oldbookbinders.co.uk

OXFORD WOMEN

SUFFRAGE

St Hugh's College
www.st-hughs.ox.ac.uk

St Hugh's College
@StHughsColl

St Hugh's College

7
North Oxford:

a new suburb & its women pioneers

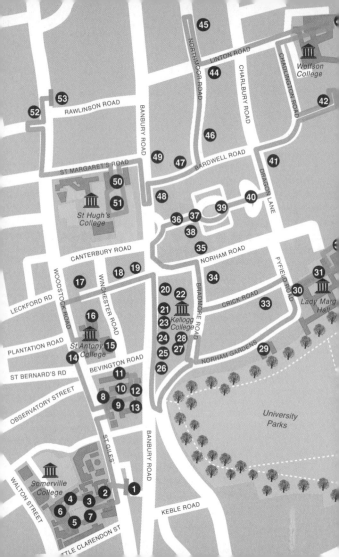

North Oxford: a new suburb & its women pioneers

Start: Oxford University Language Centre
Finish: Plaque to Dorothy Crowfoot Hodgkin
Distance: 4.5 miles

Oxford in the mid-19th century hardly extended beyond St Giles', where the city's dense mesh of streets and colleges gave way to farmland and countryside. The University was still focused on training Anglican clergy and providing higher education to the social elite, but as the century progressed, the removal of religious conditions for entry and other reforms encouraged middle-class parents to consider an Oxford education for their sons as a useful prelude to a professional or civil-service career.

The resulting demand for student accommodation prompted both merchants and professionals to sell their city-centre homes and move out to new suburbs – most notably in the area of North Oxford covered by this walk. The pioneers were wealthier tradespeople, joined by a few clergymen and University professors. Fellows of the University (until the 1880s bound to celibacy) and their families followed towards the end of the century, along with newcomers from outside the city.

A number of residents of the new suburb – many of them women – made important contributions to science, social welfare or the arts, and this walk passes several of their homes. The walk also takes in four of the women's colleges founded in the second half of the 19th century – located discreetly outside the confines of the city, initially occupying houses on North Oxford's estates – as well as a college building designed by the early 21st century's most famous female architect.

The walk starts at the south end of Woodstock Road and weaves around this and Banbury Road, the two main routes leading north from the city centre. Information about the colleges you'll pass is

given if you wish to go into them and it is possible to terminate the walk and catch a bus back to the city centre at virtually any point.

Begin the walk at the ❶ **Oxford University Language Centre** in **Woodstock Road**, a red-brick arts and crafts building dating from the first decade of the 20th century. Look carefully at the glass above the main entrance and you'll see the words 'Big Game Museum', referring to the building's origins as a home for the large collection of large animals killed by Charles Peel (1869–1931), who claimed big-game hunting was 'the greatest and grandest of all sports'. The collection, including 'Gerald the Giraffe' and an African elephant, was moved to the Royal Albert Memorial Museum in Exeter in 1918.

From 1923, this was home to the Oxford Playhouse – largely thanks to actress Jane Ellis (born Helen Olive Stockbridge), who persuaded the building's owner to rent it out and enticed director J. B. Fagan, with whom she had worked at the Royal Court in London, to set up a company. The opening performance (attended by the playwright) was George Bernard Shaw's *Heartbreak House* and early Oxford players included John Gielgud, Flora Robson, Tyrone Guthrie and Margaret Rutherford. In 1938 the Oxford Playhouse moved to a new building in Beaumont Street (see page 243). Cross the road to the entrance to Somerville College.

Somerville College
Woodstock Road, OX2 6HD
www.some.ox.ac.uk
Open term time, 9–12 and 14–16

The second of the women's colleges, Somerville was founded in 1879 by members of the Association for the Education of Women in Oxford who objected to the insistence that the first female college, Lady Margaret Hall (see below), should be exclusively for Anglican students. Beginning with just twelve members, it was named in honour of Scottish mathematician and scientist Mary Somerville (1780–1872), the first female member of the Royal Astronomical Society and the first signatory on John Stuart Mill's unsuccessful petition of 1868 for female suffrage. Alumni and college members include writers Vera Brittain, A. S. Byatt, Margaret Forster, Rose Macaulay, Iris Murdoch, Michèle Roberts and Dorothy L. Sayers; scientists Kay Davies and Dorothy Hodgkin; politicians Indira Gandhi, Margaret Thatcher and Shirley Williams; and TV presenter Esther Rantzen.

The entrance arch in the plain stone wall – designed as if to frustrate prying eyes – leads to the intimate ❷ **Front Quadrangle** flanked by cottage-like arts and crafts terraces dating from 1933. A further arch leads to a jumble of buildings around a carpark, including an ill-proportioned brick and stone residential block built in 1885 by Thomas Graham Jackson, architect of the newly completed Examination Schools in the High Street (see page 35). Another brick archway leads to a second, much larger space with a central green and an eclectic mix of buildings from brick Elizabethan revival to brutalist concrete. To your right (abutting the Jackson building) is ❸ **Walton House**, Somerville's original hall of residence, and it is presumably on the central green that the first principal, Madeleine Septima Shaw-Lefevre, recalled: 'for the first few years two cows and a pig formed part of the establishment, but these were later replaced by a pony and a donkey which might be seen disporting themselves in the field, adding to the picturesque and homely character of the place.' Lectures, shared by students from Lady Margaret Hall, were delivered in a room above a baker's shop in Little Clarendon Street, at the southern edge of the campus.

Anticlockwise from Walton House is the ❹ **library** of 1903 by Basil Champneys, who also worked at Lady Margaret Hall and designed the Rhodes Building at Oriel. Built in red brick, with an arcaded loggia topped by elegant columns and a central bow window surmounted by swags, this is the largest college library in Oxford, its early collections dating from a time when women had no access to the Bodleian. The unashamedly 20th-century residential buildings opposite both the entrance and the library are by Philip Dowson of Ove Arup, who was recommended to the principal by alumna Dorothy Hodgkin (you can see her former home at no. 94 Woodstock Road at the end of the walk) following government pressure in the early 1960s to increase women's access to the University. The ❺ **Vaughan and Fry Buildings** (1966), opposite the library, have an exposed concrete frame that provides occupants with shade and privacy while satifsying the contemporary modernist dogma to express the building's structure externally; the ❻ **Wolfson Building** (1967), opposite the entrance, offers a tougher, more brutalist variation on the same theme. The determinedly unfussy ❼ **chapel** in front of the Fry Building was added – controversially, given the college's original remit – in 1933 with funds from Baptist adventurer, writer and artist Emily Georgina Kemp (1860–1939) as a place where college members of all nationalities and religions could meet.

To the right of the college entrance on Woodstock Road is a plaque about the hospital that occupied Somerville's buildings during World War I, with patients including poets Siegfried Sassoon and Robert Graves.

Cross Woodstock Road and continue north to St Anne's College.

St Anne's College
Woodstock Road, OX2 6HS
www.st-annes.ox.ac.uk
Open daily, 9.00–17.00

The first sight of St Anne's as you walk along Woodstock Road is a sinuous pierced sandstone wall topped by a roof garden. Surprisingly, this belongs to the kitchens, built by Fletcher Priest in 2012 along with the handsome library and **❽ academic centre** – a cube with a frame of local stone punctured by uniform tall windows. The last of the women's colleges to become part of the University in 1952, St Anne's was born in 1879, when the Society of Home-Students was formed to allow female students to attend tutorials and lectures while living in lodgings across the city. The society's first physical space was a commonroom on Ship Street, and it was not until the 1930s that it took over the current site, becoming the St Anne's Society in 1942. Alumni and college members include writers and journalists Tina Brown, U. A. Fanthorpe, Helen Fielding, Zoë Heller, Penelope Lively, Melanie Phillips and Libby Purves; actress Maria Aitken; conductor Simon Rattle; politician Edwina Currie; and academic researcher Kathryna Kwok.

St Anne's is perhaps the only Oxford college without a chapel: when funding was running short, the college decided to focus on the statement **❾ dining hall**, to the right of the entrance, as this would be more welcoming to students. One of Oxford's first modernist buildings, dating from 1960, the double-height, light-filled space has a lantern roof topped by a ship, recalling the college's first home.

The rest of the campus is pleasantly landscaped between an eccentric array of buildings. The original medievalist castellated and turretted **❿ library** of 1938 is by Giles Gilbert Scott (architect of the Weston Library, see page 52) – the beavers above the columns that flank the doorway are the college

mascot, chosen by a Canadian founder because beavers work industriously within a community before returning to their own lodges to sleep. Among the notable halls of residence are the **⓫ Ruth Deech Building** opposite the library by Kohn Pedersen Fox (2005), its concrete frame punctuated by slatted wooden cladding, and two robust, linked concrete-framed **⓬ residential blocks** beyond and to its right built in the 1960s by leading 'new brutalists' Howell, Killick, Partridge and Amis that were intended to be joined by four more to form a snaking chain across the campus.

Turn right to reach the grassed quadrangle, skirt the second of the new brutalist blocks and a paved path leads to no. 27 Banbury Road, built by J. J. Stevenson, a leading proponent of the Queen Anne style, for moral philosopher **⓭ Thomas Hill Green** (1836–82) and his wife Charlotte. The high dormers, rooftop observation platform and red brick were unusual for North Oxford at this time – as was the way the terracotta monogram (accessible from Banbury Road) included both their initials in acknowledgement of their parity as householders (in fact, Green died before the house was completed and Charlotte was forced to mortgage it to her brother, John Addington Symonds, a poet, literary critic and advocate for the legitimacy of male homosexuality). A friend of both Mrs Humphry Ward and Clara Pater (see below), Charlotte was a prominent member of the branch of the Association for the Education of Women in Oxford that was instrumental in founding Somerville.

Return to Woodstock Road and walk north. On the corner of Bevington Road, on the opposite side of the street, is the former ⑭ **Horse & Jockey pub**, built in 1880 and subsequently leased to St John's College. It is said that former US president Bill Clinton was a regular during his days at Oxford in the late 1960s. The pub closed in 2002 to become student accommodation.

Moving northwards, next door to St Anne's is St Antony's.

St Antony's

62 Woodstock Road, OX2 6JF
www.sant.ox.ac.uk
(officially open only by appointment,
but porters have proved willing to allow entry)

St Antony's is a graduate college specialising in international studies. Set up in 1950 by French shipping magnate Antonin Besse, the college was originally housed in the former convent of the Holy Trinity, founded by Marian Hughes (1817–1912), who in 1841, encouraged by Oxford Movement leader Edward Bouverie Pusey (see box, page 84), became the first woman since the Reformation to take nuns' vows within the mainstream Church of England. The chapel at the south of the site, distinguished by a decorative lead spire, still houses the library. Alumni and college members include screenwriter Julian Mitchell; philosopher and writer Gillian Rose; sociologist and political activist Hilary Wainwright; and Africanist Stephen Ellis.

Two exemplary and extraordinary buildings face off to the north of the entrance: the **15 Hilda Besse Building** (1970) by Howell, Killick, Partridge and Amis and the **16 Investicorp Building** (2015), completed a year before her death by British-Iraqi architect Zaha Hadid. The former is an even more confident example of new brutalist expressionism than the practice's work next door at St Anne's, with a base raised on pilotis, a first floor featuring heavily canted square openings and a double-height hall and commonroom on the upper level clad in concrete panels and lit by a beautifully detailed modern take on a coffered ceiling (visible through the upper windows).

Built to house the Middle Eastern Studies Centre's archives, library and lecture theatre, the Investicorp Building is a sinuous, space-age, fortified tube clad in stainless-steel panels above a concrete base, with a fully glazed, screen-like end wall facing the Hilda Besse façade.

16

Continue north along Woodstock Road, where you will see the tail and body of Zaha Hadid's Investicorp Building clinging limpet-like to the nondescript Victorian houses next door. On the same side of the street, again moving north, is **⓱ St Philip and St James**, built in 1866 as the parish church of the new North Oxford suburbs by George Edmund Street, mentor to William Morris and architect to the diocese of Oxford. An imposing presence with a commanding tower constructed of rugged stone with red-brick banding, the gothic revival church now houses the Oxford Centre for Mission Studies.

Turn left along **Church Walk**, past the delightfully eclectic terraces of Winchester Road, to **⓲ North Parade Avenue**, an uncharacteristically narrow street of pubs, cafés and independent shops. Developed from former farm buildings sold off in lots by St John's College at an auction held at the Horse & Jockey (see above) in 1832, a century ago this was still the site of such grinding poverty that, according to Jan Morris, 'it first turned the schoolboy mind of [future Labour Party leader] Hugh Gaitskell towards Socialism'.

Confusingly, North Parade is a mile or so south of South Parade in Summertown: it is claimed that this is because during the siege of Oxford in the Civil War (1642–46), when Charles I made the town his new capital (see box, page 168), South Parade formed the Parliamentarian southern front and North Parade the Royalist northern front. As you will pass only one other café on the rest of the walk (the Cherwell Boathouse), this is a good opportunity to refuel, either now or as you return to this part of Banbury Road later.

The white stuccoed houses on the northern corner of North Parade, ⑲ nos 77 and 79 **Banbury Road**, also date from the first half of the 19th century: their elegant Georgian restraint stands in contrast to the extravagantly proportioned, individualistically detailed villas that were soon to populate the area.

Turn right into Banbury Road and cross to the other side. The houses in this stretch of the street exemplify the exuberant villas that make up the Norham Manor estate. Built on land leased piecemeal from St John's College, the area is described by architectural historian Geoffrey Tyack as 'one of the finest examples of Victorian middle-class suburban development in England'.

Envisaged as an irregular arrangement of neo-gothic and Italianate villas dotted through a landscape crossed by winding roads, the estate was laid out from 1860 by William Wilkinson, architect of the Randolph Hotel (see page 243) and of several country houses around his home town of Witney. Wilkinson designed many of the earliest houses himself – importing to suburban Oxford the gothic sensibility he had developed in the design of country parsonages – with others commissioned by clients from architects of their choice or built on spec by developers in line with regulations governing standards of workmanship, sanitation, finishes, boundary walls and even prospective tenants strictly enforced by St John's. Individuality in planning and detailing – whether towers, porches, bay windows or carved decoration – was sought by former residents of city terraces who were at last able to indulge their architectural fantasies in distinguishing their homes from the other red- or yellow-brick villas around them.

According to the census of 1881, some 40 per cent of households were headed by professional men, with half of these working at the University and almost half of the rest clergy. Some 20 per cent of household heads were engaged in trade and almost one-third – the vast majority women – lived on private incomes. Including servants, the ratio of women to men in North Oxford was an extraordinary 3:1.

Many houses contained two or three large reception rooms, a minimum of four or five bedrooms for family and guests, and accommodation for three or four live-in servants. Today, with most of the villas repurposed as private schools or University departments, it is hard to believe that these sprawling mansions were once middle-class family homes.

Walking south, **20** **no. 66** (formerly St Catherine's and now the Oxford English Centre), distinguished by its tall corner tower and rooftop balustrade, was designed in 1874 by Wilkinson's pupil Frederick Codd on one of the most expensive sites leased by St John's. Its first owner, Henry Fry, had spent much of his working life as a missionary in Tasmania; he died soon after moving in, leaving the house to his widow, Catherine. With its gothic porch decorated with elaborate carvings of animals and birds, **21** **no. 62** (now part of Kellogg College, a postgraduate college founded in 1990) was designed in 1865 by Edward George Bruton for Richard St John Tyrwhitt, a vicar of the Anglo-Catholic St Mary Magdalen (see page 122) known for his controversial views on homosexuality (against) and evolution (for).

It is worth walking behind the house to see **㉒ The Hub**, a café pavilion completed in 2017 by Feilden Clegg Bradley Studios. With Islamicist fretwork shading its upper level, this is the University's first building to achieve a Passivhaus certification for low energy use in its construction and running. **㉓ No. 60** (also part of Kellogg), with its unusual roofline and Rapunzel turret above the doorway, was built by Wilkinson in 1869 for a local chemist.

Designed in 1866 by John Gibbs, **㉔ no. 56** (Wykeham House, now the Oxford Careers Service) is a bizarre confection in yellow brick with a statue of William of Wykeham in a niche on the chimney. It was built for a local draper and in 1881 was bought for scientist Edward Poulton and his wife-to-be Georgina, a member of the Huntley & Palmer biscuit dynasty, as a wedding gift from her parents. Poulton, who was responsible for several additions including the tower on the left and the extraordinary porch, lived here until his death in 1943.

㉕ No. 54 (also by Gibbs) was designed in 1866 for Tom Arnold, brother of poet Matthew Arnold and father of Mrs Humphry Ward (see below): its fourteen bedrooms were intended to accommodate students for whom Arnold acted as private tutor. A decade later it was bought by a committee of evangelical churchmen, renamed Wycliffe Hall (after the 14th-century theologian) and much extended – fittingly for a theological college, the red-brick agglomeration appears

to have two chapels, one in front and one (actually the refectory) to the side. Since 1883 the college has also owned ㉖ **no. 52**, designed by Codd in 1870 as a convent for an order whose sisters ran a printing school to train young women in an alternative career to domestic servitude; for more than a decade the nuns printed all the works of Pusey.

Turn left into **Norham Gardens**. Designed by Wilkinson in 1862, the immaculately restored house at ㉗ **no. 7**, on the corner of Bradmore Road, was the first home built on the estate. The client, Regius Professor of Modern History Goldwin Smith, set a trend among his University colleagues, making the area around Norham Gardens the most popular part of the estate for Oxford academics.

Turn right into **Bradmore Road**. No. 2, a relatively modest red-brick semi designed by Codd, was from 1869 to 1885 the home of ㉘ **Clara Pater** (1841–1910) and her brother Walter (1838–94). Clara was involved in setting up the first University lectures for women: having studied Greek and Latin with other North Oxford residents including novelist Mrs Humphry Ward, who lived further down the street (see below), she became the first Classics tutor at Somerville and from 1885 the college's first resident tutor. After her brother's death she moved to King's College, London, and from 1899 to 1900 was a private tutor to Virginia Woolf, whom she inspired both in life and as the model for Kitty Malone's tutor in *The Hours*.

Regarded as a father of the Aesthetic Movement and of literary modernism, Walter Pater became a fellow of Brasenose in 1864. A literary and art critic famed for his precious prose style, he rejected religious dogma and considered the intense response to aesthetic delight to be the key to happiness. On his death, Brasenose honoured him with a plaque in the college antechapel that shows him surrounded by four of his peers – Leonardo da Vinci, Michelangelo, Dante and Plato (see page 106). During his lifetime, Pater was known for

his green cravats as well as his wit, and it is said that he and Clara introduced William Morris' wallpapers to the Oxford suburbs.

Continue along **Norham Gardens**, with its series of extraordinarily extravagant villas, mainly by Wilkinson or Codd. The largest of these, no. 13 is a rambling red-brick mansion with Tudor-style chimneys designed in 1869 by Wilkinson for a tutor at The Queen's College. At the start of the 20th century it belonged to ㉙ **William Osler** (1849–1919), the first physician to introduce ward-based practice to medical training, exorting his students to 'listen to your patient; he is telling you the diagnosis'. Osler and his American wife Grace added an enormous drawing room and master bedroom to the garden front as well as bathrooms and central heating: thanks to their generous hospitality, their home became known as 'The Open Arms'. Lord Nuffield of Morris Motors (see box, page 228) became a friend when as a young man he came to fix Osler's car – and it was in part thanks to Osler's influence that Nuffield was later to donate so much of his personal fortune to medical science. At the end of the street is Lady Margaret Hall or LMH.

Women at Oxford

In 1873 A. M. A. H. Rogers won scholarships to Balliol and Worcester, having come top in the Oxford school examinations – offers that were withdrawn once it was realised that A. M. A. H. stood for Annie Mary Anne Henley (Balliol sent an edition of the works of Homer as a consolation). Rogers gained the equivalent of a first-class degree in University examinations for women in Classics in 1877 and Ancient History in 1879 but it was not until 1920 that women were awarded degrees. Rogers became one of Oxford's first official female graduates in a ceremony described by fellow graduate Vera Brittain as 'tense with the consciousness of a dream fulfilled'.

Unsurprisingly, Rogers had become involved in the Association for the Education of Women in Oxford (AEW), founded in 1878 by a group that included North Oxford residents Charlotte and Thomas Hill Green. Since 1873 North Oxford women including Mrs Humphry Ward, Clara Pater and Lavinia Talbot had been organising lectures for female students, known as 'Lectures for Ladies', and in 1875 the University agreed to set examinations for them – as taken by Rogers. The AEW worked to establish women's halls – initially in North Oxford houses – but split acrimoniously when Lavinia and Edward Talbot insisted that the first of these, Lady Margaret Hall, be open only to Anglicans.

Somerville was swiftly established as a non-denominational women's college and the Society of Home-Students (later to become St Anne's) catered for those who lived outside college accommodation. St Hugh's was founded in 1886 and St Hilda's (like the others outside the confines of the city, this time to the east of Magdalen Bridge) in 1893. The four women's halls were formally recognised by the University in 1910 and the first female medical students were admitted in 1916.

Prejudice and unequal treatment persisted, however: in 1926 the all-male Oxford Union passed a motion that all women's colleges should be levelled to the ground and the following year new regulations ensured that women students made up no more than 25 per cent of the total intake, with a ban on new women's colleges. In 1932 Merze Tate became the first African-American woman to attend Oxford (at St Anne's).

Following World War II there was some liberalisation, and government pressure led to the abolition of the quota in 1957, encouraging a wave of new building at the women's halls. In 1959 these were given full collegiate status, in 1962 women were admitted to the Oxford Union and in 1969 St Hilda's provided the first female crew to qualify for the Summer Eights boat race.

Co-education was not introduced until the 1970s, however, with Brasenose, Hertford, Jesus, St Catherine's and Wadham all admitting their first female students in 1974: other colleges soon followed suit, though Oriel held out until 1980. Lady Margaret Hall and St Anne's reciprocated by admitting male students in 1979 and 30 years later St Hilda's was the last college to embrace mixed education.

In 2015 political scientist Louise Richardson became the University's first female vice-chancellor and three years later women undergraduates at Oxford outnumbered men for the first time.

Lady Margaret Hall
Norham Gardens, OX2 6QA
www.lmh.ox.ac.uk
Open daily, 10–dusk

Named after Lady Margaret Beaufort, mother of Henry VII and the patron of two Cambridge colleges, LMH was founded in 1878 by Edward Talbot, the warden of Keble College and later an Anglican bishop, and his wife Lavinia: their insistence that it was open only to Anglicans led to a split in the Association for the Education of Women in Oxford and the foundation of non-denominational Somerville. The first principal – with just nine students – was Elizabeth Wordsworth, great-niece of the poet. The college became the first women's college to admit

male students in 1979 and in 2016 became the only college in either Oxford or Cambridge to offer a Foundation Year for students from disadvantaged backgrounds. Alumni and college members include writers Gertrude Bell, Caryl Churchill and Antonia Fraser; politicians Benazir Bhutto, Michael Gove and Ann Widdecombe; chef Nigella Lawson; comedian Josie Long; and Save the Children founder Eglatyne Jebb. Nobel Peace Prize laureate Malala Yousafzai became a student in 2017.

From the Norham Gardens approach, LMH resembles a barracks more than an Oxford college. At the end of the open **30** **Laetare Quadrangle** is a starkly forbidding, bare red-brick wall punctured by a series of small windows, leaded as if barred, with a plain, pedimented stone archway at its centre. Its architect, Raymond Erith, hoped it would 'do something to rest the eyes and nerves of North Oxford', and the contrast with the wildly proportioned villas of the Northam Manor estate could not be greater. Completed in 1961, it must have inspired the military aesthetic of the twin entrance lodges: added in 2017 by architect John Simpson, these seem modelled after guardhouses, with overlarge porticos supported on squat Doric columns. If Erith's new range and the library beyond it use classical proportions and elements in a stripped-down form appropriate to the modern era, Simpson's postmodern additions exaggerate decorative motifs drawn from classicism to a level of whimsy, as in the lampposts or over-fussy detail of friezes and doorways.

To the right of the quadrangle is the 'Old Old Hall', a typical Norham Gardens villa that provided accommodation for the first students. The house was extended by the addition of the 'New Old Hall' by Basil Champneys (architect of Somerville's library) in 1884: unlike in male colleges, which favoured a staircase plan, Champneys provided rooms flanking corridors on the principle that 'you cannot turn girls out into the air when they pass from room to room'.

Beyond Erith's 1961 block is the Wolfson Quadrangle: the library that forms its northern range, again of barracks-like simplicity, with an arcaded base and lunette windows on the upper floor, is by Erith but the other two sides were largely built by Reginald Blomfield in the first two decades of the 20th century. All have beautifully detailed brickwork. Most notable is the **31 Talbot Building** opposite the entrance, its grandiosely pedimented front and cupola once terminating the view from Norham Gardens. The colonnade at the north-eastern corner of the quadrangle leads to a further quadrangle with buildings to your right designed in the 1930s by Giles Gilbert Scott (architect of St Anne's library): the large neo-byzantine **32 chapel** has a delicately carved porch with a frieze of art deco angels.

Return through the Wolfson Quadrangle to the gardens, where you can appreciate the magnificent glazing of the other face of the Talbot Building and the charmingly informal landscaping. Studded with an impressive variety of ancient trees and topiary (as well as benches!), the gardens lead past a boathouse and sports fields to the River Cherwell.

From the front of LMH, turn right up **Fyfield Road**. Turn left along **Crick Road**: no. 11, on the left, was home during the last decade of the 19th century to scientist  **John Scott Haldane** (1860–1936), his wife Louisa and their two infant children – future geneticist John Burden Sanderson Haldane and novelist Naomi Mitchinson. Haldane's research was concerned with respiration and the body's use of oxygen: interested in applying his findings to real-life situations, he conducted several experiments on himself and his family that led him to invent the first gas mask, to pioneer the use of canaries to detect carbon monoxide in mines and to devise a scheme of staged decompression for deep-sea divers. Much of this work was done in a private laboratory in the grounds of his next home in Linton Road (demolished to make way for Wolfson College, see below).

Turn right up **Bradmore Road**. The large yellow-brick villa with the gothic porch at no. 17, on the right, was built in 1872 (again by Codd) for Mary Arnold Ward – aka **Mrs Humphry Ward** (1851–1920) – her husband Thomas Humphry and their three children, who lived here until 1881 (for her reminiscences of this time, see box, page 323). A niece of poet Matthew Arnold and aunt of novelist Aldous Huxley, Ward was instrumental in establishing education for women at Oxford, becoming the first secretary of Somerville and even suggesting its name.  During her lifetime she was best known for 26 moralising novels – most notably the 800-page *Robert Elsmere* (1888) – that explored social issues and religious faith: by the turn of the century she was the world's best-selling novelist, amassing vast sums in royalties that more than compensated for her journalist husband's lack of earning power. After moving to London, she founded the Mary Ward Centre in Tavistock Place to provide public education and social services, established the first school for disabled children and instigated the Play Centre movement to provide children with after-school care. As she grew older, Ward became increasingly conservative, founding the Women's National Anti-Suffrage League in 1908, a move that caused Somerville to disown her.

Continue to **Norham Road**. Immediately opposite is the **35 Maison Française**, a research centre founded in 1946 to promote academic and cultural exchange between France and the UK. Its present premises – a series of simple modern boxes, with the only rhetorical flourish a cantilevered awning – was designed in 1963 by Jacques Laurent. The statue in the garden is Aristide Malliol's *La Flore, nue* (1910–11).

Life in North Oxford

For nine years, till the spring of 1881, we lived in Oxford, in a little house, north of the Parks, in what was then the newest quarter of the University town... We had many friends, all pursuing the same kind of life as ourselves, and interested in the same kind of things. Nobody under the rank of a Head of a College, except a very few privileged Professors, possessed as much as a thousand a year [about £100,000 today]. The average income of the new race of married tutors was not much more than half that sum. Yet we all gave dinner-parties and furnished our houses with Morris papers, old chests and cabinets, and blue pots. The dinner-parties were simple and short. At our own early efforts of the kind, there certainly was not enough to eat. But we all improved with time; and on the whole I think we were very fair housekeepers and competent mothers. Most of us were very anxious to be up-to-date, and in the fashion, whether in aesthetics, in house-keeping, or education. But our fashion was not of that of Belgravia or Mayfair, which indeed we scorned! It was the fashion of the movement which sprang from Morris and Burne-Jones. Liberty stuffs very plain in line, but elaborately 'smocked,' were greatly in vogue, and evening dresses, 'cut square,' or with 'Watteau pleats,' were generally worn, and often in conscious protests against the London 'low dress,' which Oxford – young married Oxford – thought both ugly and 'fast.' And when we had donned our Liberty gowns we went out to dinner, the husband walking, the wife in a bath chair, drawn by an ancient member of an ancient and close fraternity – the 'chairmen' of old Oxford.

Mrs Humphry Ward, *A Writer's Recollections*, 1918.

Return to Banbury Road, turn right and take the first right into **36** **Park Town**. Laid out in 1853–55 by city surveyor Samuel Lipscomb Seckham, this was the first of North Oxford's suburban developments, intended for 'parties of limited income' – pegged at between £500 and £1,000 per year (corresponding roughly to the salary of an Oxford tutor and professor respectively). A pair of elegant crescents in Bath stone and a less elegant terrace at the far end are interspersed with detached and semi-detached villas, mostly less elaborate versions of the kind that were to characterise the area's future development. At the entrance to the crescent is Oxford's oldest **37** **Victorian postbox**, a Hexagonal Penfold model (named after its designer, John Penfold) dating from 1866.

No. 10 – a handsome red-brick villa with a monkey-puzzle tree surrounded by ruined stone columns in the front garden – was the home of pioneering colour photographer **38** **Sarah Acland** (1849–1930) for the first three decades of the 20th century. Acland's father

Henry was instrumental in setting up the University Museum of Natural History (see page 135): his children were close friends of Alice Liddell and her sisters, and like them were photographed by Charles Dodgson (Lewis Carroll). Another family friend was John Ruskin, and Sarah studied with Ruskin at the newly formed Oxford School of Arts in the late 1860s, later becoming his assistant and close friend.

Sarah ran the family household in Broad Street between the death of her mother in 1881 and that of her father just over twenty years later. She was given her first camera in the early 1890s and her photographic portraits of visitors such as Ruskin and prime minister William Gladstone earned her a place as the first female member of the Oxford Camera Club. From 1900, after her move to Park Town – where the house's wooden superstructure may have served as a studio – she experimented with techniques for producing colour prints. Credited with inaugurating colour photography 'as a process for the travelling amateur', her groundbreaking images of two trips to Gibraltar gained her a fellowship of the Royal Photographic Society in 1905.

Continue around the crescent to no. 42, former home of Russian scholar ㊴ **William Morfill** (1834–1909) and his wife Charlotte Maria from 1863 until their deaths in 1909 and 1881 respectively. A graduate of Oriel, Morfill taught himself Slavonic languages by travelling extensively across Eastern Europe, compiling dictionaries, grammars and cultural histories and becoming the UK's first Professor of Russian and Slavonic Languages. His Park Town home became an unofficial faculty for local and visiting scholars and he hosted Sunday salons in the expansive drawing room.

'The Jungle'

The Terrace

If footsore, at this point you can return through Park Town to Banbury Road, turn right and resume the walk at **48**, see page 332. Or, if you would like a longer walk (a further 1.2 miles) past the Cherwell Boathouse café and restaurant, the riverside gardens of Wolfson College and the former homes of author J. R. R. Tolkien, continue along the path through the small garden at the end of the street to the stone archway (marked '1855 The Terrace').

40

At the end of the garden, opposite the archway, is a stone set into the path with an inscription to **40** **Charles Elton** (1900–91), an ecologist who helped to invent the concept of the food chain and pioneered research into animal population cycles, biological invasion and nature conservation. He lived

for many years in one of Park Town's semi-detached villas with his wife, poet E. Joy Scovell, and their two children, maintaining this small green space, 'The Jungle', for 30 years.

Go through the archway and turn left down Dragon Lane, then right along **Bardwell Road** past the ④ **Dragon School**, set up in 1877 as Oxford Preparatory School by a committee of dons wishing to educate their own children in a way that would today be described as progressive. It has been said that the committee was headed by Mr George, giving the school its nickname and subsequently its name, reflected in the dragons above the entrance to the last building on Bardwell Road and on the gates beyond. The initial mortgage for the premises came courtesy of Edward Poulton (see above) and alumni include writers John Betjeman, Naomi Mitchison (from 1904 to 1911 the only girl at the school), Nevile Shute and Christopher Tolkien; scientist John Burden Sanderson Haldane; politician Hugh Gaitskell; philosopher Alain de Botton; actors Hugh Laurie and Emma Watson; and tennis player Tim Henman.

Turn right down a track at the junction of Bardwell and Chadlington roads that leads past the school playing fields, with a war memorial and cricket pavilion at the far end, to the ㊷ **Cherwell Boathouse**, a riverside café and restaurant where you can hire punts from mid-March to mid-October. The picturesque building, with carved wooden barques flanking an ornate clock on its prominent gables, still houses a boat-repair shop.

Return along the lane and turn right into **Chadlington Road** then right along **Linton Road** (both dating mostly from the first decade of the 20th century) to ㊸ **Wolfson College** (open daylight hours). Wolfson began life in 1965 as a home for fellows without a college; grants from the Wolfson and Ford foundations later enabled it to build a campus on its present site. Its buildings – unusually uniform for an Oxford college and containing the University's first accommodation for married students – were completed by Powell & Moya in 1974.

The entrance from the street has the typically forbidding aspect of a traditional Oxford college, but unusually you can access the grounds simply by walking through the carpark to your right. Here a series of highly articulated blocks with rough-cast reinforced concrete frames punctured by large, deeply recessed windows steps down to the Cherwell, where the architects created an artificial island and lake as a haven for wildlife. A left turn through a gap between buildings leads to the hall with its pyramid roof and the River Quadrangle with its expansive views.

Return along Linton Road. **44** **St Andrew's**, on the left, was established as an evangelical church in conjunction with Wycliffe Hall in the first decade of the 20th century. To see the houses where author **45** **J. R. R. Tolkien** (1892–1973) and his wife Edith lived from 1926 to 1930 (in the charming Hobbit hole of no. 22, for which they held the first lease) and 1930 to 1947 (in the somewhat dull no. 20, which they bought from bookseller Basil Blackwell), turn right up **Northmoor Road**.

Orphaned at the age of twelve, Tolkien met Edith when he was sixteen and she was nineteen and both were lodging in the same boarding house. His guardian, Father Francis Morgan, forbade further contact because Edith was a Protestant, but on attaining his majority Tolkien persuaded her to marry him, despite the fact that she was engaged to someone else. They wed in 1916, before Tolkien was sent to the Western Front. The first of three sons was born in 1917 and their only daughter in 1929.

For most of his time in Northmoor Road, Tolkien was Professor of Anglo-Saxon and a fellow of Pembroke College. A member of the Inklings, a group of literary and fantasy enthusiasts that met in the Eagle and Child pub in St Giles' (see page 118), he wrote *The Hobbit* (published in 1937) and the first two volumes of *The Lord of the Rings* (published 1954–55) during his time here.

Return down **Northmoor Road**. Though the houses in the northern section were the last of the Norham Manor estate to be completed, dating from the 1920s, the red-brick villas in the southern section were mostly designed by Wilkinson's nephew Harry Wilkinson Moore around the turn of the 20th century. Particularly notable is **46** no. 2, a wonderfully eclectic mix of Queen Anne-style red brick, arts and crafts detailing around the doorway and a hint of art nouveau in the double-height bow at the front, designed in 1903 for Charles Firth, Regius Professor of Modern History, by another local architect.

Turn right along **Bardwell Road**: the **47** **Oxford High Preparatory School** on the right is a branch of the city's oldest girls' school, opened in 1875 with Ada Benson, aunt of *Mapp and Lucia* author E. F. Benson, as its first headmistress. Alumni include writer Rose Macaulay; actors Miriam Margolyes and Maggie Smith; comedian Mel Giedroyc; and politician Margaret Hodge. On the left is Wychwood School for Girls, founded in 1897 and at its current location since

1918. A plaque on Banbury Road honours former pupil **48** **Honor Fell** (1900–86), a biologist working mainly in Cambridge who pioneered the organ culture method that allows scientists to grow living cells within the laboratory.

Turn right into **Banbury Road**: at no. 78 is a postbox installed specifically to serve the needs of **49** **James Murray** (1837–1915). Appointed editor of the first *Oxford English Dictionary* in 1873, Murray generated huge volumes of correspondence with an army of volunteers who sent in slips for individual words following an 'Appeal to Readers' issued via libraries and bookshops (his most prolific contributor, William Chester Minor, an army surgeon and murderer, sent 12,000 slips from Broadmoor).

For three decades from 1885, when no. 78 was built, Murray, his wife Ada and various of their eleven children lived in the Banbury Road house, with a 'Scriptorium' in the garden acting as office and archive. Publisher Oxford University Press expected the dictionary to take ten years and to run to four volumes; it was finally published in twelve volumes in 1928, over a decade after Murray's death, with 414,825 words using 1,827,306 citations to illustrate their meanings.

Cross the street and walk along **St Margaret's Road** to St Hugh's College (official policy is to apply before visiting, but in practice the porters have helpfully allowed entry).

St Hugh's College

St Margaret's Road, OX2 6LE

www.st-hughs.ox.ac.uk

Open: apply before visiting or try asking at porter's lodge

St Hugh's College was founded in 1886 by Elizabeth Wordsworth, the first principal of Lady Margaret Hall, with the aim of opening up an Oxford education to women 'who find the charges of the present halls at Oxford and Cambridge (even the most moderate) beyond their means'. Annual fees for board and lodging were £45, compared to £60 at Somerville and £75 at Lady Margaret Hall. The college was funded with money left to Wordsworth by her father, the Bishop of Lincoln, and was named after St Hugh of Avalon, one of the bishop's 13th-century predecessors (the swan on the gates, the college emblem, was chosen because Hugh claimed to have a guardian swan).

The first principal was Charlotte Moberly (1846–1937), an academic and writer who became known for the best-seller *An Adventure* (1912), an account of a trip to Versailles with her vice-principal Eleanor Jourdain (1863–1924) during which the two women claimed to have met leading figures from the French Revolution including Marie Antoinette, who chatted to them while she sketched the park. Alumni and college members include writers Patricia Duncker, Mary Renault and Joanna Trollope and politicians Aung San Suu Kyi, Barbara Castle and Theresa May.

St Hugh's opened with four students lodged in a house at 25 Norham Road; the current **50 main building**, designed to accommodate 71 students, was completed in 1916. Unusually for an Oxford college, the building is fully visible from the street – a reassuringly domestic-style two-storey red-brick range, its only flourishes a pair of octagonal turrets and a taller central pavilion with a scrolled door surround, elegantly arched window, pediment and cupola. The porter is housed in one of the two stone lodges that flank the gate – an arrangement that perhaps inspired the recent additions to Lady Margaret Hall.

Because the main building of St Hugh's fronts the campus, you have to pass through it to access the gardens at the rear – a rare instance of visitors being allowed inside a college. Behind it, a generous terrace with benches allows you to sit and appreciate the grounds, parts of it laid out in the last ten years of her life by Annie Rogers (1856–1937), the University's first female graduate and a tireless campaigner for equality of education at Oxford as well as for female suffrage: the **51** **sundial** on the terrace bears the inscription 'Floribus, Anna, tuis faveat sol luce perenni' (Annie, may the sun favour thy flowers with perpetual light) and there is also a bench dedicated to her memory behind the University Church of St Mary (see page 103). According to Vera Brittain, 'If the women of Oxford could be said to owe their triumph to any one individual, the credit is hers. She was their forerunner, their expert, their champion, and the symbol of their struggle.'

After taking a tour of the campus – a collection of Victorian houses and modest 1960s brick blocks dotted within attractive gardens – return to the entrance through a door in the western side of the main building then continue left along St Margaret's Road to Woodstock Road.

Cross **Woodstock Road**, turn right and on the first corner is **2 Polstead Road**, the home of **52** **T. E. Lawrence** (Lawrence of Arabia, 1888–1935) from 1896 to 1921. Built in 1890 by Harry Wilkinson Moore, the nine-bedroom, red-brick semi-detached house was on the market for almost £3 million at the start of 2018. Lawrence's parents were Thomas Chapman, a married Anglo-Irish aristocrat, and Scottish governess Sarah Junner: having moved several times to escape the stigma of 'living in sin', using the

assumed names 'Mr and Mrs Lawrence', they eventually settled in North Oxford, where they attended the evangelical church of St Aldates and brought up their five sons (Thomas Edward, or Ned, was the second).

At the back of the house, clearly visible on Google Earth but not from the street, is the arts and crafts bungalow built for Lawrence when he was a teenager. It was here that he lived between stints as an archaeologist and on army missions to the Middle East in the 1910s and where he probably wrote *Seven Pillars of Wisdom*, his account of his experiences as a liaison officer with rebel forces during the Arab revolt against the Ottoman Turks from 1916 to 1918. He and his brothers all attended Oxford Boys' High School (see page 234) and he went on to read history at Jesus College, where he was eligible for a scholarship because he was born in Wales; his thesis on Crusader castles is still in the library and there is a bust of him in the chapel (see page 76). In 1919 Lawrence was granted a fellowship at All Souls, which funded him to work on *Seven Pillars of Wisdom*; according to Jan Morris, he organised a successful strike of scouts there in the 1920s.

Recross **Woodstock Road** and continue north to no. 94, where Nobel Prize-winning scientist **53 Dorothy Crowfoot Hodgkin** (1910–94) lived from 1957 to 1968. To enable Dorothy's husband Thomas, a Marxist educationalist and African historian, to be based in Ghana for three years reforming the country's universities and Dorothy to travel to meet scientists in the Soviet Union, China and India, the Hodgkins and their three children shared the substantial double-fronted red-brick house with Dorothy's younger sister Joan, an archaeologist who catalogued the Ashmolean's Ancient Egyptian collection, and Joan's family of five.

Dorothy was born in Cairo (her father John worked for the Egyptian ministry of education) but spent most of her childhood with her grandparents near Beccles, where John insisted she attend the local grammar school rather than being privately educated. She read chemistry at Somerville from 1928, having crammed privately to pass the requisite Latin exam, and in 1932 became only the third woman to be awarded a first-class degree by the University. Four years later she became Somerville's first fellow and tutor in chemistry, a post she held until

1977: her students included Margaret Thatcher, who was to hang a portrait of Hodgkin in Downing Street, despite the fact that her heroine was a lifelong Labour supporter. Between 1945 and 1969, using X-ray diffraction techniques, Hodgkin determined the structures of penicillin, vitamin B12 and insulin. She became a Nobel Laureate for Chemistry in 1964 and is still the only British woman to have been awarded a Nobel Prize for science. In 1975 she became President of the Pugwash Conferences on Science and World Affairs, campaigning against nuclear weapons.

From here, you can either walk or get a bus down Woodstock Road to the city centre. ●

Visit...

Cherwell Boathouse
Bardwell Road, OX2 6ST
www.cherwellboathouse.co.uk

Eat/Drink...

Brew Coffee Shop and Retailer
75B Banbury Road, OX2 6PE
www.brewoxford.co.uk

Gardeners Arms
8 North Parade, OX2 6LX
www.gardnersarms-northparade.com

**Taylors Gourmet
Sandwich & Deli Co.**
31 St Giles', OX1 3LD
www.taylorsoxford.co.uk

The Rose & Crown
14 North Parade Avenue, OX2 6LX
www.roseandcrownoxford.com

Vinny's Cafe
10 North Parade Avenue, OX2 6LX

The Thames with college boathouses

8
Along the Thames:
power & pleasure

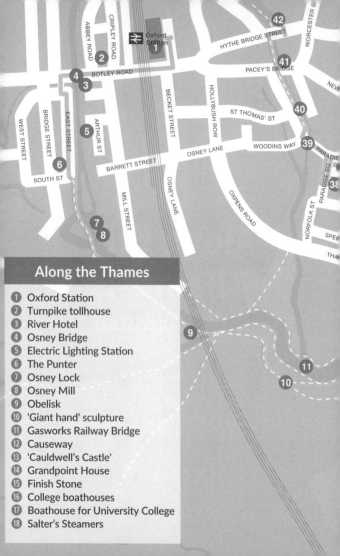

Along the Thames

1. Oxford Station
2. Turnpike tollhouse
3. River Hotel
4. Osney Bridge
5. Electric Lighting Station
6. The Punter
7. Osney Lock
8. Osney Mill
9. Obelisk
10. 'Giant hand' sculpture
11. Gasworks Railway Bridge
12. Causeway
13. 'Cauldwell's Castle'
14. Grandpoint House
15. Finish Stone
16. College boathouses
17. Boathouse for University College
18. Salter's Steamers

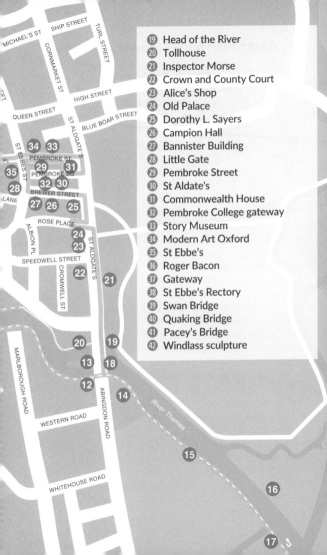

Along the Thames: power & pleasure

Start: Oxford Station
Finish: Windlass, Hythe Bridge Street
Distance: 3.5 miles

'We have had regularly a boat on the Isis and explored all the streams about, which are more in number than your eye-lashes.'
John Keats to his friend John Hamilton Reynolds,
21 September 1817

Situated roughly equidistant from the south, west and east coasts, Oxford is notoriously low-lying and flood-prone, with a climate deemed dank and unhealthy. Some 6 miles long but only just over a mile wide, its shape is determined in part by the contours of the gravel bank it was built on, bounded to west and east by the Thames and Cherwell, which meet at the city's southern tip. From Anglo-Saxon times until the late 19th century, the Thames was a major thoroughfare, bringing in goods and travellers from London and from the rural areas to the north: on reaching Oxford, it splits into a complicated network of backwaters and streams that once powered mills and fed breweries, before converging again to the south of the city.

This walk traces the course of two of Oxford's major waterways: the Thames itself and Castle Mill Stream, a backwater that leaves the main river near Walton Well Road in Jericho (see page 281) and runs alongside it about half a mile to its east before rejoining it some 3.5 miles later to the west of Folly Bridge. You can easily extend the walk by following the Thames further south towards Iffley or by continuing north up the Oxford Canal at the end.

In Oxford (and indeed from here to its Cotswold source), the Thames is known as the Isis in acknowledgement of its ancient name of Tameisis, but for familiarity's sake the name Thames is used throughout the text.

The walk starts at ❶ **Oxford station**, established in 1852 and today an undistinguished 1970s gateway to the city with a major redevelopment planned. The railway first arrived in Oxford in 1844 with a station at Grandpont, just south of Folly Bridge (see below): this was a terminus for a branch line that ran south to Didcot, where it met the mainline Great Western Railway route from London to Bristol. The introduction of the railway had been fiercely resisted by the University, whose members feared easier access to London would provide unwelcome temptations for students as well as drawing a mass of common visitors to the city. In 1850 a line north to Banbury was opened: this was extended to Birmingham two years later, at which point the new through station here was built and Grandpont became redundant.

Turn right from the station and right again under the railway bridge in **Botley Road**. The squat stone building on the right beyond the bridge was built by the Great Western Railway to replace the ❷ **turnpike tollhouse** demolished to make way for the Banbury line. It served for only 18 years before being converted into a pub – and it is still a bar and restaurant. The single-storey extension to the east with the complicated roof was added in 1902.

On the left is the ❸ **River Hotel**, a substantial (if ugly) brick house built in 1878 and occupied from 1889 by Thomas Henry Kingerlee, twice mayor of Oxford and owner of a construction company that built several streets of houses to the north of Botley Road as well as the Jam Factory opposite the station (see page 215). The largest building firm in Oxford in the last decades of the 19th century, when it was the second biggest employer after Oxford University Press, Kingerlee's (now based in Kiddlington) is still headed by a family member.

Cross ❹ **Osney Bridge**, built in 1888 after floods swept away the central arch of a crossing whose stones were re-used in the construction of the bases of the balustraded abutments. The new bridge with its single iron span was designed by the city engineer and you can see shields bearing the arms of the University and City of Oxford and the names of the chairman of the Oxford Local Board (wine and spirit merchant C. J. Laker) and engineer W. H. White attached to the decorative ironwork. The bridge has the lowest headroom of any across the navigable Thames.

Turn left at the far side of the bridge and cross the narrow iron footbridge into the area known as Osney Town, developed by solicitor and town clerk George P. Hester from 1851, mainly to provide housing for railway workers. The sluice gates around the bridge control the flow of water to stop the low-lying area from flooding. Despite the rigid grid of streets, individual houses vary subtly in size, some with the chequerboard brickwork characteristic of contemporary workers' housing in Jericho. Built in 1881 as a family home and the largest building on the island, the West Oxford Democrats Club on the corner of East Street and North Street was opened as a social club in 1939 by two Osney residents after their local pub closed: despite the name, it has no formal political affiliation.

OXFORD LOCAL BOARD

1888

Follow the Thames Path along **East Street**. On the opposite bank is the former ❺ **Electric Lighting Station**, created in 1892 to satisfy increasing demands for electricity from both the town and the University. Built to impress, with three gables and ornate red-brick blind arcading at first-floor level, it was opened with much civic ceremony – as well as a University-run poetry competition to mark the occasion. Hillaire Belloc's (unsuccessful) entry, submitted under a pseudonym, ran as follows:

> ...Descend, O Muse, from thy divine abode,
> To Osney, on the Seven Bridges Road;
> For under Osney's solitary shade
> The bulk of the Electric Light is made.
> Here are the works; – from hence the current flows
> Which (so the Company's prospectus goes)
> Can furnish to Subscribers hour by hour
> No less than sixteen thousand candle power,
> All at a thousand volts. (It is essential
> To keep the current at this high potential
> In spite of the considerable expense.)
> The Energy developed represents,
> Expressed in foot-tons, the united forces
> Of fifteen elephants and forty horses.

Designed by Thomas Parker of Wolverhampton, an electrical engineer and industrialist known as the 'Edison of Europe', the power station used steam-driven turbines, fuelled by coal delivered by barge, and pioneered a method of delivering electricity that became known as the 'Oxford System'. The small northern extension was added in 1905 as an office for the chief engineer: the oriel window allowed him to check on the arrival of coal barges. Because water used to cool the turbines was pumped back into the river, local people swam and bathed in warm water all year round, with a makeshift diving board on the opposite bank and children daring each other to swim under the outlets to emerge in the substation

itself. The power plant closed in 1968 and the building was acquired as lab space by the University. It is currently being developed into a Global Leadership Centre by the Saïd Business School, founded by Syrian-Saudi businessman, political fixer and arms dealer Wafic Saïd.

At the far end of East Street is ⑥ **The Punter**, Osney Island's only surviving pub, founded as the Waterman's Arms in 1871 with stables along South Street for the horses that pulled the coal barges. On the South Street façade is a plaque for Morland Brewery, based from the 1880s until 2000 at nearby Abingdon: the depiction of an artist with a palette in one hand and a tankard in the other was inspired by popular genre painter George Morland (1763–1804; in fact no relation to the brewing family), known for a dissolute lifestyle of excessive drinking and what his biographer John Hassell described as a 'foppish puppeyism' embodied in a signature outfit of velvet coat, leather breeches and an extravagant hat 'to which was attached a short thick tail, not unlike a painter's brush'.

Continue along the towpath to ⑦ **Osney Lock**, first built using prisoner labour in 1790, when the millstream dug by the monks of Osney Abbey (see below) in the early 13th century was developed into the main navigation channel of the Thames, linked to the newly established Oxford Canal to the north. The glass-fronted wooden pavilion with solar panelling before the lock is the community-owned Osney Lock Hydro, completed in 2015 to generate electricity for local homes, with surplus fed back into the national grid. The complex also incorporates a 'fish pass', so for the first time for more than 200 years fish can move freely upstream. On the opposite bank just before the lock gates are marked the record flood levels of 1894, 1947 and 2003. The stone house behind the booth from which the lock-keeper still emerges to operate the electrically powered gates bears the crest of the Thames Conservancy, set up in 1857 to manage the river.

On the opposite bank is ⑧ **Osney Mill**, an important source of income for Osney Abbey, one of four substantial monastic houses established in Oxford in the course of the 12th and 13th centuries (the others were St Frideswide's, which was subsumed into Christ Church College; Rewley, just north of the station; and Godstow, further upstream). Osney was allegedly created after Editha, the wife of Norman governor Robert d'Oilly, founder of Oxford's castle, was disturbed by a flock of noisy magpies that her religious advisor Ranulph claimed were souls in purgatory demanding the establishment of a monastery so they might be saved by prayer. Ranulph became the abbey's first prior. Following the monastery's dissolution in 1539, the abbey church briefly served as Oxford's cathedral until that honour – along with much of the surrounding land as well as the bell now called Great Tom (see below) – was transferred to Christ Church. Chaucer has the cuckolded husband in 'The Miller's Tale' (*c.* 1380) engaged at the abbey ('And so bifel it on a Saterday / This carpenter was goon til Osenay') while his wife and her lover plot future assignations.

The present mill building dates from the 1840s and was run as a water-powered flour mill for almost a century until it switched to electricity because the neighbouring power station was taking so much water from the river. Disastrously, the flour clogged the circuitry, resulting in a devastating fire. Left empty for 60 years, the site was converted into flats in 2012.

Continue across the bridge, with Osney Pool, from which the Environment Agency runs the barges that maintain the river, on your right. On the opposite bank is Osney Mill Marina, with moorings for 40 boats in a basin dug out in the 1960s from the former mill race by the owner of the derelict mill. A little further on, Boney's footbridge (perhaps named in reference to Napoleon) crosses the now neglected Bulstake Stream, until 1790 the main Thames navigation channel. An **9** **obelisk** marks the spot where in 1889 21-year-old Edgar George Wilson drowned while saving two boys who had got into trouble while fishing. The first of the two railway bridges just beyond the footbridge was built in 1850 to carry the line from Didcot to the new station to the north; the second was added in 1887.

10

Take the footpath that branches to the right and runs uphill between trees before emerging in a meadow. Now Grandpont Nature Park, the area was formerly part of the Oxford and District Gas Company Works, established in St Ebbe's on the north side of the river in 1818. As gas usage increased for street lighting as well as domestic and University heating and cooking, the works stretched across a 7.5-hectare site, expanding on to the south bank in the 1880s. Over-excited by T. S. Eliot's 'The Waste Land' (1922), fellow poet W. H. Auden is said to have thought the industrial complex was the most beautiful place on earth.

The last gasometer was demolished in 1968 and in 1985 the 3 hectares south of the river – considered too polluted to be developed – were transformed into a park. The ⑩ **'giant hand' sculpture** to the rear of the meadow – with fingers and thumb either emerging from or sinking into the ground – was created in 1997 by local schoolchildren working with artist Diana Bell (see Bonn Square, page 230) to express the ambiguous relationship between humankind and the environment. The impressively wide footbridge was originally the ⑪ **Gasworks Railway Bridge**, built in 1886 to link the two sites, with a single rail spur from the main line as well as a footpath and cart-road. From the bridge looking north you can see the point where Castle Mill Stream joins the Thames.

Return to the towpath beyond the bridge and look back towards it. Its sections assembled on this side of the river and floated into position on barges, it is supported on massive decorated central piers with pepperpot caps, with end piers of Staffordshire brick. From below the bridge you can see the gas pipes that ran underneath. The reach of the gasworks site can be gauged by the distance to the skeletal pipe bridge further downstream, built in 1927 to carry pipes from one side of the site to the other. The fortress-like frontage just before it belongs to the Sir Geoffrey Arthur Building, student accommodation for Pembroke College (see below) designed in the late 1980s by Maguire and Murray.

Follow the towpath to Folly Bridge, site of the Anglo-Saxon ford for driving cattle across the Thames that gave Oxford its name. On the right as you approach the bridge you can see two arches set within a battered (outward-sloping) rubble wall: this was once part of a 2-mile **12** **causeway** (or *grand pont*) built by Robert d'Oilly c. 1085 to cross the marshy ground approaching Oxford's first masonry bridge. To the south, Abingdon Road runs above the causeway's remains; to the north, St Aldate's leads to Carfax, the city's central crossroads. The 'folly' after which the bridge was named was probably a hexagonal tower with a portcullis and drawbridge built to defend the southern approach to the city and used as an observatory by alchemist, philosopher, scientist and Franciscan friar Roger Bacon (c. 1220–92; see below). The current bridge dates from 1825.

Demolished in 1779 so the road could be widened, the tower no doubt provided inspiration for ⓭ **'Cauldwell's Castle'**, the eccentric house on Folly Island just before the bridge. The crenellated brick building, decorated with plaster statues of bishops and draped maidens, was created in 1849 for mathematician Joseph Cauldwell. A couple of years after its completion, its owner shot and injured one of a group of students who were dragging the cannons in his forecourt into the river: he was cleared after his defence counsel accused the perpetrators of 'luxuriating at a cricket club supper, smoking cigars and drinking beer' before setting off to 'despoil his premises, for the sake of gratifying a morbid and wicked disposition'. In 1911 the house was bought by Robert Gunther, first curator of the History of Science Museum (see page 62).

On the other side of the bridge is Hertford College Graduate Centre, student accommodation designed in 2000 by Architects Partnership: continue along the towpath and look to your right to see that the building oversails a stretch of water in a nod to older structures that were supported on arches above water or waterlogged ground. A few metres further on is ⓮ **Grandpont House**, also raised on arches that in this case obviously predate the house. The charming if somewhat ill-proportioned building – with canted bays, a central Venetian window and a glorious fanlight – was created in 1785 for town clerk William Elias Taunton. From the 1860s until his death in 1887, it was home to town councillor, former mayor and tailor Thomas Randall, who was possibly the inspiration for the Mad Hatter in *Alice's Adventures in Wonderland*.

Author Charles Dodgson (aka Lewis Carroll, 1832–98) started the story as entertainment for Alice Liddell, whose father was dean of Christ Church, where Dodgson lived for 47 years as a student and then mathematics don: many characters and locations were based on people and places that would have been familiar to both of them. Since the 1950s Grandpont House has been a residential centre for religious organisation Opus Dei.

14

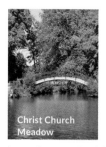

Christ Church
Meadow

On the opposite bank is Christ Church Meadow, a triangle of flood-prone pasture bounded to west and east by the Thames and Cherwell and grazed in summer by English Longhorn cattle. On this bank are the Queen's and Brasenose sports grounds with a picturesque cricket pavilion: having already played for Kent County Cricket Club as a schoolboy, Colin Cowdrey was awarded a scholarship to Brasenose in 1951, soon becoming captain of the University team and playing for England for a decade from 1954. On the towpath approximately in line with the pavilion is the ⑮ **Finish Stone**, marking the end point of the annual Torpids and Summer Eights races (see box, page 357). It is inscribed in memory of aptly named Colin Cox, who worked as a waterman, responsible for the repair and maintenance of college boats, for Oriel, Lincoln and Queen's.

On an island beyond the meadow are the ten ⑯ **college boathouses** that superseded the magnificent barges which previously served as clubhouses for the rowing teams. Accommodating 24 college clubs, with boat sheds below and viewing terraces above, the buildings – each adorned with college crest(s) – range from recent (the first is shared by Wadham, St Anne's and St Hugh's) through pioneering

15

lightweight modernist 1950s pavilions to the older red brick of Christ Church, with its dignified arched window. This end of the island is where the Cherwell joins the Thames. The forbidding black box beside the towpath is the ⑰ **boathouse for University College**, a hectoring architectural statement in comparison with the modest pavilions across the river. Shared with Wolfson, St Peter's and Somerville, it was designed by Belsize Architects in 2007 after its predecessor was destroyed in an arson attack.

MEN'S 1ST VIII

2003

Bumped

MERTON · ST. PETER'S
KEBLE · BRASENOSE

Oxford Boat Races

The Oxford–Cambridge Boat Race, contested annually in March or April, is a key English sporting event, but less well known are the Oxford intercollegiate Torpids (held at the start of March) and Summer Eights (held over a week in May). Because of the narrowness of this stretch of river, these are bump races, which means the boats start in single file (based on the results of the previous day or for the first day the previous year), about a boat and a half's length apart, with each aiming to catch (or 'bump') the boat in front and so move up a place in the starting hierarchy. The goal over a week of racing is to reach the front of the line, known as the 'head of the river'.

The tradition began with a race between Brasenose and Jesus in 1815, with the boats (each with a crew of eight plus a cox, as today) racing upstream from Iffley Lock to a point just before Folly Bridge – still the start and end points of the races today. Allegedly, the staggered start was the idea of students who would leave a pub downstream in Sandford at different times and see who could get home first. For the early races, teams had to haul their boats up a ramp to get out of the lock, creating a natural gap between them.

Originally watched from college barges moored on the banks of the river, today races are followed from the roofs and terraces of the college boathouses. Winning crews are rewarded with a college binge and their triumph is recorded in chalk on the walls of the college quadrangle.

Retrace your steps to Folly Bridge. Facing you on Folly Island are the offices of ⑱ **Salter's Steamers**, founded in 1858 and soon a leading builder of racing boats (their craft still hold the most speed records in the Oxford–Cambridge boat race), college barges and canoes as well as paddle steamers and naval vessels. Salter's also pioneered the idea of passenger trips and holiday boat hire – and you can still rent punts or power boats or take a cruise from the wharf in front of the offices. Salter's boatyard was the starting point for a rowing trip to Godstow during which 24-year-old Charles Dodgson entertained ten-year-old Alice Liddell and her two younger sisters with the tales that were to become *Alice's Adventures in Wonderland*, eventually published ten years later, in 1865.

Emerge on Folly Bridge and turn right to cross it. The ⑲ **Head of the River** pub – in front of which you can still see a loading crane – was built in the 1820s as a warehouse on a wharf created in 1638 and occupied by Salter's from 1858 to the 1970s. With tables with river views both inside and out, it is a good place to stop for lunch. The pub takes its name from the title awarded to the winning boat at the end of each day of the annual Summer Eights intercollegiate race (see box, page 357).

Between the pub and Christ Church Meadow, crossed by a bridge with blue and white balustrading, you can glimpse the mouth of Trill Mill Stream, a finger of water than runs beneath central Oxford from Castle Mill Stream, near Hythe Bridge Street. Filled with sewage and garbage from the workers' housing in St Ebbe's, it was covered over in the 1860s to minimise the risk to public health. In 1908 future archaeologist, army officer and diplomat T. E. Lawrence (aka Lawrence of Arabia, 1888–1935), then studying history at Jesus College, led a fleet of canoes along the culvert, firing blank shots through the gratings to frighten people in the streets above. In the early decades of the 20th century the remains of a Victorian punt with three skeletons was allegedly discovered in the waterway.

Trill Mill Stream

Opposite the Head of the River is a small pedimented **⑳ tollhouse** built to collect dues from those arriving at Grandpont Station to offset the cost of the bridge's construction. By the 1850s the costs had been met and the tollhouse became redundant.

Continue walking north up **St Aldate's**. Low down on no. 61 on the left – formerly a pub – is another plaque for Morland Brewery depicting artist George Morland. On the opposite side of the street, to the left of the vehicle entrance to the Thames Valley Police headquarters, is a much more modest acknowledgement of another beer enthusiast, **㉑ Inspector Morse**. Unveiled in 2006 by author of the detective series Colin

Dexter, the plaque commemorates a decade from the mid-1980s when TV crews would regularly film actor John Thaw pulling up outside in the inspector's beloved red Jaguar. Opposite is the extension to the ㉒ **Crown and County Court**, with a plaque featuring a portrait of motor manufacturer William Morris. The main court building beyond was converted in 1985 from a showroom built for Morris Motors (see box, page 228) in 1932, when the company was Britain's largest car manufacturer. A confident mix of classicism and art deco, it features a frontispiece with giant fluted Ionic columns flanking a curved pressed-metal window.

At no. 83, on the same side of the street, is the diminutive ㉓ **Alice's Shop**, the model for the Old Sheep Shop in *Alice's Adventures in Wonderland* sequel *Through the Looking Glass* (1871), when Alice finds herself: 'in a little dark shop, leaning with her elbows on the counter, and opposite to her was an old Sheep, sitting in an arm-chair knitting'. It is believed that the shop was formerly the grocery where Alice Liddell would buy her favourite barley sugars. The metal gates opposite lead to Christ Church Memorial Garden, commemorating college members killed in World War I, as well as the college visitor entrance (see page 170 for information and a tour) and Christ Church Meadow. Step into Rose Place, just beyond Alice's Shop, to see the elaborate plasterwork on the northern elevation of the ㉔ **Old Palace**, built in the 1620s by Thomas Smith Jr, twice mayor of

Oxford and a member of an important brewing dynasty, as an extension to his twin-gabled home to the right. Named from an earlier house said to have belonged to Robert King, first Bishop of Oxford, it features strange carved figures – including un-ecclesiastical cloven-hoofed hybrids – supporting the oriel windows.

Continue north up St Aldate's: the junction with **Brewer Street** marks the site of the former south gate of the city, demolished in the mid-17th century (it is possible that 'Aldate' took its name from a contraction of 'old gate' rather than an obscure Gloucestershire saint). The stone house at nos 1–2 was created in two parts: no. 2, still with its original paired Tudor windows, was built in 1596 by brewer Thomas Smith Sr, with no. 1 added by his son Oliver (father of Thomas Smith Jr) in the early 1600s. Beside the fine Georgian doorcase is a blue plaque to crime writer ㉕ **Dorothy L. Sayers** (1893–1957), whose father was chaplain of Christ Church and headmaster of the neighbouring Cathedral School, transferred from the college grounds to Brewer Street by Dean Liddell in the 1890s. From 1912 to 1915 Sayers studied at Somerville (at at time when women could not yet be awarded degrees), drawing a nostalgic if unflattering portrait of the college in *Gaudy Night* (1935) when detective writer Harriet Vane revisits her alma mater. Beyond the arts and crafts Cathedral School premises, built by North

Brewer Street

361

Oxford architect Harry Wilkinson Moore, is the Jesuit **26** **Campion Hall**, designed in 1935 by Edwin Lutyens and his only Oxford building. The austere stone Brewer Street elevation is relieved only by a deeply recessed arched doorway and a series of small regular windows – including the arched leaded lights of the upper-floor chapel, their arrangement allegedly inspired by a cardinal's biretta. At the far end of the building is the Georgian doorway to the much older Micklem Hall, a lodging house that had belonged to a succession of brewing families.

The glass bridge that oversails the street links the 21st century Rokos Quad of Pembroke College (see below) with the main campus to the north. The **27** **Bannister Building** – dedicated to neurologist Roger Bannister (1929–2018), who served as master of Pembroke from 1985 to 1993 but is best known for becoming the first athlete to run a mile in under four minutes at the track in Iffley Road in 1954 – was converted from 18th-century town houses with street-level shops. The massive wall opposite is part of the medieval city boundary that ran between South Gate and Little Gate on **St Ebbe's Street**. Its site marked by an inscription on the modern wall opposite the junction with Brewer Street, **28** **Little Gate** is said to have been built for the convenience of the Franciscans, who in 1224 had established a friary just outside the city limits.

Turn right into St Ebbe's Street and take the first right. The **29** **south side of**

Pembroke Street has a notable run of attractive and varied houses, with no. 28 (the first, cream-painted house) to no. 15 (painted pink) now forming the northern range of Pembroke's North Quad. Like many of the others, no. 23 (with green-painted upper storeys and a shopfront on the ground floor) dates from the late 16th or early 17th centuries, with a 17th-century top-floor oriel supported on scrolled brackets. The smaller house next door – also with an 18th-century shopfront – has a shallow bow window lighting the first floor; next to it is a later, flat-fronted house with variegated brickwork followed by a smaller house with an overhang and single sash at first-floor level below the royal arms of Queen Victoria – but no front door. Following two more houses without front doors is a pair of much restored stone houses with gables and bays dating from the early 17th century. Finally, the extraordinary house at nos 13–14 (the penultimate building before the snicket) was built in 1641 by Richard Hannes, whose father was an Oxford mayor and brewer, with the ground and first floors constructed in stone and the timber-framed storeys above stuccoed to resemble masonry. The smaller of the two central doorways is original, with the larger and grander pedimented entrance added later.

Turn right along the snicket to reach **Pembroke Square**. On your right you can glimpse the surprisingly jettied and gabled garden façade and fine woodwork of nos 13–14 Pembroke Street. The evangelical – and very popular – church of ㉚ **St Aldates** on the left was established in the 12th century but was almost completely rebuilt in the 1830s by Henry Jones Underwood, who also expanded the prison complex in Oxford Castle, before being remodelled again in the 1860s. At the side is a glazed entrance added *c.* 2000 during a refurbishment that included removing pews to accommodate an expanding congregation. Between the church and Pembroke Street, to your left, is a collection of graves – floor slabs, stacked headstones and freestanding monuments – from what was once the Pembroke College cemetery. They stand seemingly at random in front of the long block of ㉛ **Commonwealth House**, run by an organisation allied to the church that offers accommodation to international students.

In the corner of the square is the ㉜ **gateway to Pembroke College** (open to the public only on open days or by appointment), its ornate gothic oriel, with an angel surmounted by richly carved masks and foliage, added by builder Daniel Evans (see page 115) *c.* 1830. Named after the third Earl of Pembroke, chancellor of the University and benefactor of the Bodleian Library (where his statue stands, see page 198), the college was founded in 1624. Alumni include dictionary compiler

Samuel Johnson; chemist James Smithson, the aristocratic founder of the Smithsonian Institution in Washington DC; politicians Maria Eagle, Michael Heseltine and Senator William Fulbright; journalists Miranda Sawyer and Katherine Viner; King Abdullah II of Jordan; and poet Patience Agbabi. J. R. R. Tolkien was a fellow for two decades from 1925. Johnson, forced through poverty to abandon his studies in 1729 after only four terms (spent, by his own admission, regularly downing three bottles of port a night courtesy of University College), had rooms on the second floor above the entrance.

Turn left and walk along the side of the church to **St Aldate's**. Christ Church College, on the far side of the street, was founded by Cardinal Wolsey in 1525, with its entrance embellished through the addition of Tom Tower, designed by Christopher Wren, in 1680 (see pages 164–165). Great Tom, the bell from Osney Abbey, strikes 101 times at 21.05 each evening: the number represents the 100 students of Henry VIII's foundation plus an additional place funded later; 21.05 signals the student curfew according to Oxford time, which is five minutes behind Greenwich Mean Time.

Tom Tower

Turn left into St Aldate's, past the east end of the church and the front of Commonwealth House – its ground floor George & Danver's ice-cream parlour – then left back along **Pembroke Street**. ㉝ The **Story Museum** at no. 42 began life as a Victorian inn with stables, a barn and a courtyard behind before being converted into a sorting office and staff accommodation for the Post Office in St Aldate's. The museum opened in 2014. Nos 39 and 38, with double overhangs and gables, date from 1690 and Pembroke House beyond, with a gateway to a courtyard at the rear, from the 18th century.

㉞ **Modern Art Oxford** at no. 30 occupies premises built in 1888 for Hanley's City Brewery as stores and a 'square room', where fermentation was carried out in square open-topped stone vessels. The architect was the inappropriately named Harry Drinkwater, who also modernised the Lion Brewery for Morrell's (see below) at around the same time. Opened in 1966, the gallery is an early example of repurposing an industrial building.

On the opposite side of **St Ebbe's Street** is the church of ㉟ **St Ebbe's**, the oldest documented parish church in Oxford. The present building dates mainly from the early 19th century, with the south aisle with its tracery window added in the 1860s by George Edmund Street to serve an expanding population of workers from the gas plant who lived in the surrounding terraces.

A memorial tablet facing the street at the southern end commemorates James Grainge, a churchwarden and mayor who ran a pawnbroking business from one of the houses in Brewer Street that is now part of the Bannister Building. Walk along **Penny Farthing Place**, skirting the north side of the church, turn left and on the west wall is an arched portal decorated with beakheads and chevrons said to have been installed as a penance by Norman governor Robert d'Oilly after he received a vision

of the Virgin Mary urging him to nourish the poor and rebuild or embellish Oxford's churches. The beakheads were thought to represent evil spirits lying in wait to pluck the good seed from those leaving the church.

Most of the workers' housing in St Ebbe's – an area described in the mid-19th century as 'a swamp converted into a cesspool' with housing displaying 'a degree of neglect and filth rarely witnessed' – was demolished in the 1960s, with the area to the west developed as the Westgate Centre, which received a total makeover in 2017 (see page 227). Turn left before Sainsbury's into **Roger Bacon Lane**, an unprepossessing alley named after the Franciscan friar, polymath and pioneer of scientific empiricism whose *Opus Majus*, written at the command of Pope Clement IV in 1267, was a summary of contemporary human knowledge. After several years in Paris – including a period spent under house arrest because of his radical beliefs – Bacon (aka Rogerius Baconus or Doctor Mirabilis) returned to Oxford in 1278 to spend his final fifteen years at the St Ebbe's friary.

Turn Again Lane

Turn right into **Turn Again Lane**: the three cottages on the right, dating from the 17th century, have been restored by Oxford Preservation Trust, which uses no. 10 as its offices. Continue along Turn Again Lane past an art installation named 'Paradise Garden' to the shopping mall: on your right at the entrance is a plaque in English and Latin acknowledging ㊱ **Roger Bacon** as the 'Wonderful Doctor who by the Experimental Method [empiricism] extended marvellously the realm of science'.

Walk through the Westgate Centre to Castle Street and cross the road into **Paradise Street**. The Castle pub on the corner was rebuilt in the 1890s by Drinkwater, who began his career as an assistant to Street and thereafter divided his time between commissions for the Church of England and for Oxford's many breweries. The richly carved ㊲ **gateway** on the left, topped by a cartouche of foliage flanked by scrolled volutes, leads to a courtyard between the two houses whose side elevations create the street line: dating from the 17th century, the larger house nearest the Castle pub has a glorious shell porch embellished with similar motifs. Also built in the 17th century, with twin gables and an overhang, the Jolly Farmers next door claims to be the oldest continuously operating pub in Oxford – and Oxford's oldest gay venue.

Turn left along Paradise Square and left again: the handsome stone house with mullioned windows and a medievalised stair turret at the rear is the former **38** **St Ebbe's Rectory**, designed by Street in the 1850s, a decade before he began work on the church. The surrounding garden is all that remains of the grounds of the medieval Franciscan friary, described as 'a large plot partly enclosed by a rivulet and whereon was so pleasant a grove of trees, divided into several walks, ambits and recesses... that by the citizens of Oxon was called Paradise'. The building is now the Oxford Centre for Anxiety Disorders and Trauma. On the side wall is a blue plaque to vicar John Stedwell Stansfeld (1855–1939), a civil servant and occasional medical practitioner from Bermondsey in London who took holy orders at the age of 55 and from the age of 72 spent three years setting up a mission school in Kenya. In the interim, as vicar of St Ebbe's, he bought 8 hectares of land in Headington to give local children the opportunity to spend a holiday camping in the countryside. The adjacent brick building, also by Street, was the parish school, much altered and with the ecclesiastical porch added by another architect in 1868.

Return to Paradise Street and turn left: the Victorian house on the corner is Peace House, the Oxford headquarters of the Fellowship of Reconciliation, founded in 1914 by an English Quaker and German Lutheran to oppose war. On the right is an entrance to Oxford Castle (see page 223), which served as a prison until 1997 and is now a hotel. The battered base of the round tower – part of the city's defences – dates from c. 1235.

Cross Castle Mill Stream at ㊴ **Swan Bridge**, named after Swan's Nest Island, just to the south. Skirted by Castle Mill Stream and a small tributary, this was the site of the Swan Brewery – one of many in an area amply supplied with water and water power. Founded in 1646, Swan's was taken over in 1795 to become Hall's, whose logo of four tiles with an image of a hare is still found on many Oxford pubs. From the bridge you get a good view of the castle's St George's Tower, possibly originally part of the city's Saxon west gate and certainly part of the Norman castle's defences, which D'Oilly reinforced by diverting Castle Mill Stream to form a moat. Castle Mill, straddling the stream in front of the tower, where a

Castle Mill Stream

sluice now stands, may have dated back to Saxon times: rebuilt in 1781, it was not demolished until 1930. You can still see the mill pond immediately to the north.

Follow Castle Mill Stream to ⓸ **Quaking Bridge**, a crossing dating from at least the early 13th century when it was used by the canons of Osney Abbey to reach the chapel of St George, attached by D'Oilly to St George's Tower and annexed to the abbey in 1199. Cross St Thomas' Street into **Fisher Row**. The low three-storey building on the opposite bank is Fox's Malthouse, designed with a large floor area to spread out the grain but just enough floor-to-ceiling height for a man to stand to shovel and turn it. The malthouse was owned by Edward Tawney, founder of the Lion Brewery just west along St Thomas' Street: after selling the brewery to the Morrell family in the 1790s he built the handsome three-storey brick house at no. 1 Fisher Row. Three times mayor of Oxford, he also founded an almshouse next door to his home (if in somewhat less grand style). A plaque on the gable gives the date (1799) and name of the founder.

Continue to walk alongside Castle Mill Stream, until the middle of the last century lined with terraces housing a thriving community of bargemen, fishermen and boat repairers. Cross Park End Street at ㊶ **Pacey's Bridge**, established in 1770 and rebuilt in its present form in the 1920s: a plaque on the far side states that from 1661 to 1715 this was the site where Oxford's Baptists baptised new members.

Continue along the riverside path. The next crossing, Hythe Bridge, is known to have existed in the early 13th century, probably in the form of a wooden bridge also built by the monks of Osney Abbey. The present iron structure dates from the early 1860s. Emerge from the riverside path and turn right to cross the bridge: the carpark and Nuffield College to your right are on the site of wharves that served the Oxford Canal – one for coal and the other (beneath the carpark) for building materials and manufactured goods. The canal was linked via Castle Mill Stream to the Thames at Isis Lock, just to the north, providing a route from the coalfields and factories of the Midlands to London. Unfortunately its success was short lived as the Grand Junction Canal, opened fifteen years later in 1805, provided a faster route between London and Birmingham.

Take the path on the left at the far side of the bridge to see where the canal – home to a community of narrow-boat dwellers – now terminates. At its truncated conclusion, a ㊷ **sculpture in the form of a windlass** commemorates its 200th anniversary.

To return to the station, walk west down Hythe Bridge Street. ⬤

42

Visit...

Story Museum
42 Pembroke Street, OX1 1BP
www.storymuseum.org.uk

Modern Art Oxford
30 Pembroke Street, OX1 1BP
www.modernartoxford.org.uk

Eat/Drink...

The Punter
7 South Street, OX2 0BE
www.thepunteroxford.co.uk

Head of the River
Folly Bridge, St Aldate's, OX1 4LB
www.headoftheriveroxford.co.uk

The Roof Terrace
Westgate, Oxford OX1 1TR
www.westgateoxford.co.uk/roof-terrace

Index

*Street names are indexed
together under Streets, etc.*

Index

Index

Index

Index

Index

Index

Index

Index

Index

Oxford Castle Mound

Image credits

Front Cover; carvings at Magdalen College Oxford © Alamy Stock Images; Author photograph opposite page 1 © Kat Kwok; page 43 © All Souls; pages 77, 78, 79 © Lincoln College; pages 130, 131 @ St John's College; pages 136, 137, 139 © Oxford University Museum of Natural History; pages 154, 155 © Keble College; page 157 © Kat Kwok; page 228 © MG Car Club; page 236 (36) © Kat Kwok; page 249 (52) Niall McLaughlin Architects; page 252 (56) © Oxford Audio Consultants; page 279 (18) © Kat Kwok; page 281 (bottom) © Kat Kwok; page 311 (21) © Kat Kwok; pages 318, 320 © Lady Margaret Hall; page 348 (top) © Kat Kwok.